Designing Photo Mosaics and more

Fast and Fabulous Pages Using a Simple Grid System

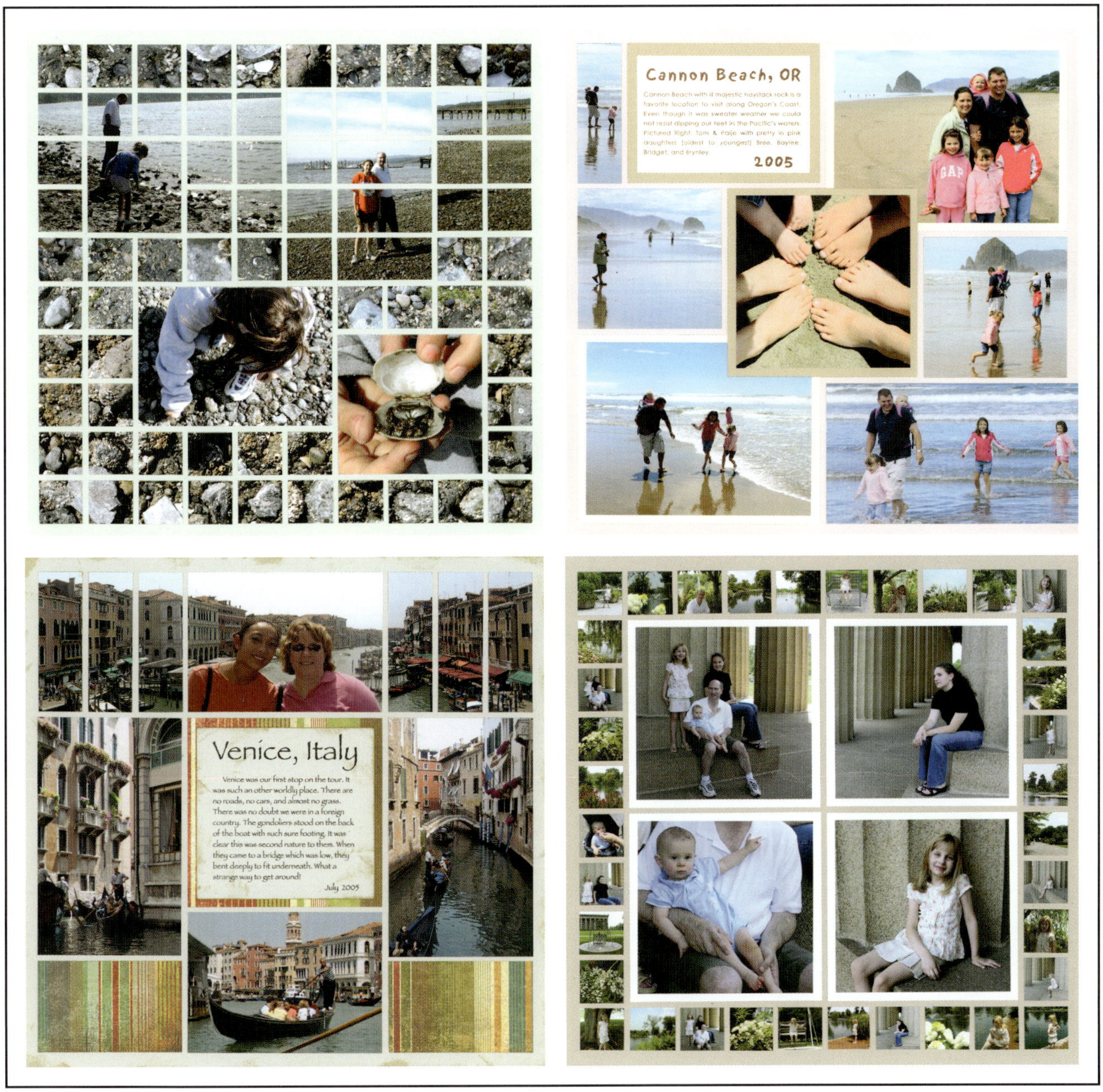

written by Tami Potter

Acknowledgements

My deepest gratitude to a wonderful group of friends: Angela Andrews, Anita Czajkowski, Joan Hess, Shannon Johnson, Sandi Keene, Keila Underwood and Jaime Zenger, who came through with photographs, time, and fabulous mosaic creations.

Sincere appreciation to extended family members who tolerate my incessant camera clicking and personal photo pilfering.

Undescribable thanks to the love of my life, Kevin, and our children. They are the direct links to all inspiration and joy in my life.

Special gratitude to those who find new knowledge or creative inspiration, it is for you that these pages exist.

Designing Photo Mosaics and More

www.tamipotter.com

Published by Wish in the Wind, LLC
PO BOX 5852
Williamsburg VA 23185
757 564 6400
www.wishinthewind.com

ISBN 0-9719403-1-2

First Edition Printed in USA
Second Printing October 2007

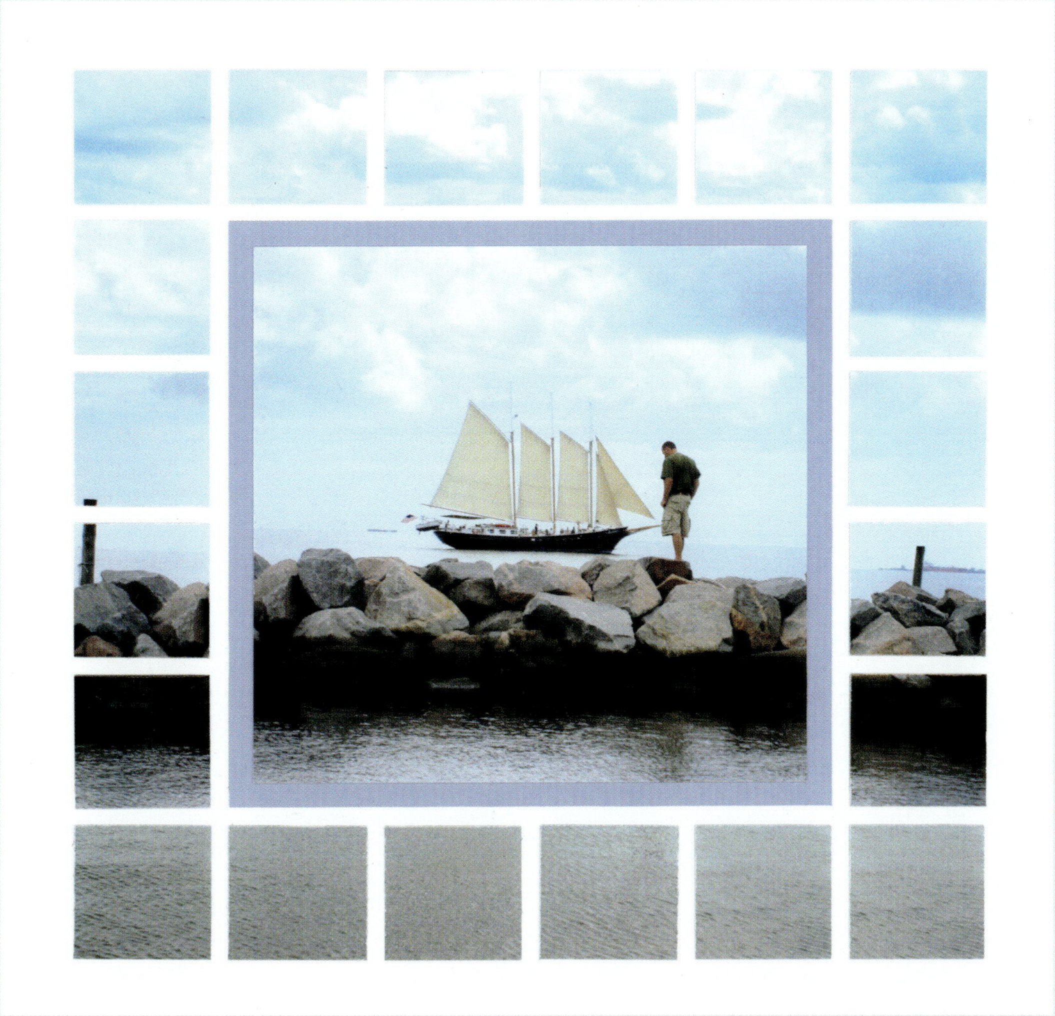

Dedicated with loving thanks to Ruth Palmer, my mother, who put up with scribbles on her walls, provided me with plenty of paper, and encouraged my creative talents.

Riverside: by Shannon Johnson

Table of Contents

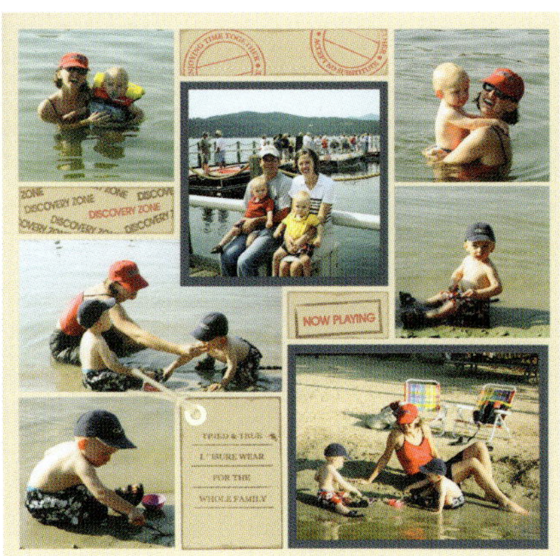

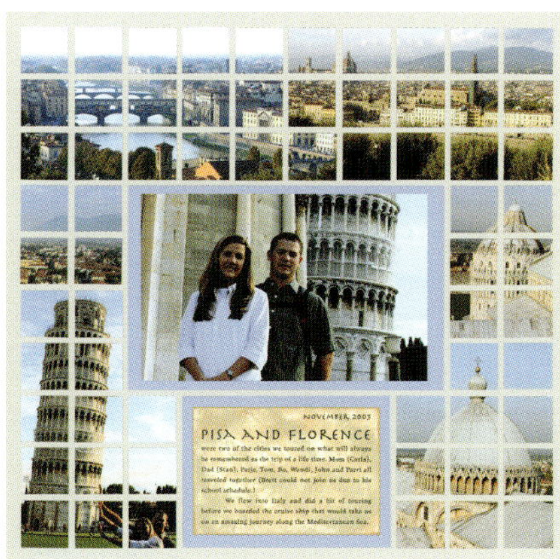

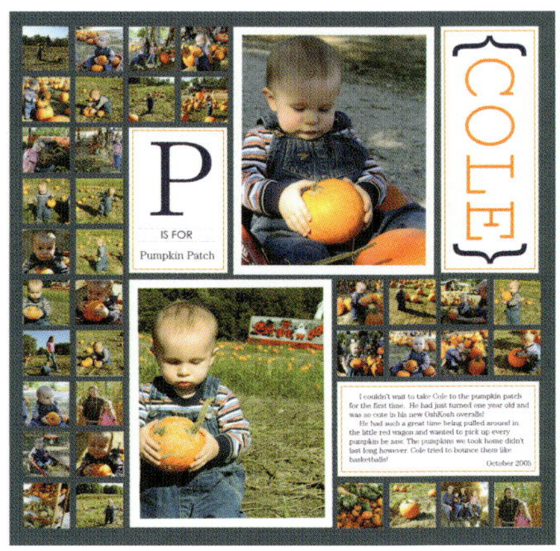

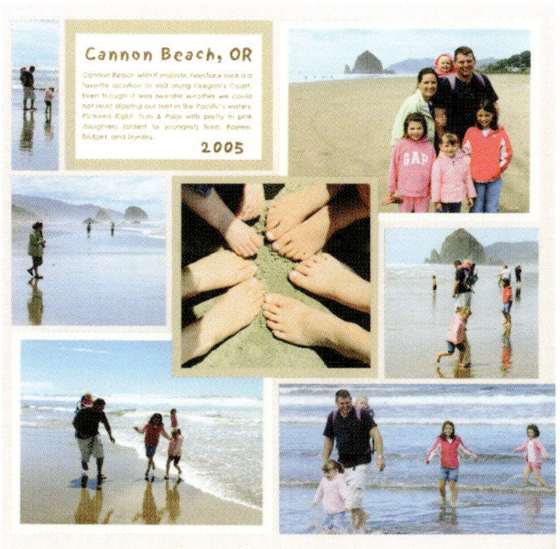
Cannon Beach, OR
2005

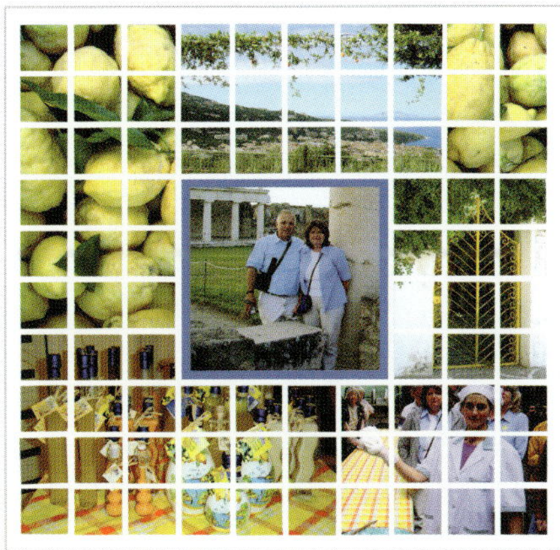

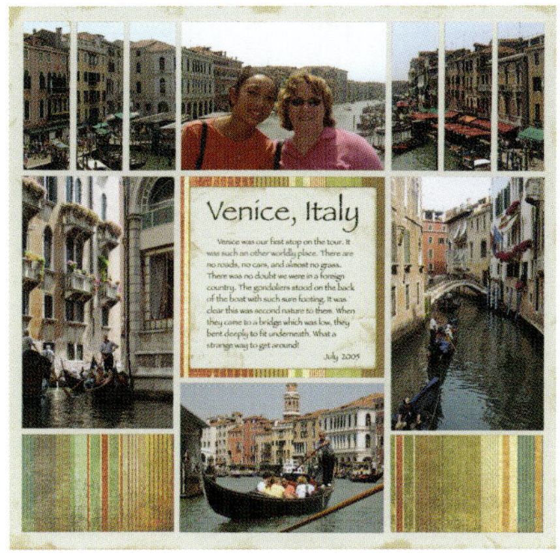
Venice, Italy

Introduction

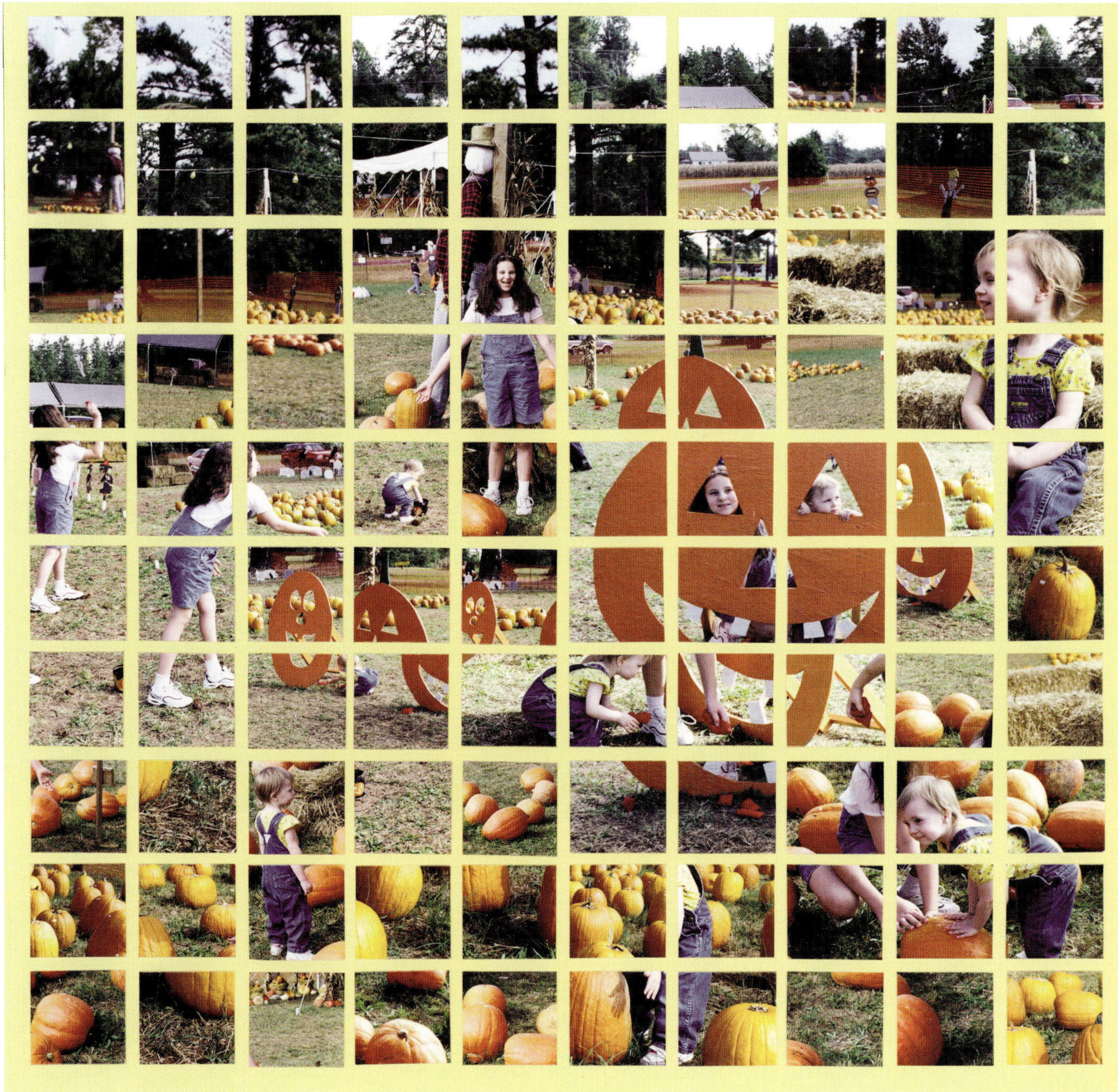

Pumpkinville: Tami Potter
number of photos: 10-12

Beginnings

Several years ago, my husband and I took our daughters to the pumpkin patch. I had recently purchased a new camera and was quite excited to use it. My husband (who didn't like the new camera) brought our old camera along. So, there we were at the pumpkin patch, each of us with the "best" camera in hand.

The pumpkin patch is a great place to take pictures. Children, dressed in denim, surrounded by vibrant orange pumpkins "beg" for a photographer's attention. In a wink and a flash, our fingers had clicked through several rolls of film. I thought I had some great pictures, and a few pumpkins to dress up our holiday. Little did I know where that day would actually take me.

When I got my pictures, I laid them out trying to decide which ones I would use to make a scrapbook page. There were so many fun moments! How could I decide? Here I was, trying to capture an hour of movement and activity on a 12x12 page.

I remembered a film I watched in college about a photographer who had taken a bunch of pictures over a period of time in a defined space (in a room and a backyard.) He displayed his photographs in overlapping layers that mimicked viewing the entire space. I thought it was intriguing how it showed the movement of people/subjects over time. His fascinating methods were the inspiration for my first Mosaic Moment™.

TAMI POTTER

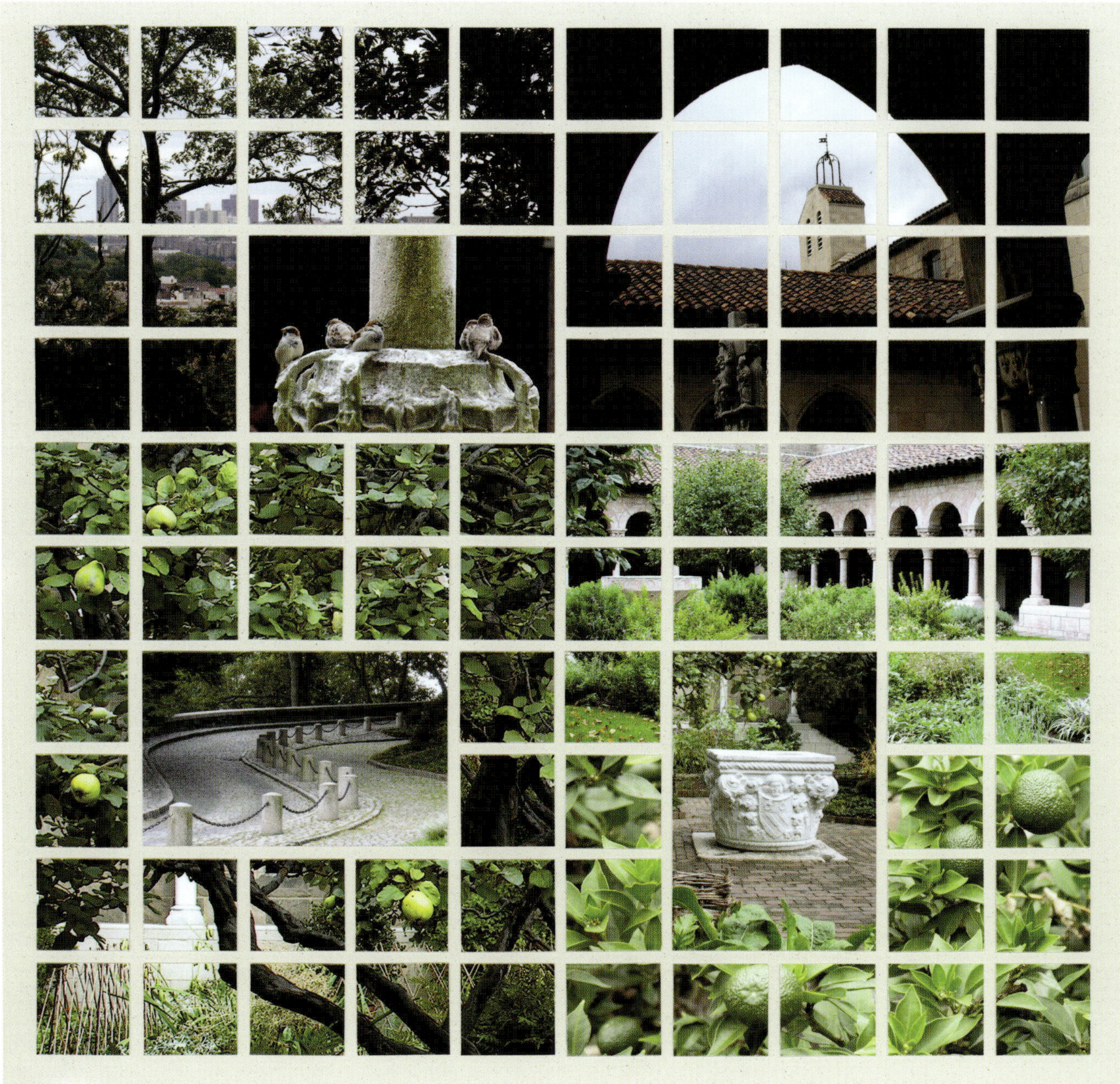

The Cloisters: Tami Potter
number of photos: 8

Method to My Madness

When I made that first photo mosaic, I didn't know how it would all come together. I just drew a grid on a sheet of 12x12 cardstock and started cutting up pictures. In the course of cutting, I started noticing little shadows, objects, and areas of interest that I hadn't noticed when the photo was in one big piece. It made the whole process very interesting to me. I enjoyed the challenge of blending things, making it difficult to see where one picture ended and another one began. It was fun, like putting together a puzzle with all square pieces.

After I had been making photo mosaics for a while, I started planning them in advance. I would see something and would think, "that is going to make a great photo mosaic," as I snapped pictures. Making things look like they were one big picture became my new goal.

Designing photo mosaics has really changed the way I take pictures. I think about getting both portrait (vertical) and landscape (horizontal) shots. I try to get a variety of angles, shoot both close up and distant shots, and take pictures of things I would have never considered taking pictures of before. Thank goodness for digital cameras!

Another thing that happened along the way...

I discovered that grid paper makes great scrapbook pages, even when I am not making a photo mosaic. I began using it for all my pages - it is spectacular for easy aligning - no more measuring from the edge of a page with a ruler to make sure my photos are straight or square with the page. I simply cut the photos into pre-determined sizes, use the grid marks to line them up, and voila! everything fits together.

In this book, I have included thoughts and tips to help you consider your photo taking habits, as well as tips for designing and organizing your pages. I am so excited about this system for scrapbooking. It truly makes my life easier. My pages go together faster and they look fabulous *every* time.

I hope you will enjoy it as much as I do.

Getting Started

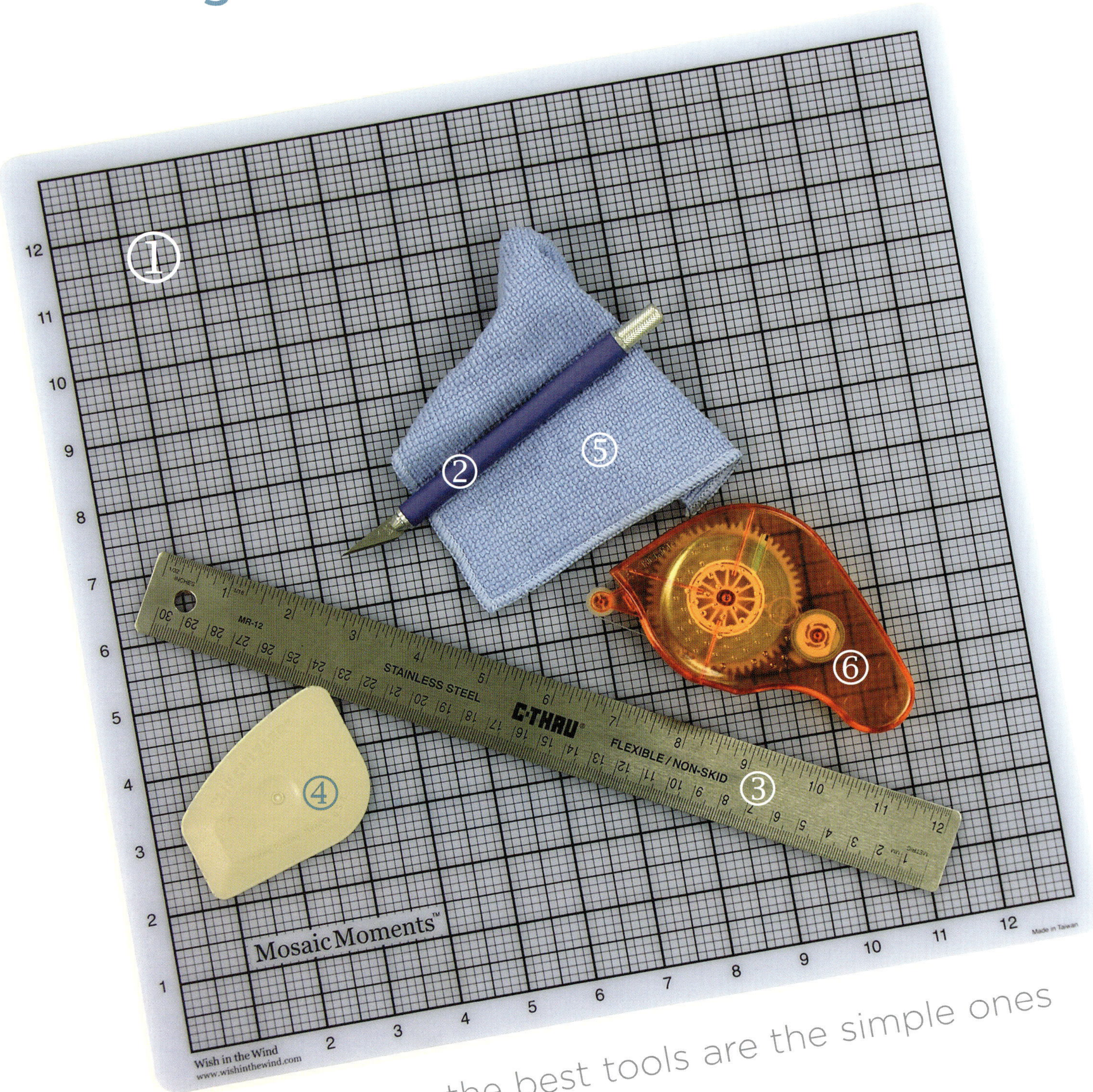

Sometimes the best tools are the simple ones

Tools

Things have come a long way since making that first photo mosaic but there is one thing that has not changed, the tools.

Mat

① Use a Mosaic Moments™ mat with self-healing surface and grid marks every 1/8 inch for flexibility in cutting.

Craft Knife

② Make sure you use a knife with a #11 blade as shown. Do not use a swivel blade knife or a box cutter. Be sure to sharpen or change blades frequently. Make sure your knife is sturdy and sharp!

Ruler

③ A metal ruler with non-slip cork backing is essential. The cork backing will help prevent the ruler from slipping out of place while you are cutting. Avoid using non-metal rulers. A craft knife will cut into the edge of plastic and wood rulers.

Lil´Chizler™

④ The beveled edge on the Lil´Chizler™ helps get under photos to lift them off of the mat without damaging edges.

Photo Cloth

⑤ Use a clean photo cloth to wipe finger prints off of photos when the project is finished.

Adhesive

⑥ Herma Dotto™ *removable* adhesive works great.

Mosaic Moments™ Grid Paper

⑦ Preprinted grid paper (pictured page-13) is a wonderful time saver. It is available in a wide range of colors. Go to www.tamipotter.com for more information about where Mosaic Moments™ Grid Paper can be purchased.

Mosaic Moments™ Quick Glance Cutting Guide

⑧ A transparent grid overlay is helpful when you are determining where to make those first cuts. (See page 93.)

■ Tip

Clean your mat with Goo Gone® and a paper towel. Use a Lil´Chizler™ to scrape up stubborn adhesive residue.

Do not use solvents on the printed surface. Do not use abrasive cleaning products or materials.

It is easiest to clean the mat immediately after completing a project. The longer the adhesive stays on the mat, the more aggressive the "sticky" gets.

Using the Mosaic Moments Mat

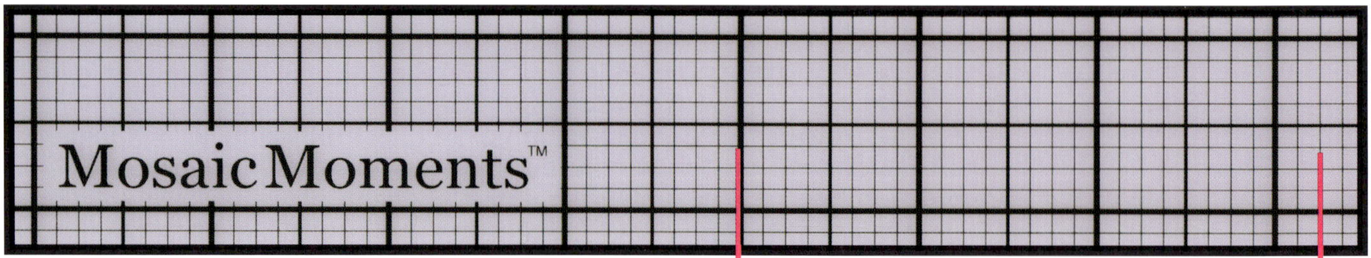

Mosaic Moments™ Mat thick/thin line detail

to cover 3 squares, count 3 thick lines + 2 thin lines

When using Mosaic Moments™ grid paper in combination with the Mosaic Moments™ mat, a simple "no measure" technique makes creating a variety of pages quick and easy.

The distance between each of the thick lines on the mat is equal to one square on your Mosaic Moments grid paper (or 1 inch.) Each of the thin lines is equal to the small gaps (or one eighth inch spacing) between the squares.

Note: mat detail image shown 90% of actual size- floral image shown 57% of actual size.

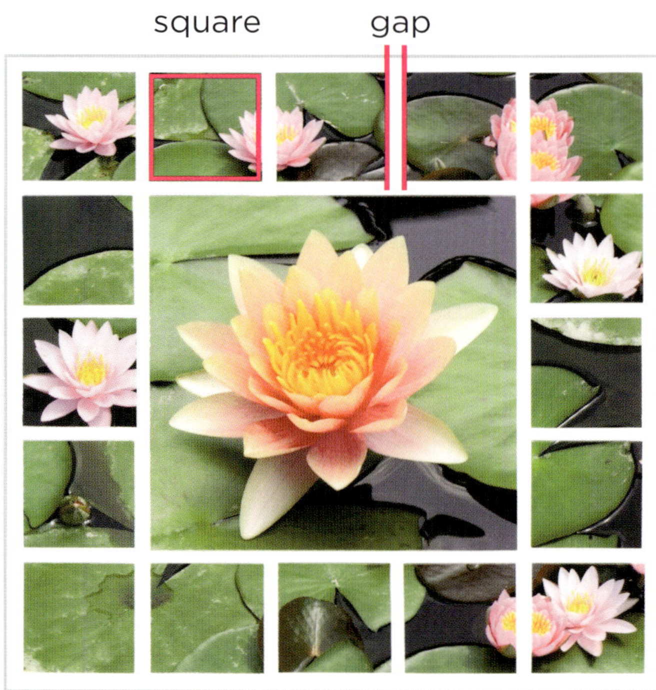

To cover more than one square at a time it is necessary to account for the entire length or width of the area - both the squares and gaps. In the image above notice that the center flower covers three squares and two gaps in both height and width. To fit this space, simply count three thick lines and two thin lines on the Mosaic Moments mat before you cut.

Mosaic Moments™ Count and Cut System™

■ Cover	■ Count
1 Square	1 sq + 0 gaps
2 Squares	2 sq. + 1 gap
3 Squares	3 sq. + 2 gaps
4 Squares	4 sq. + 3 gaps
5 Squares	5 sq. + 4 gaps

■ Tip

Notice that there is always one less gap than squares to be covered.

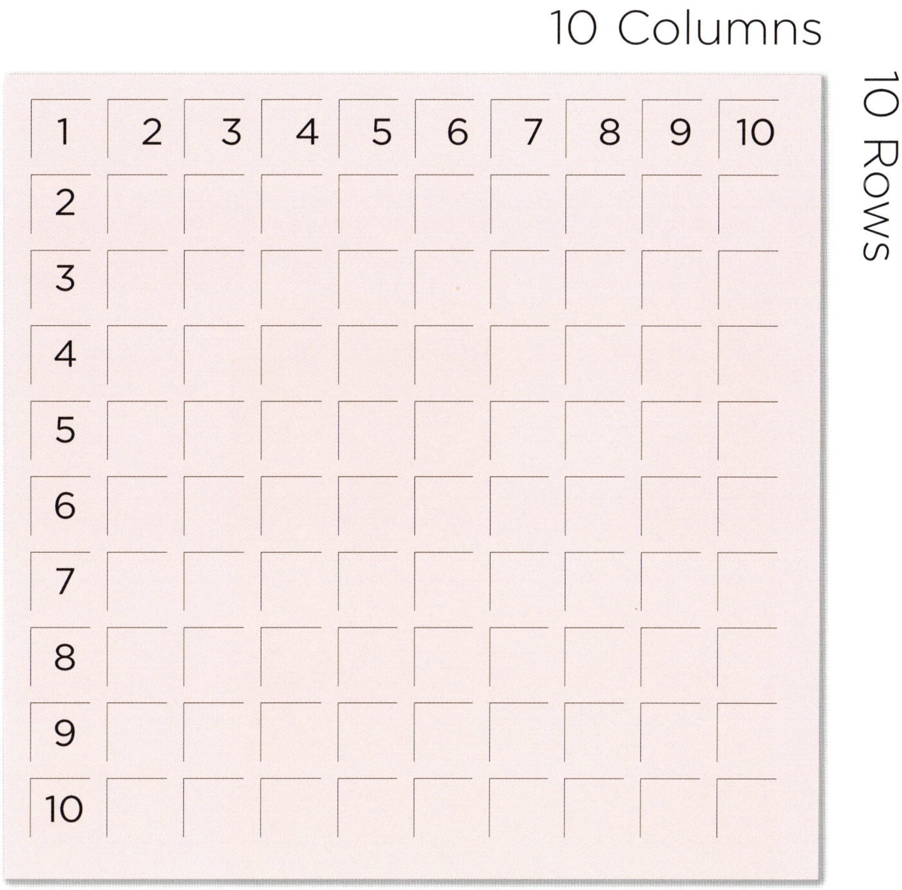

Mosaic Moments™ grid paper is designed with one inch columns and 1/8 inch gaps (space between columns.)

The options, when creating on grid paper, are endless. Your finished pages can be anything you want them to be. Mosaic Moments™ Grid Paper can be used whole or in part. It is a product designed to provide you with a foundation that enhances your creative style.

Drawing your own grid

Pre-printed grid paper, available in many colors, is the easy choice; however, there may be a time when you would need to draw your own. Place a sheet of 12x12 cardstock over your Mosaic Moments™ Mat lining it up with the grid lines.

Use a ruler to draw your first line 3/8 inch from the top of your page. Move your ruler down 1 1/8 inch and make your second line. Continue drawing lines in 1 1/8 inch increments until you have drawn 10 lines.

Turn your page 90 degrees and repeat the process - again starting your lines 3/8 inch from the top of the page.

Place your cut photo squares in the upper left corner of any space on your grid to cover drawn lines. Small segments of the drawn lines will be visible after the photo squares are placed on the paper. These can be erased, if desired.

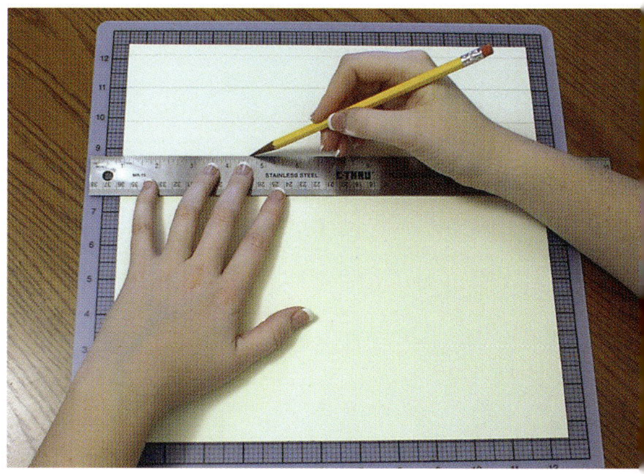

Tip

Be sure to use a very light hand when drawing grid lines. Lines will be easier to erase or may be left if they are not too distracting.

Step by Step

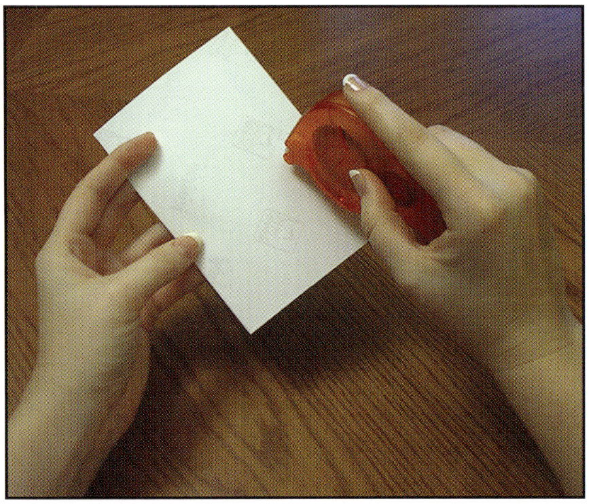

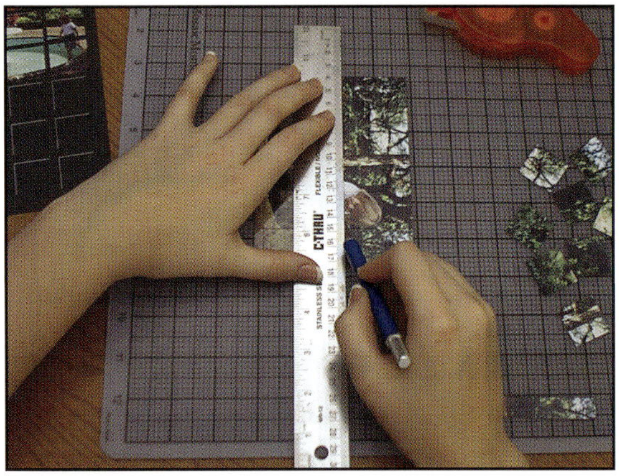

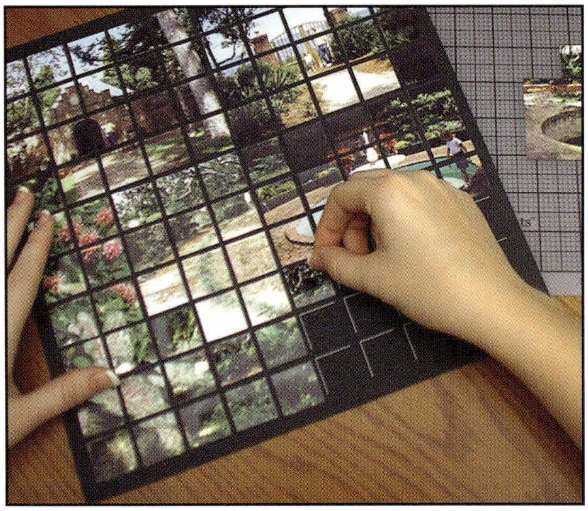

Making a photo mosaic is easier than it looks. Three basic steps will help guide you through the process.

Step One:

■ Apply adhesive.

Put removable adhesive on the back of your photo before you place it on the mat. Be sure to get adhesive on each square inch. Four lines running horizontally across the back of a 4x6 photograph will do the trick. Adhesive will keep your photo from shifting or moving out of place during the cutting process.

Step Two:

■ Cut photos.

Place photo on your mat lining it up with the grid lines. Use a metal straight edged ruler to determine where the cut will be made. Cut using a sharp craft knife with a #11 blade (as pictured on page 10.) Determining where to make your first cut is discussed in more detail on pages 16-17.

Step Three:

■ Transfer squares to grid paper.

Using your Lil´Chizler™ lift cut photo squares off of your mat and transfer them to your grid paper.

If you change your mind about placement, you can easily lift and reposition the photo squares because you used removable adhesive.

As you transfer the photo squares, check each piece to be sure there is enough adhesive to keep it in place. If not, simply roll on a bit more.

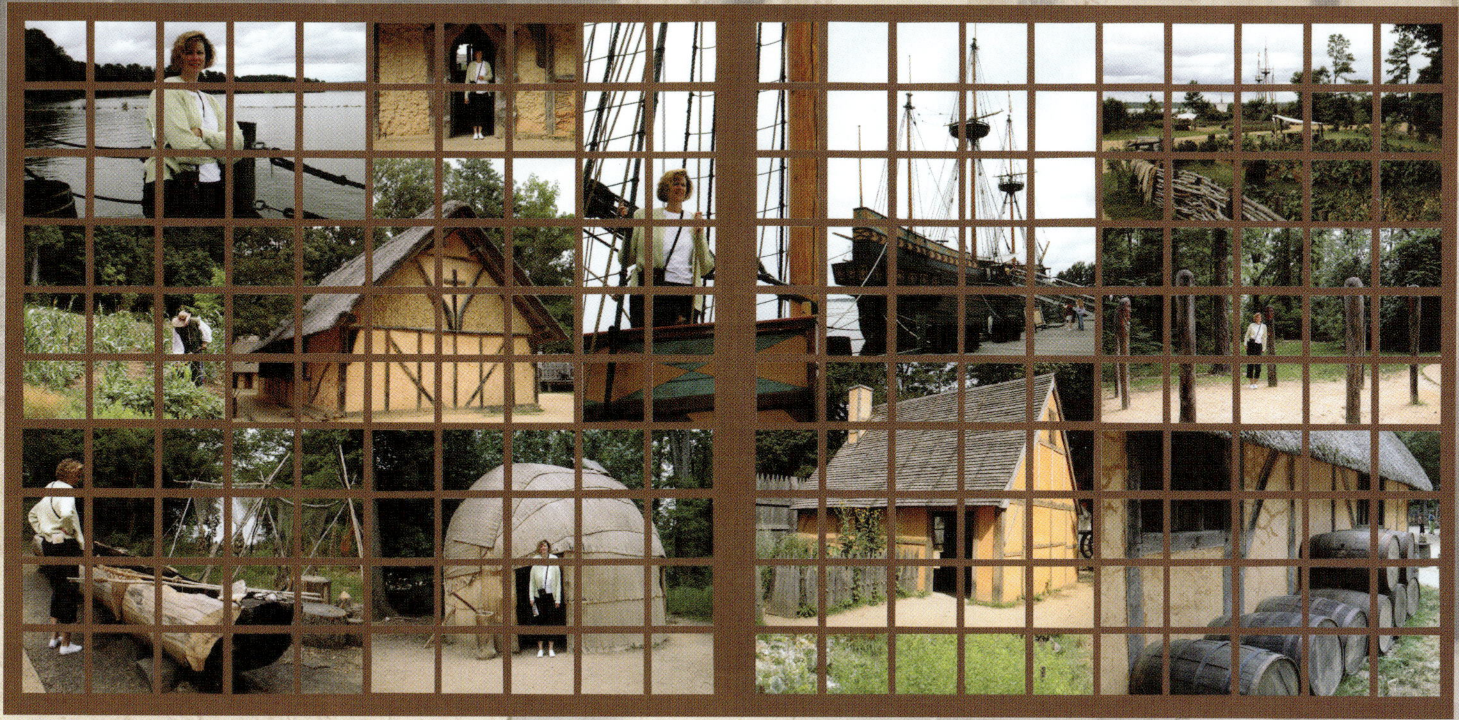

Jamestown: Tami Potter
number of photos: 12

Cutting and Cropping

Each time I line up my ruler and take my craft knife in hand, the little adage "measure twice, cut once" comes to mind. Thankfully, digital photos are easy to reprint when the need arises; however, it always feels better to get it right the first time.

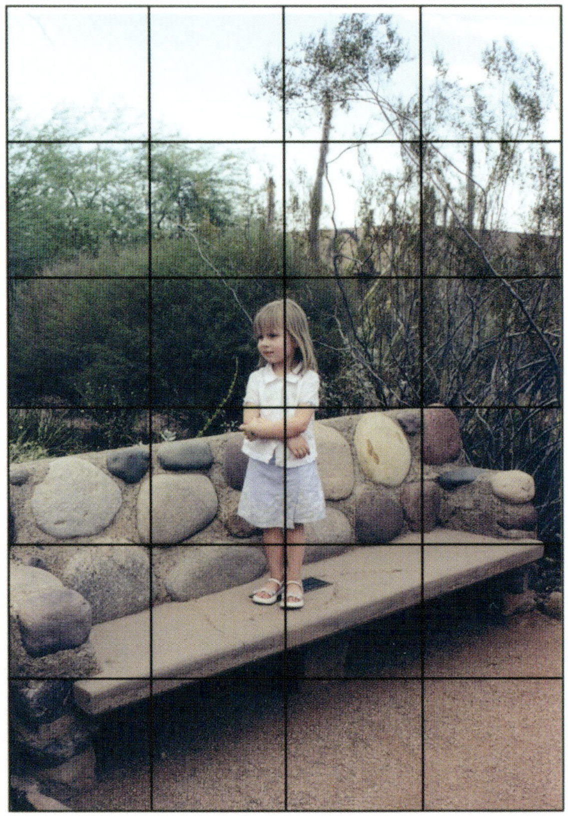

I find it handy to have a transparent overlay printed with a one inch grid to see exactly where cuts will fall. *(See page 93 for grid overlay pattern.)*

Using a transparent overlay (see image right) I can see that my standard system of cutting will not work on this photo. If I cut the photo into four even strips, I will cut right through the middle of the child's head.

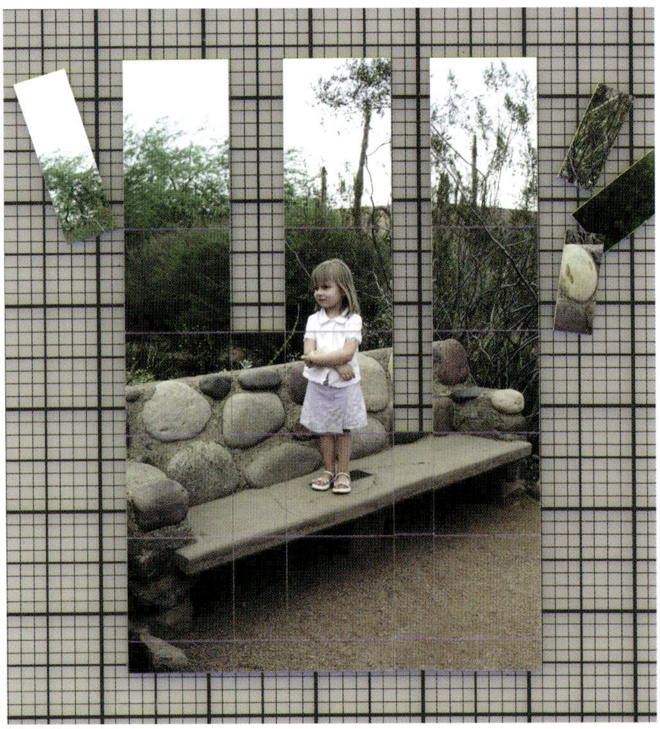

My typical solution for this problem is to center the subject's head between cuts; but, in this case, the sides of the photo (where the arms of the rock bench are located) are important as well. That made the situation a little more complex but not impossible.

By eliminating a small strip of photo from each side of the subject, I was able to keep everything I wanted in my mosaic. Each preserved section is one inch wide. I was able to save the arms of the rock bench and keep my subject's face in one square. In the finished page, (pictured right) the eliminated pieces of the photo are not missed.

■ Tip

Do not pre-crop photographs! It is not necessary since the mosaic process is all about cutting and cropping. You never know when you might need that little bit of picture.

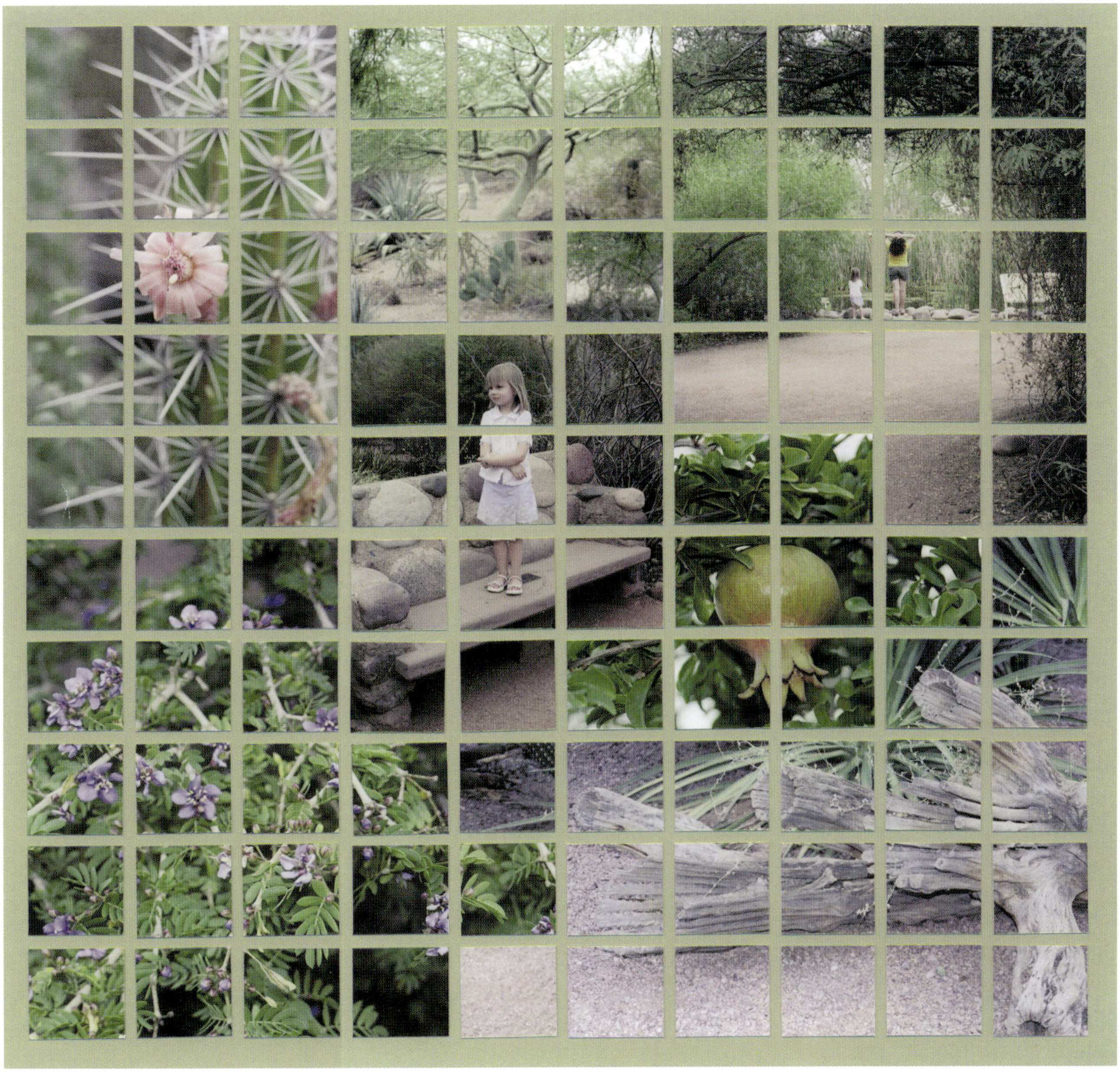

Desert Garden: Tami Potter
number of photos: 7

Tip

Before cutting or cropping, determine where to make your first cut. Using a transparent grid overlay is very helpful to this process. (See page 93 for Mosaic Moments™ Quick Glance Cutting Guide™.) As you are cutting, you may want something to fit in one square - such as a person's head. Before you cut, determine the focal point of the photo. Begin cutting in a place that will leave important aspects of your focal point intact. Cut the remainder of the photograph in one inch increments from that point.

Get The Picture

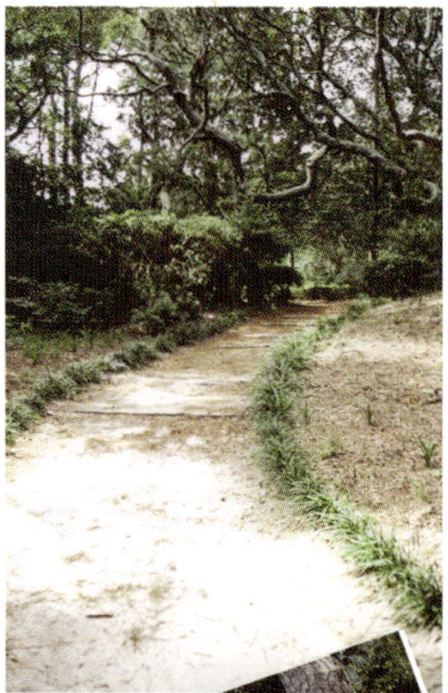

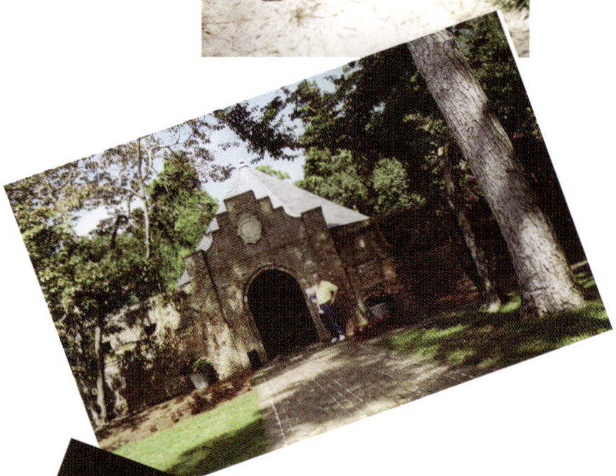

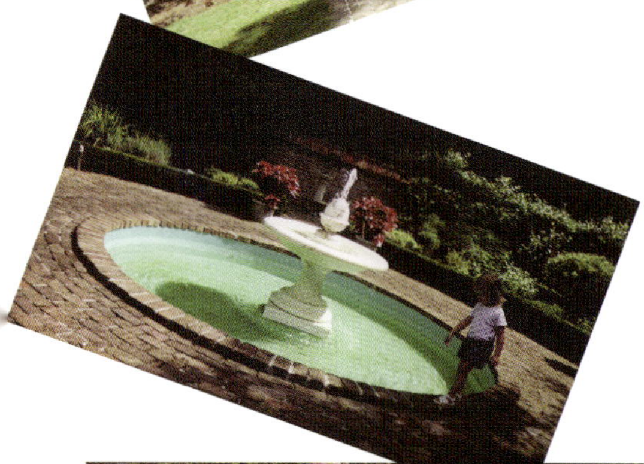

Photographs

Finding the right photos to work with grid paper is simple. Grid paper offers a great foundation for a wide range of subjects from a wedding day to a baseball game, to baby's first year, or holidays. You name it and it can be done on grid paper. Here are some things to consider when choosing your photos:

Lighting When choosing pictures for your photo mosaic, it is best to look for photographs with similar lighting.

Subjects Many photographic subjects are enhanced by the mosaic process. Scenic outdoor photographs work especially well. Photo mosaics can bring to life photos of activities such as skiing, Easter egg hunts, snowman building, or choosing the perfect pumpkin.

People Photographs with just a couple of people are easiest to work with when cutting photos into one inch squares. I prefer to use photographs where the subject's head is no larger than one inch in size so that I can keep their entire head in one cut square.

Close-ups Keep in mind that photographs will be cut into smaller pieces. Close up shots of people may not work well when cut into one inch squares. You may want to consider using those photos for focal points within your mosaic.

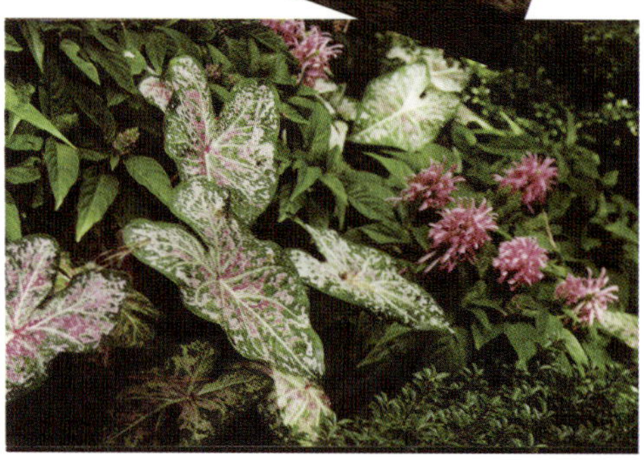

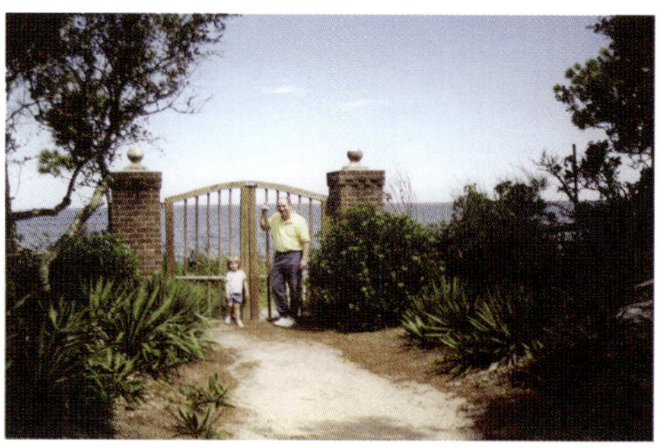

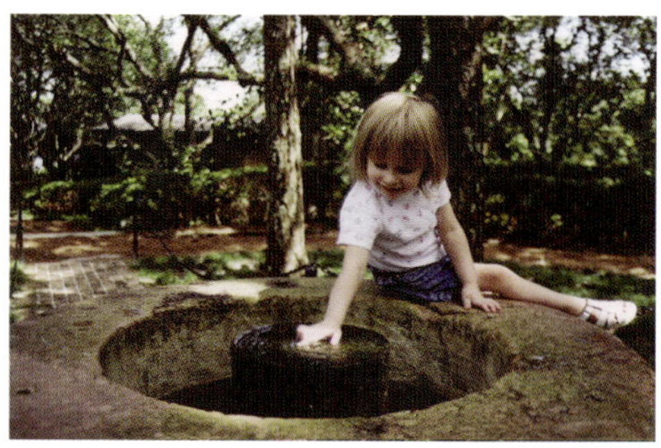

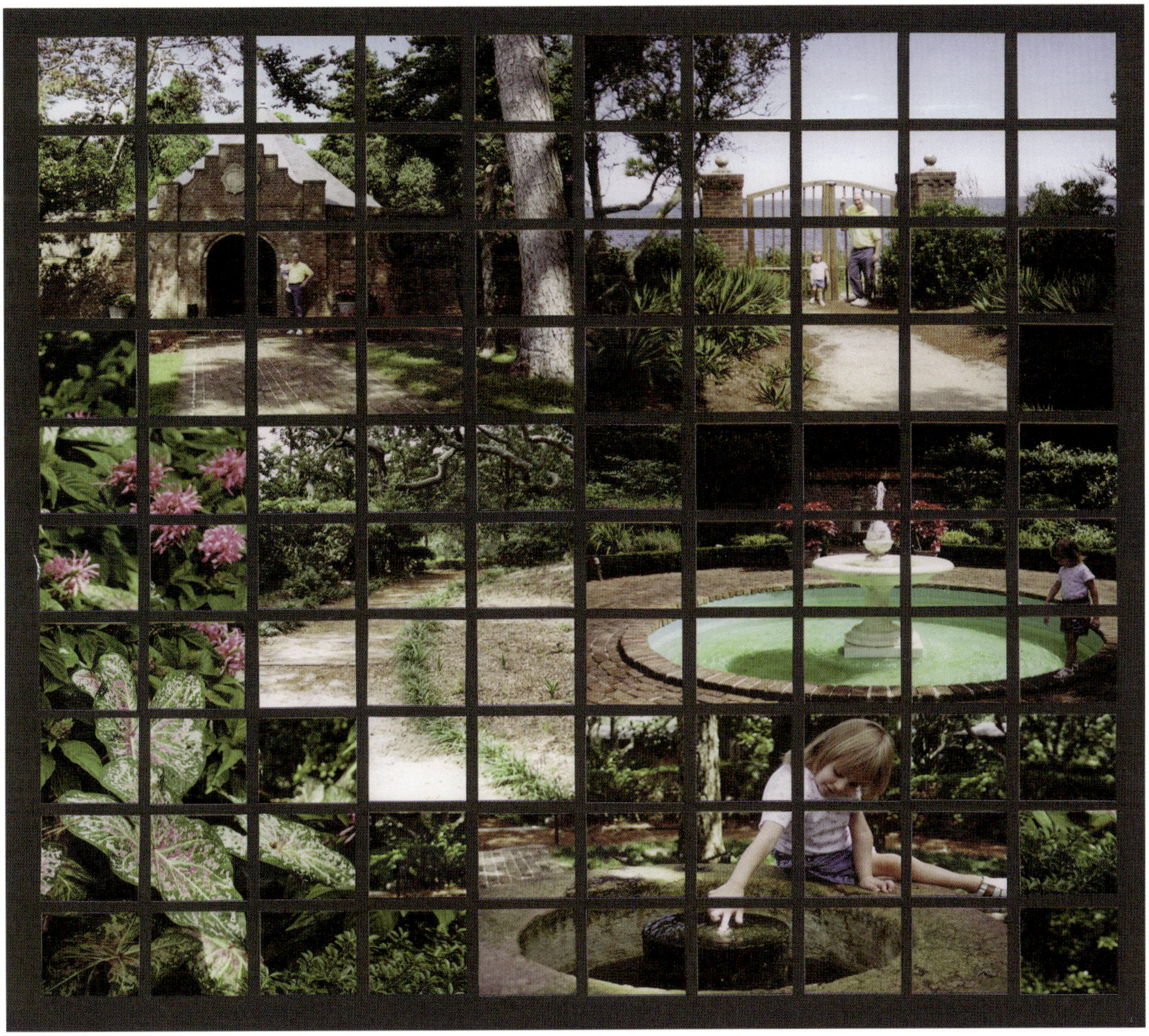

Elizabethan Gardens: Tami Potter
number of photos: 6

Six photos were used to make the above mosaic. Notice how the pathway and large fountain were cut and placed to emphasize their common curves. The photograph of the plant was cut and rearranged to fill an empty space.

Tip

Place distant shots at the top of the mosaic (in the background) and close up shots toward the bottom of the page (in the foreground.) This gives the mosaic a feeling of spatial perspective - almost as if it had all come from one large photo.

Rethinking Your Snap Habits

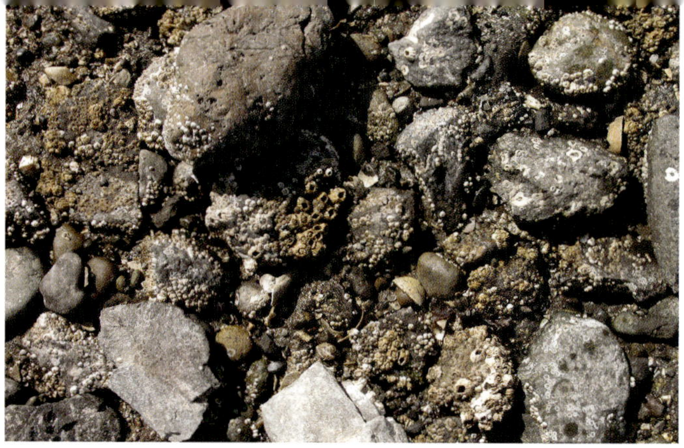

Take more pictures – we are in the digital age, after all. You can always delete later.

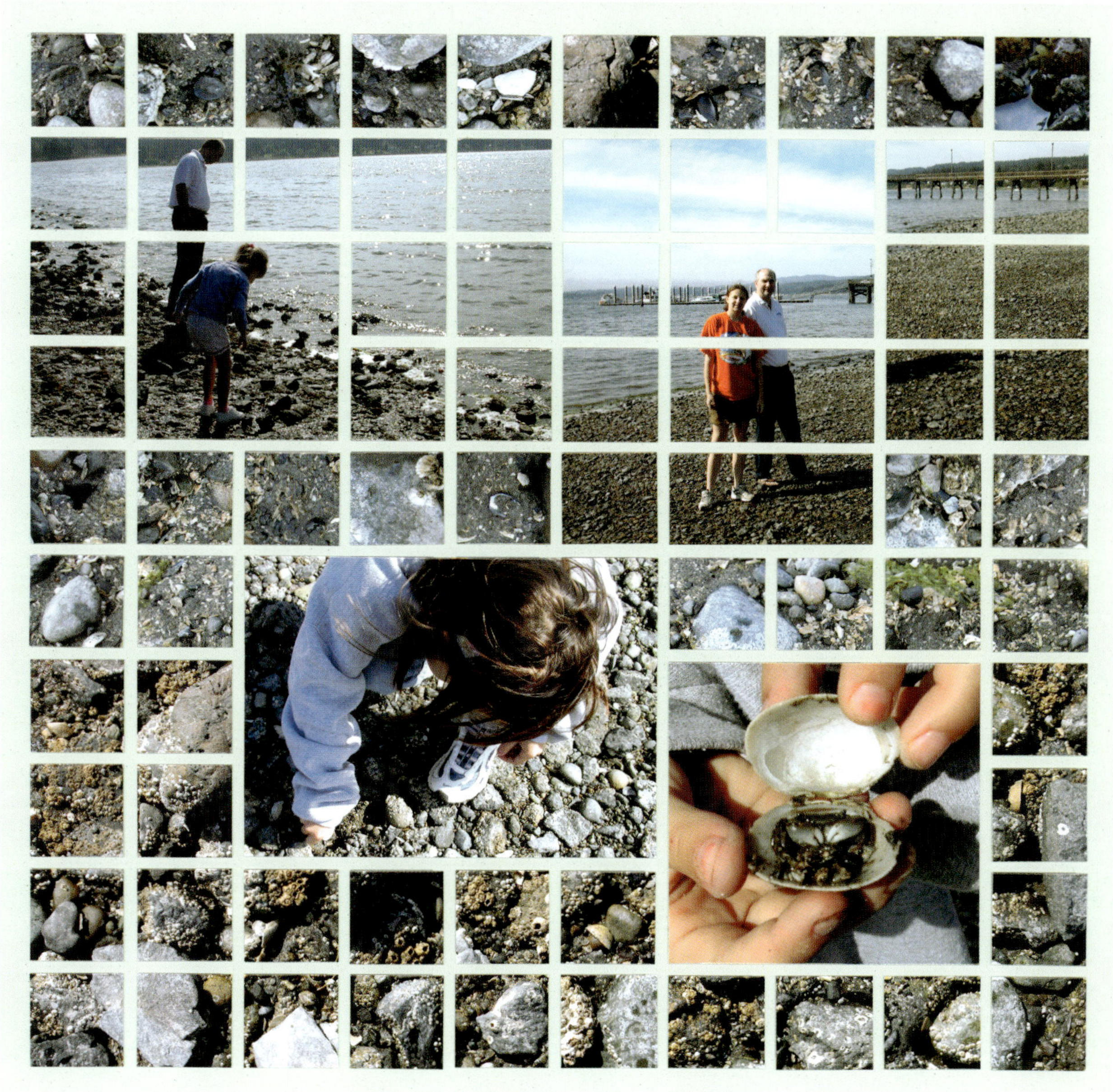

Rocky Shore: Tami Potter
number of photos: 6

Whatever you see around you - snap away!

What may seem like an uninteresting photo could be just the thing you need for a great mosaic! Theme parks have very inventive ways of "hiding" the things they don't want us to see. The "stick" fencing at Tampa's Busch Gardens caught the photographer's eye and became a great addition to this scrapbook page.

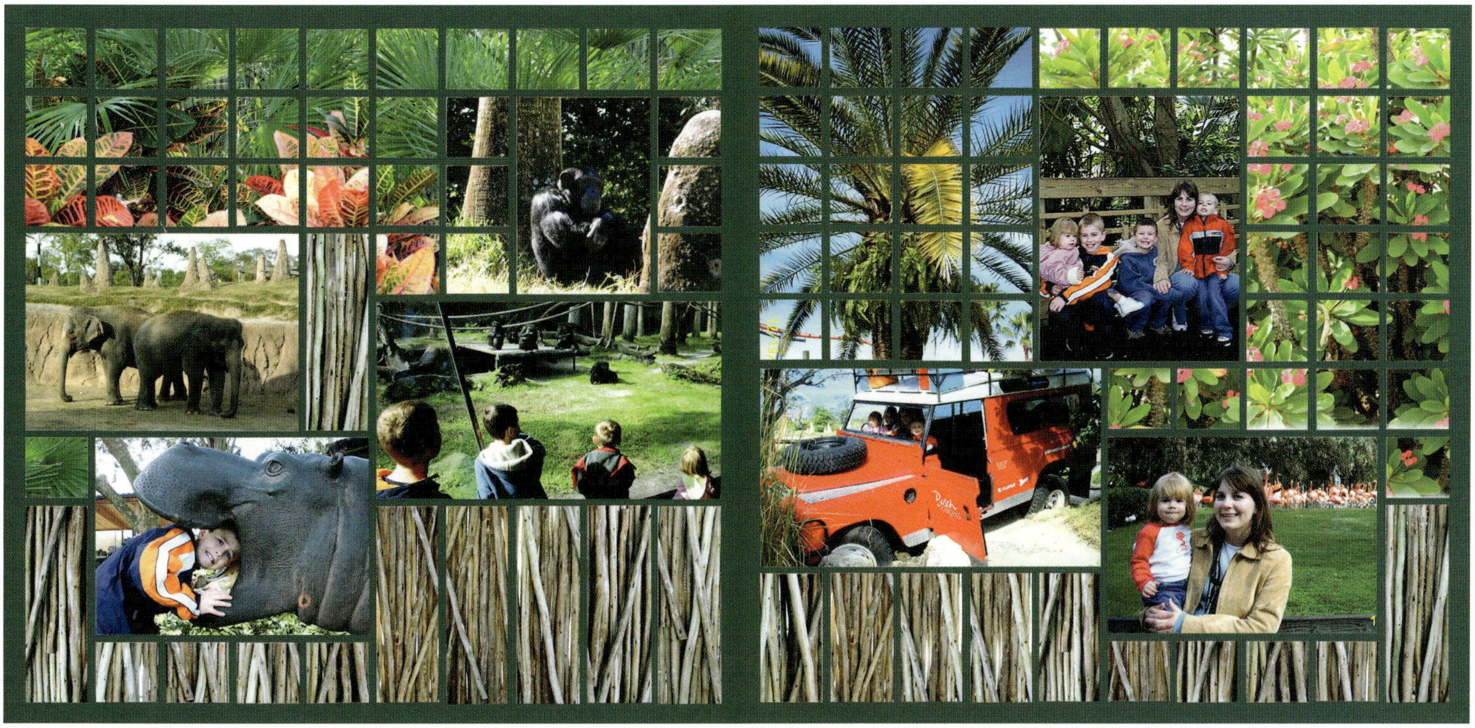

Busch Gardens Tampa: Tami Potter
photos: Shannon Johnson
number of photos: 11

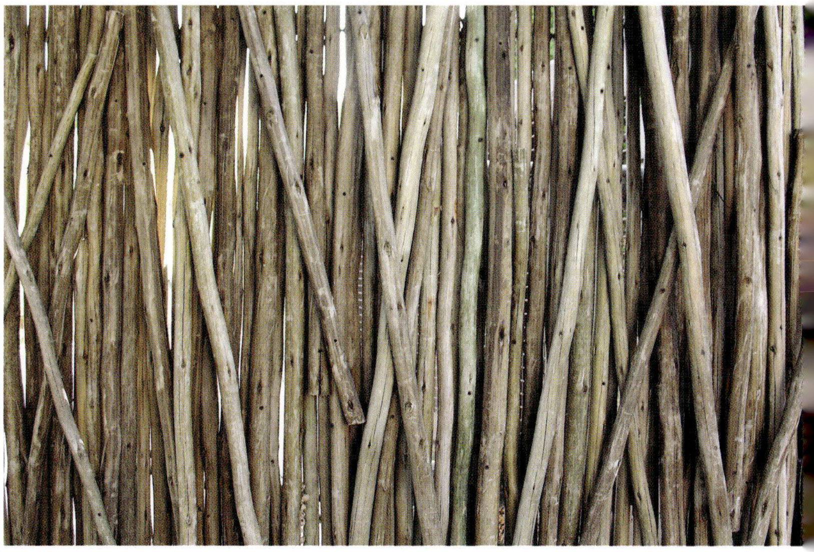

■ Tip

Surrounding larger photo blocks with smaller photo mosaic tiles creates a framing effect that brings added focus to the larger block.

In the Washington Rocky Shore page, pictured left, close up shots are embedded in a mosaic made from photographs of rocks. The rock photos add detail and help to highlight the larger photo blocks while filling in the space.

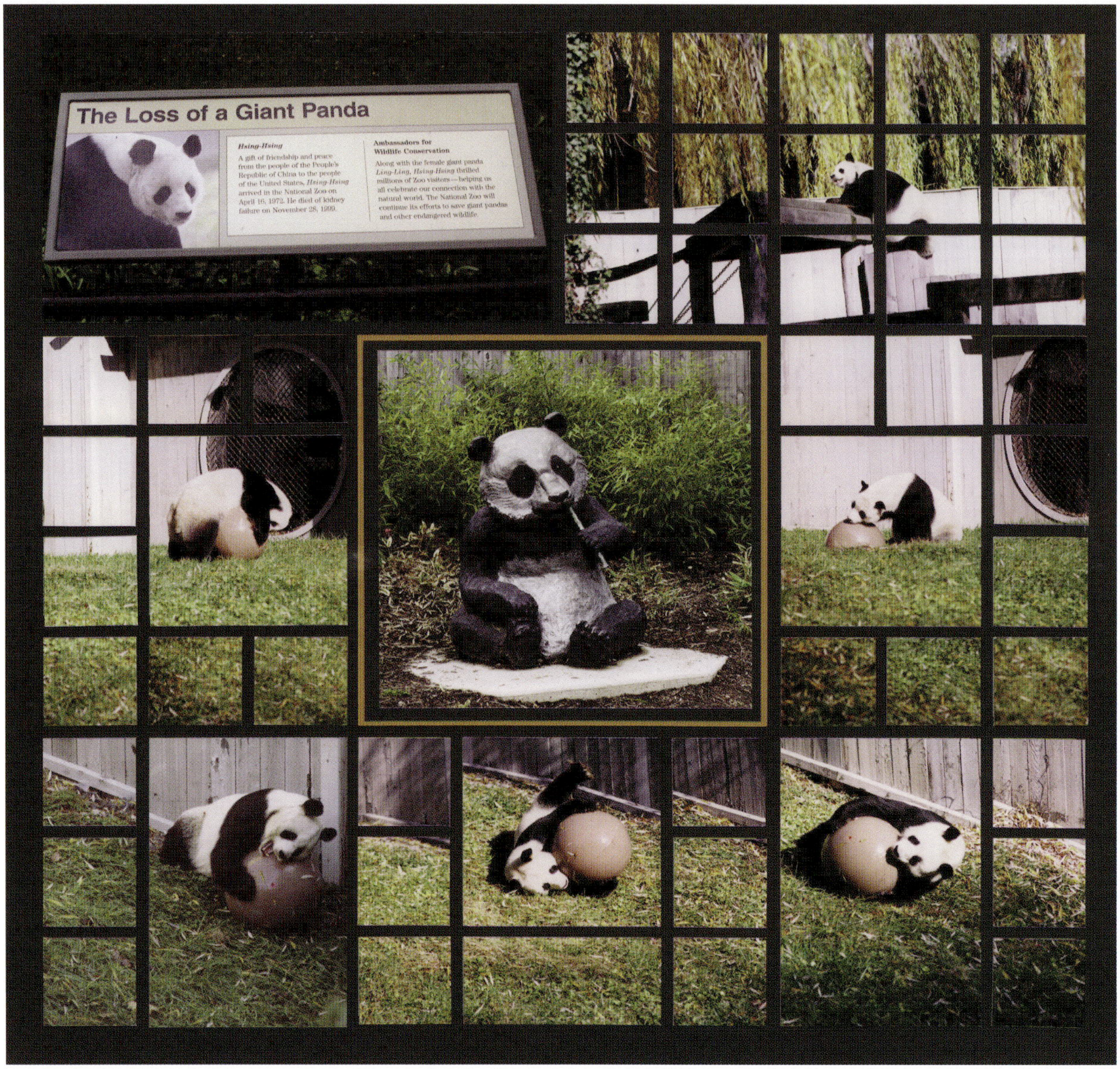

Giant Panda: Tami Potter
number of photos: 8

Looking for Signs

Sometimes, when we are lucky, someone has written just what we want to say on a sign - take a picture! Even if you do not use the photograph of the sign on your scrapbook page, it might be a great reference for your journaling.

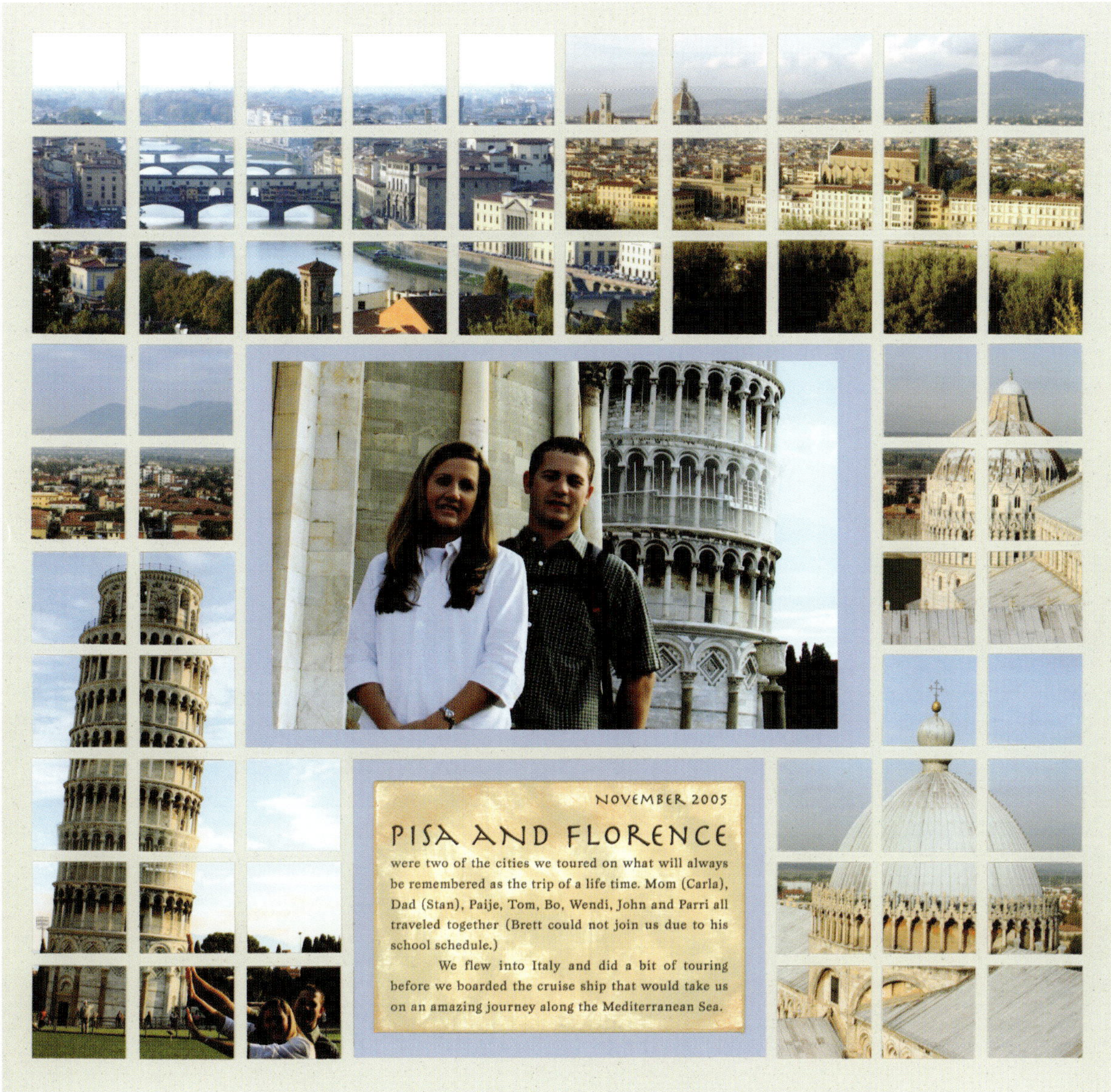

Pisa and Florence: Tami Potter
photos: Stan Palmer
number of photos: 6

Architectural Structures

Buildings, gates, fences, bridges, railing, piers - many man-made structures are the focus of our attention. However, though they are often photographed, they are frequently left in storage boxes to make way for those more important "people" shots. Try filling the space around the faces with those brilliant structure shots. After all, aren't they part of the reason you traveled all the way to Italy?

Detailing your life - what surrounds you?

I was at a convention giving mosaic demonstrations using the photos seen in the pages below. A woman asked, "What does a photo of people on a ferry have to do with fruits and vegetables at a market?" I had to laugh. Until then, it hadn't occurred to me that it might seem like an odd combination.

Each page has it's own unique story. This story is about a family who rode a ferry to Seattle to go to the public market. After visiting the market, they drove home and caught a fabulous view of Mount Rainier along their way.

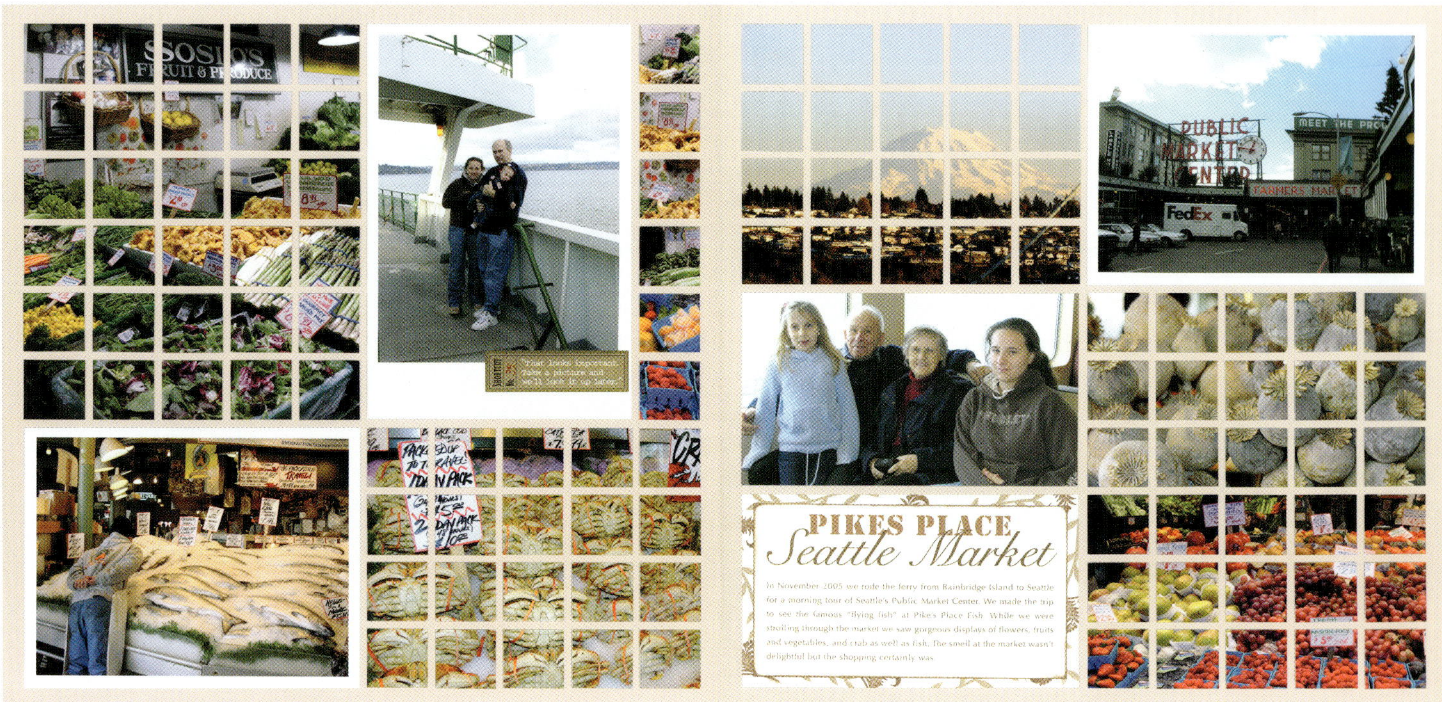

Photographic details make great photo mosaics; so, if you are photographing a sport, don't forget to focus on the sidelines. Take photos of balls and gear: a row of helmets waiting to be worn. Taking a trip? Photograph your camping gear, beachballs, or road trip "survival supplies." While you are at the pool, take pictures of the pool toys, a row of lounge chairs, decorative pool tiles and accessories. Snap the long distance shots to get the full view and then get in close to capture the details.

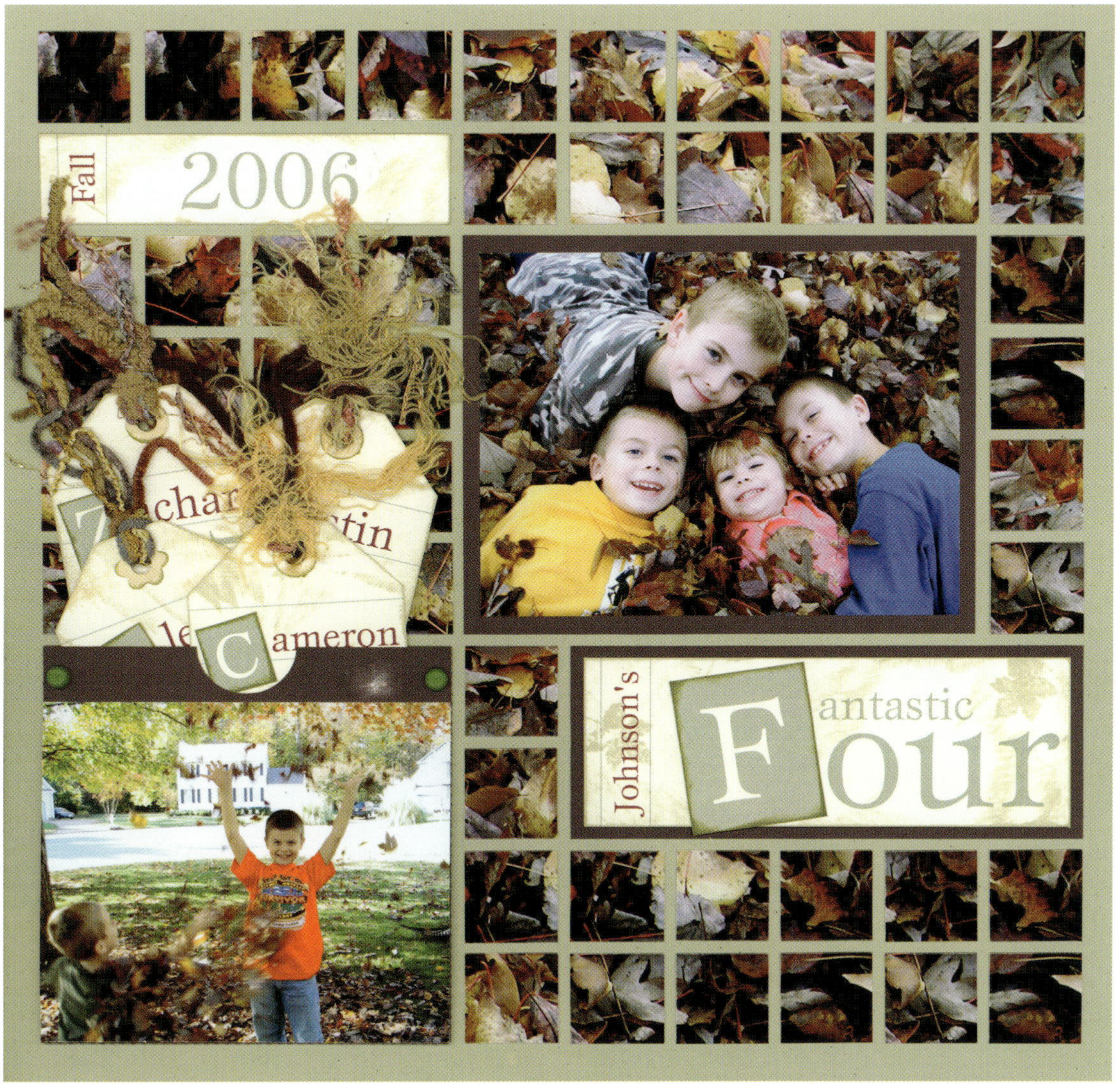

Fantastic Four: Tami Potter
photos: Shannon Johnson
number of photos: 5

A Closer Look

Need an embellishment to fill your page? Look for interesting elements in the photos you've taken. This page included five photos total - two originals and three duplicates of the leaf image - a blown up view of the top corner, as shown to the right.

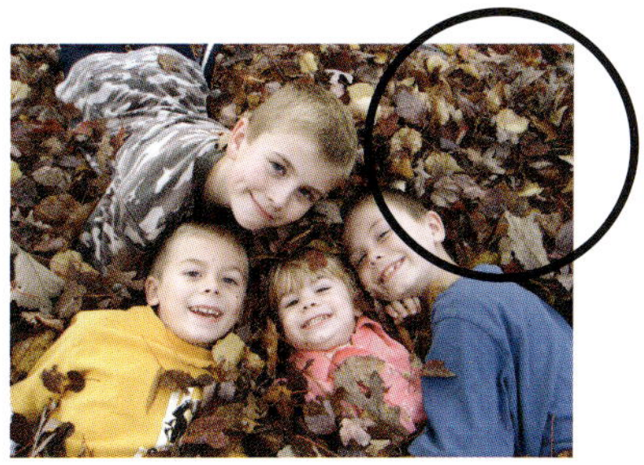

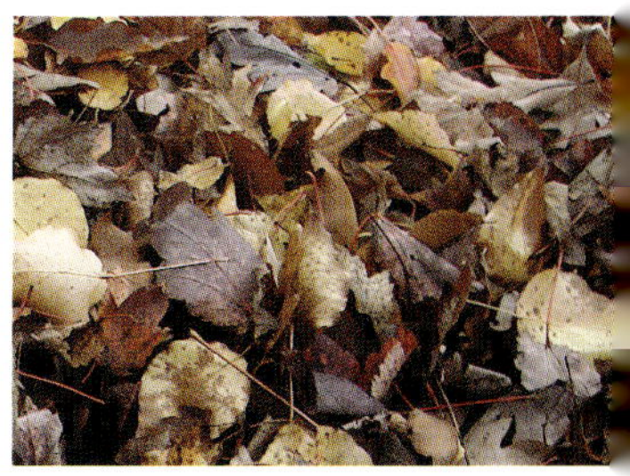

The top corner of this photo became the leaf detail shown in the page above.

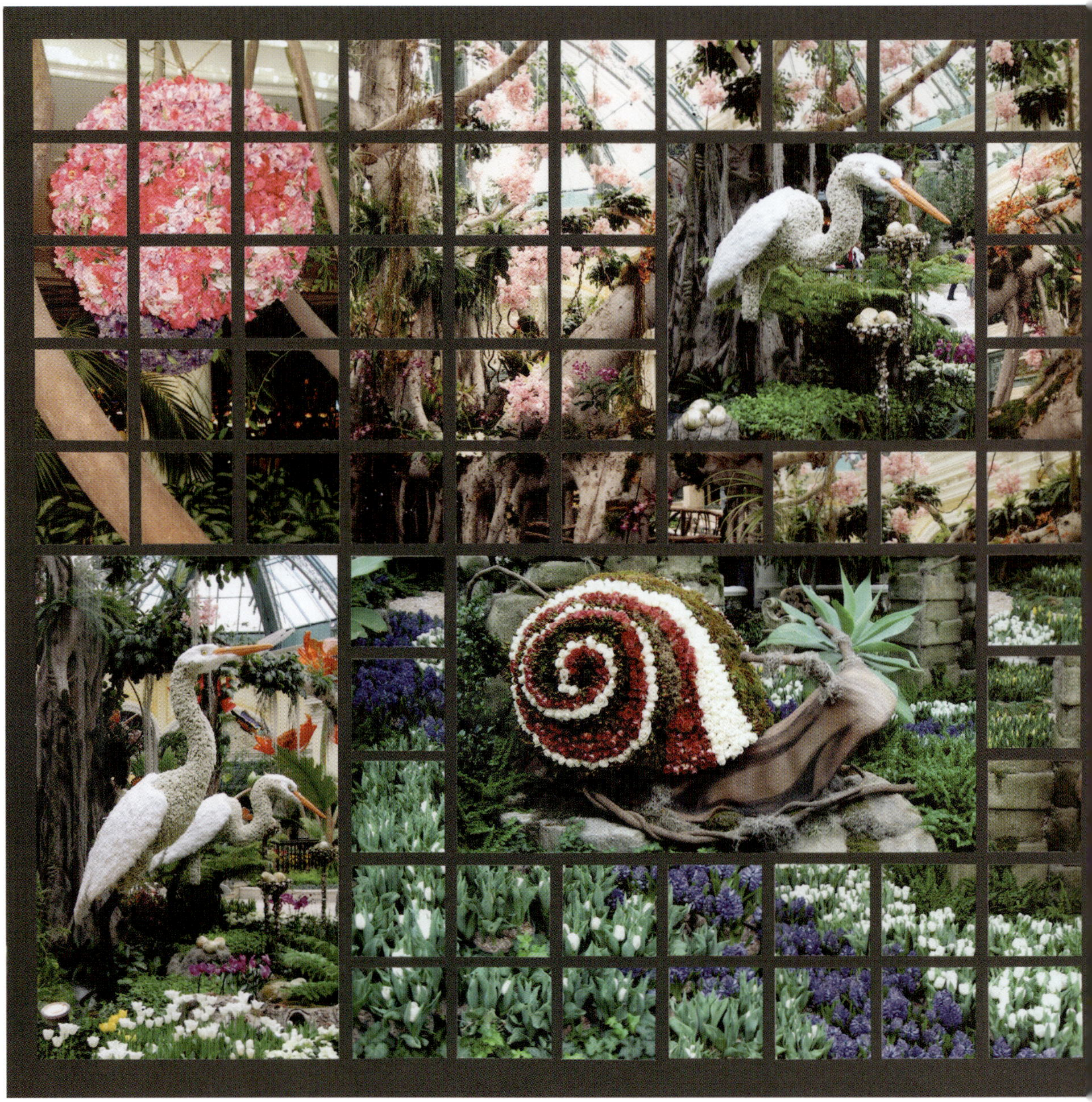

Color & Composition

These photographs of floral arrangements offer a symphony of color and texture to be explored. With such vibrant colors and so much going on, it is important to give the viewer direction.

The triangle, as a compositional tool, is evident in the work of the old masters. Creating groups of three focal points provides the artist/designer with a method for moving the viewer's attention through the artwork. The eyes are drawn and cannot help from moving between those points. In the spread above, notice how the three white birds make a triangle. Another group of three can be seen in the correlation between the snail, lady bug, and frog.

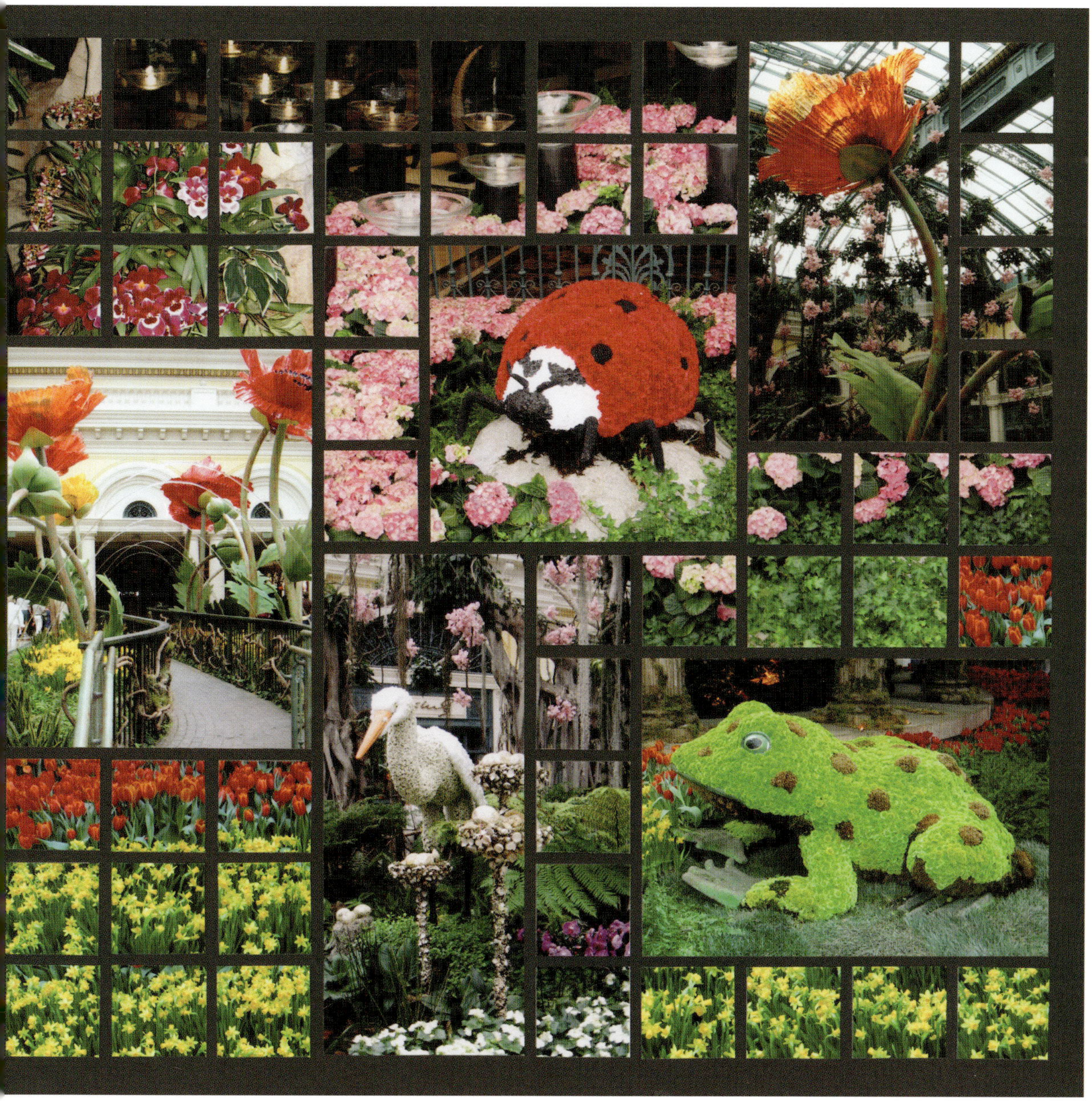

Bellagio Botanical: Jaime Zenger and Tami Potter
photos: Jaime Zenger
number of photos: 14

- **Turn the focus inward.** Notice that the floral characters (i.e. the snail and the frog) face into the center of the page - not off the page. It keeps the viewer inside the artwork discovering the things they haven't yet noticed.

- **Color can move the eye** along or stop it cold. Notice how the lady bug and the red tulips create a triangular flow on the right hand page leading your eye down, across the page, and back up to greet the lady bug again.

- **Embedding larger photo blocks** into sections of photos cut into 1x1 inch squares creates multiple layers of interest.

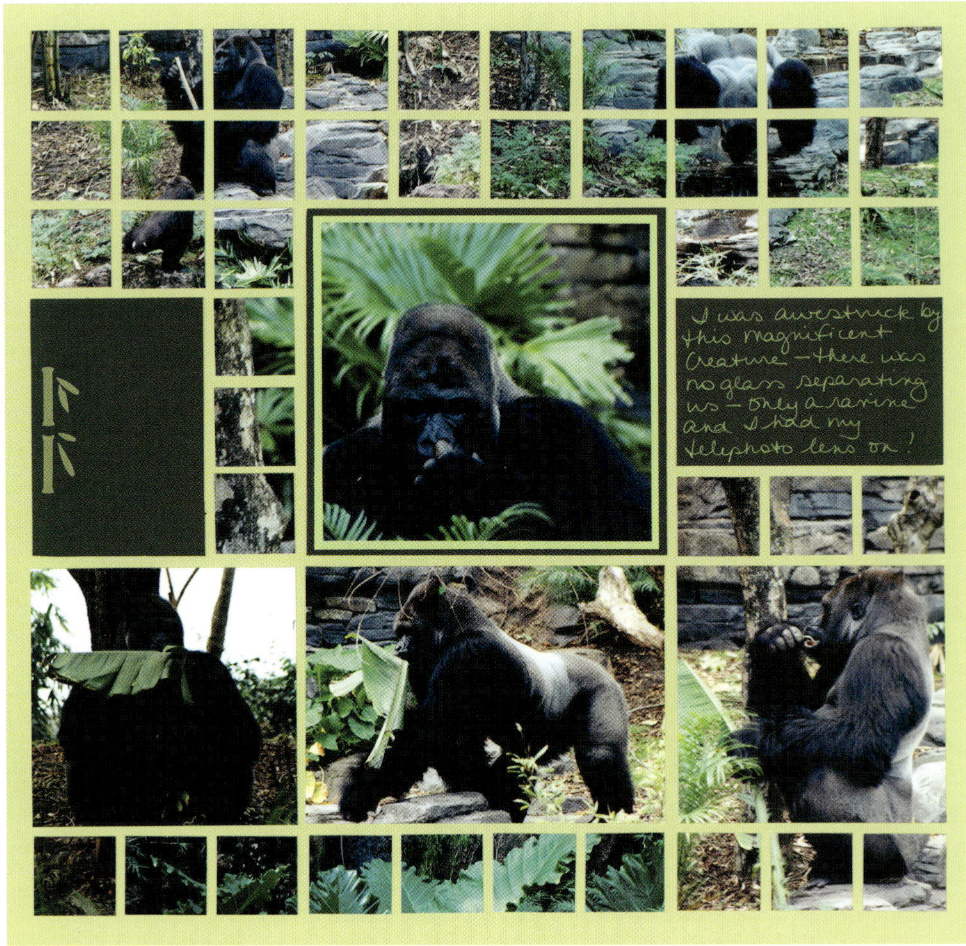

Gorilla: Angela Andrews
number of photos: 6

Norfolk Botanical: Sandi Keene
number of photos: 6

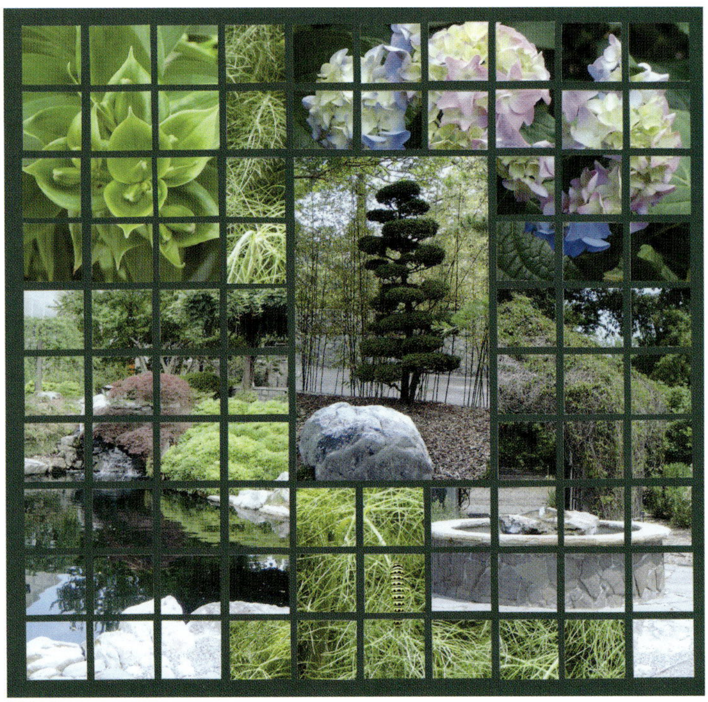

Gestalt

There are many things that capture our attention when we are looking through the view finder of a camera. Some of my favorite subjects to photograph are far from human. Flowers don't blink or smirk at me. Mountains can stand still for hours.

Taking photographs allows us to see a subject from several angles at the same time or bring together things that are located in different places.

Photos of buildings, animals, scenery, or inanimate objects might seem dull or uninteresting when they are individually mounted in an album. However, when several photographs are used to create a photo mosaic, the image as a whole becomes greater than the sum of its parts.

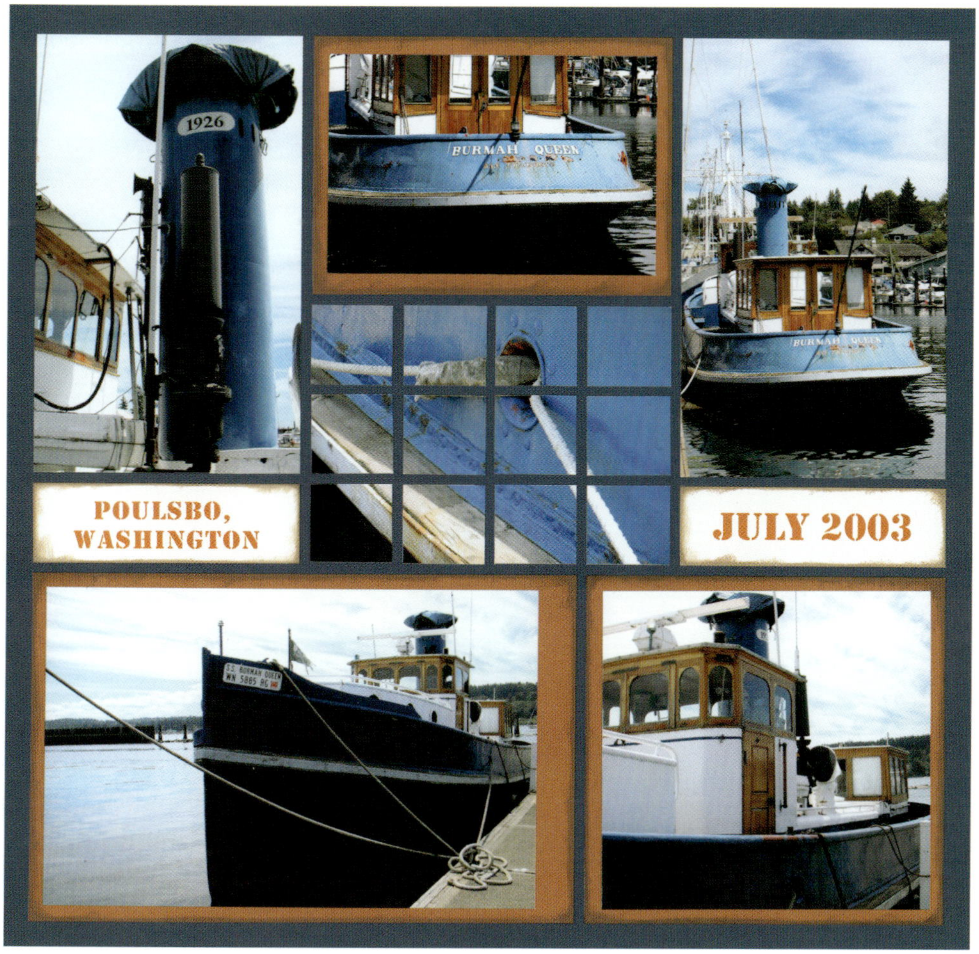

Burma Queen: Tami Potter
number of photos: 6

Love at Home: Tami Potter
number of photos: 7

Cape Hatteras: Tami Potter
number of photos: 6

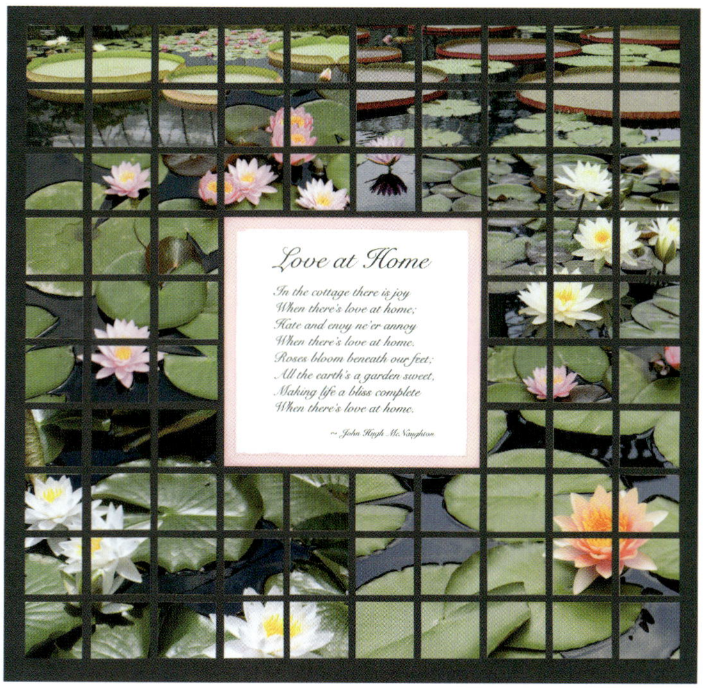

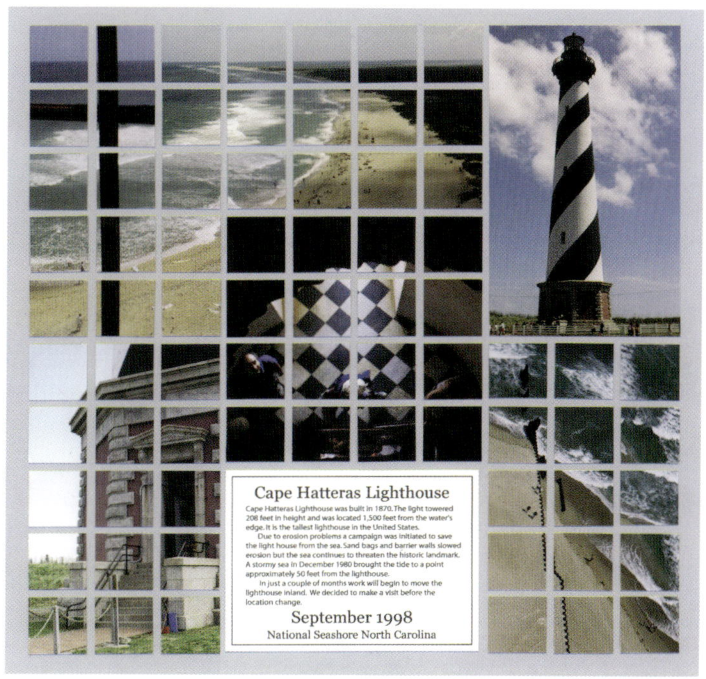

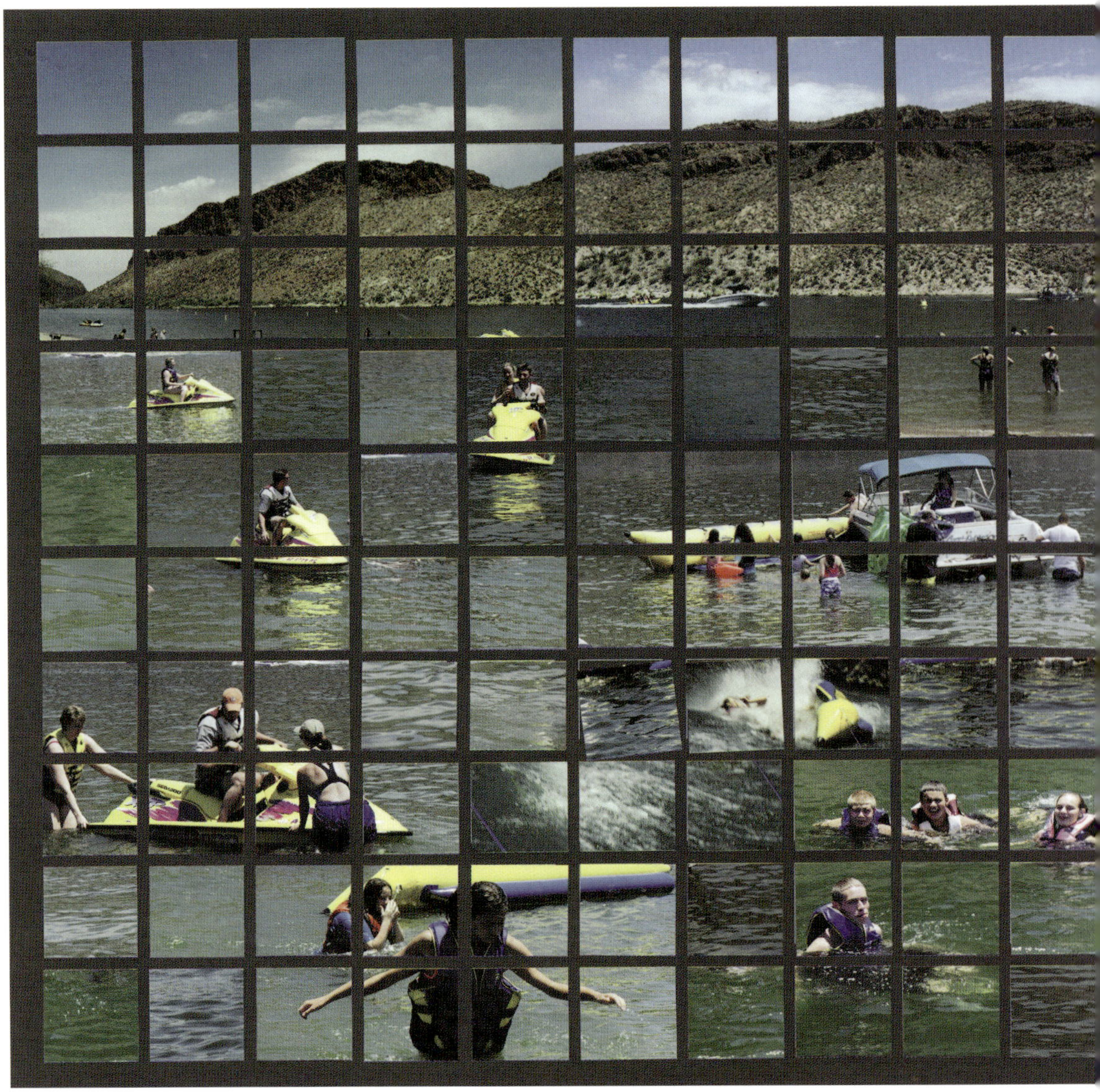

One Big Picture

No, this isn't really one big picture. However, at first glance, it looks like one. Accomplishing this photo mosaic effect is easy; it takes just a bit of planning in advance. To make your page look like it came from a blown up photograph, you need to establish a horizon line. You can create a horizon for your page by taking 4-5 landscape view photos in a horizontal line (like the photos of hills shown in the spread above.) Your digital camera may have a panoramic function to help you keep everything lined up as you click, click, click. If you do not have a panoramic function, do not fret. You can always make adjustments later. (See page 52-53) for more information on mending horizons.

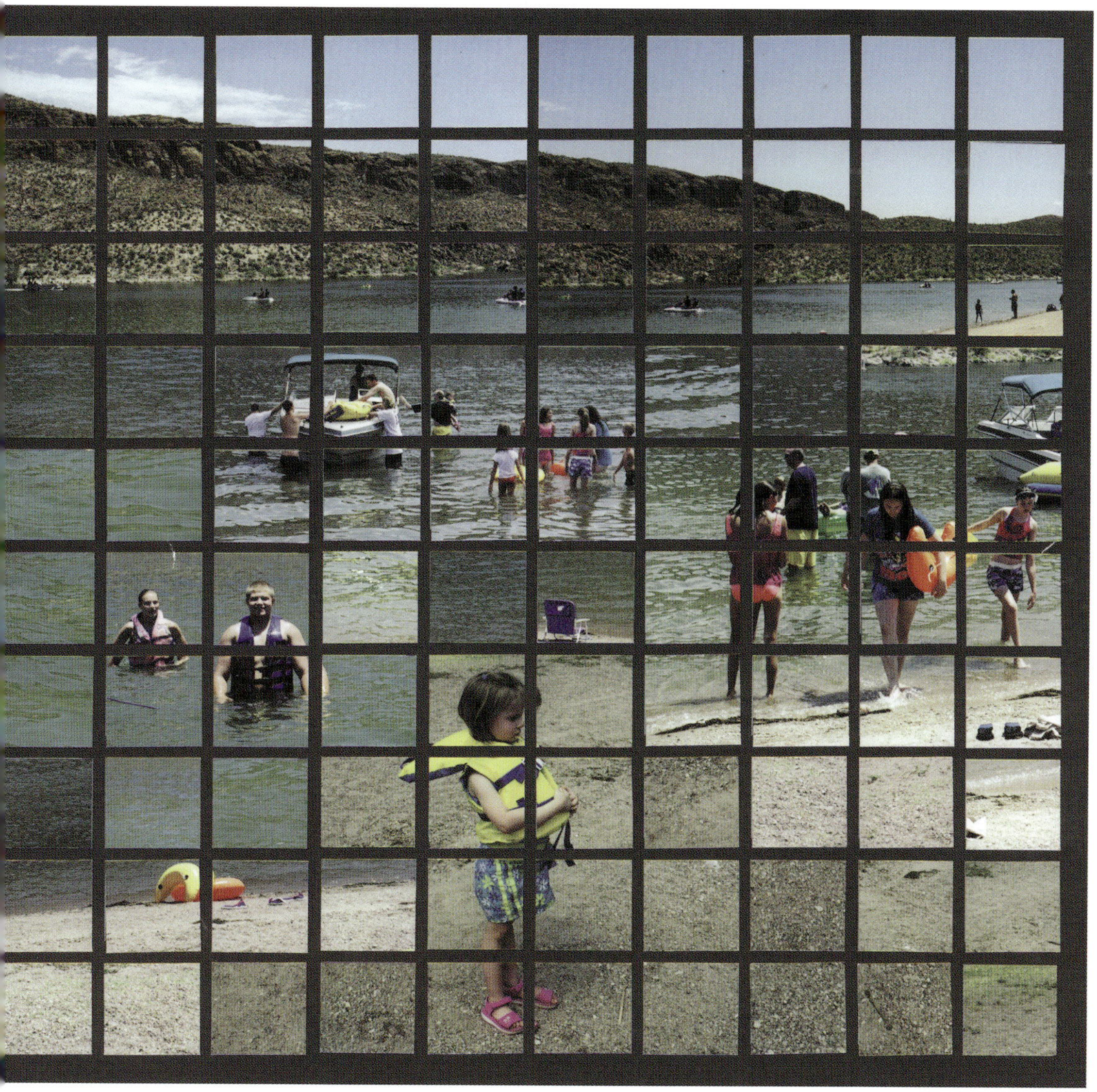

Arizona Lake: Tami Potter
number of photos: 20

■ Tip

Saving excess pieces of sky, water, grass, sand, etc., will help fill in gaps between photos.

Making One Big Picture

- **Photograph a series of landscape view photos.**
- **Cut landscape shots into one inch pieces and establish a horizon line** across the top of your page. Use the grid lines on your cutting mat to make corrective adjustments *before* you begin cutting.
- **Cut additional photos into one inch squares** and arrange them on the page with the close up shots in the foreground (toward bottom of the page) and the more distant shots near the horizon (top of page).
- **To obtain a blended look intermingle pieces from multiple photos.**

Blending Basics

As you are looking through your camera's view finder, pay attention to the location of the horizon line. Taking photos without an obvious horizon makes it easy to blend several photos together to give them that "one big picture" look. Try taking some of your photos from a higher angle. Surround the subject with water, grass, sand, or wildflowers.

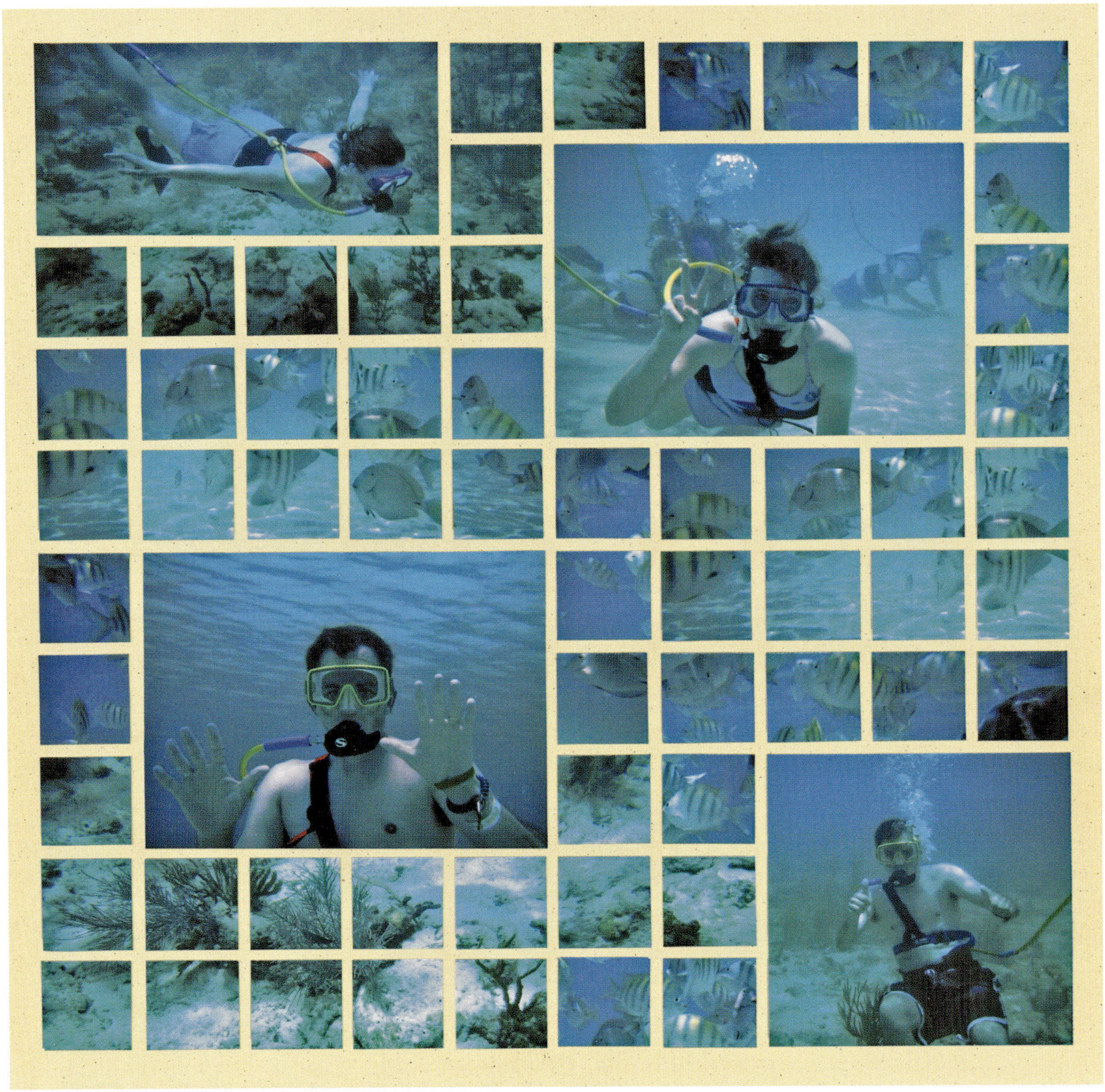

Underwater: Shannon Johnson
number of photos: 6

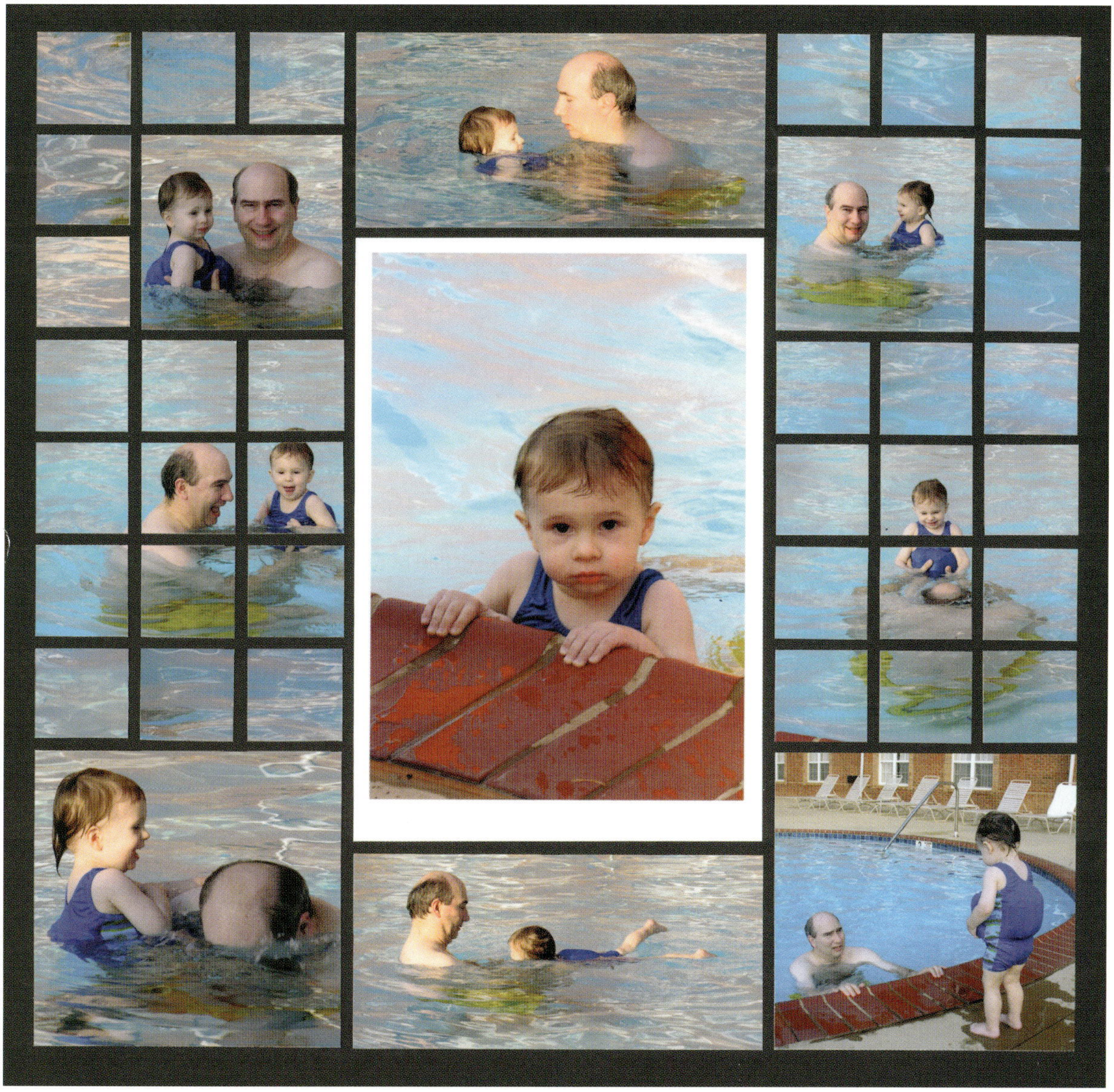

First Pool Time: Tami Potter
number of photos: 9

In the example shown above, compare the photograph in the lower right corner to the rest of the photos shown. Shooting the photos from an angle that surrounded the subjects with water, was an essential forethought to creating continuity between the photos on this page. Consider how different it would look if every photo taken had shown the building, furniture, and pool edge.

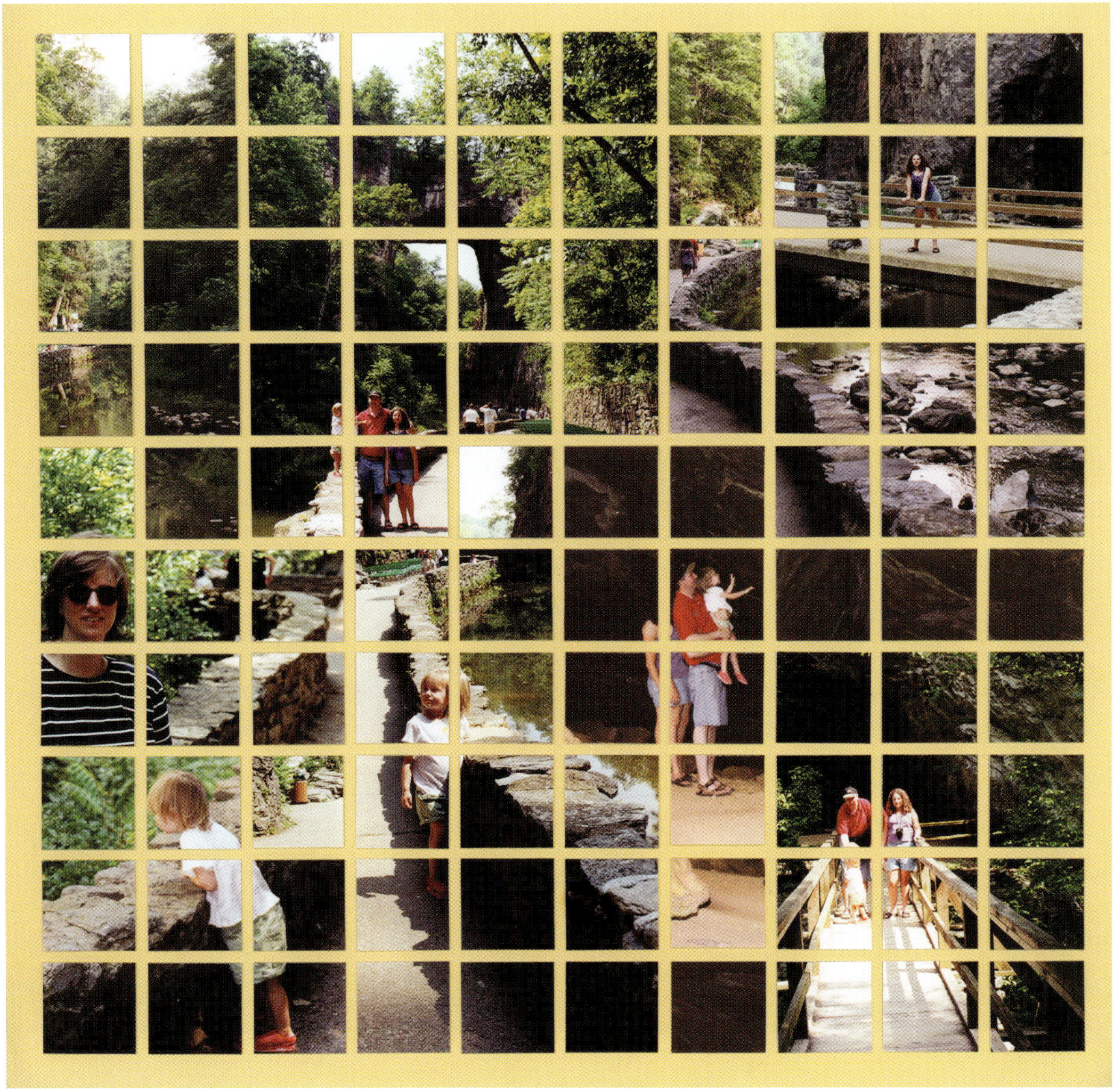

Natural Bridge: Tami Potter
number of photos: 9

Complex Blending

During the photo mosaic process, capturing the essence of a national historic site or scenic treasure becomes a puzzle-like game. Choosing the photographs, deciding where to make cuts, which pieces to retain, and which to set aside, makes each photo mosaic a unique creative experience. In the sample shown above, a blended effect was accomplished through thoughtful positioning of color, texture, and lighting.

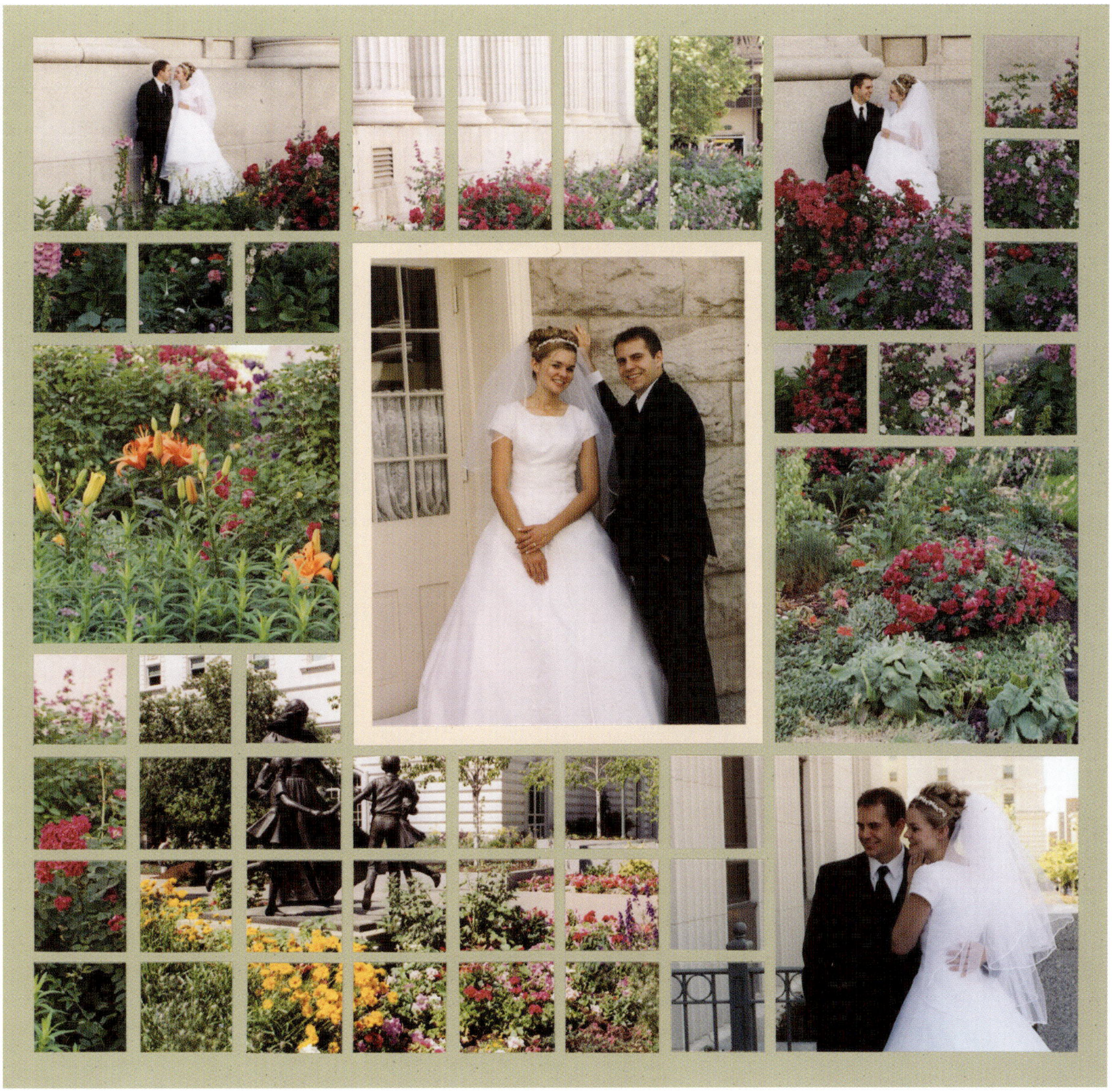

Moon Wedding: Tami Potter
number of photos: 8

Successful Blending

It is easier to blend photos that have something in common. It may be a similar subject, similar colors, or similar lighting that brings the photos together. In the page above, blending is successful thanks to similar lighting and color balance. Notice how bright flowers and the dark statue bring balance to the page.

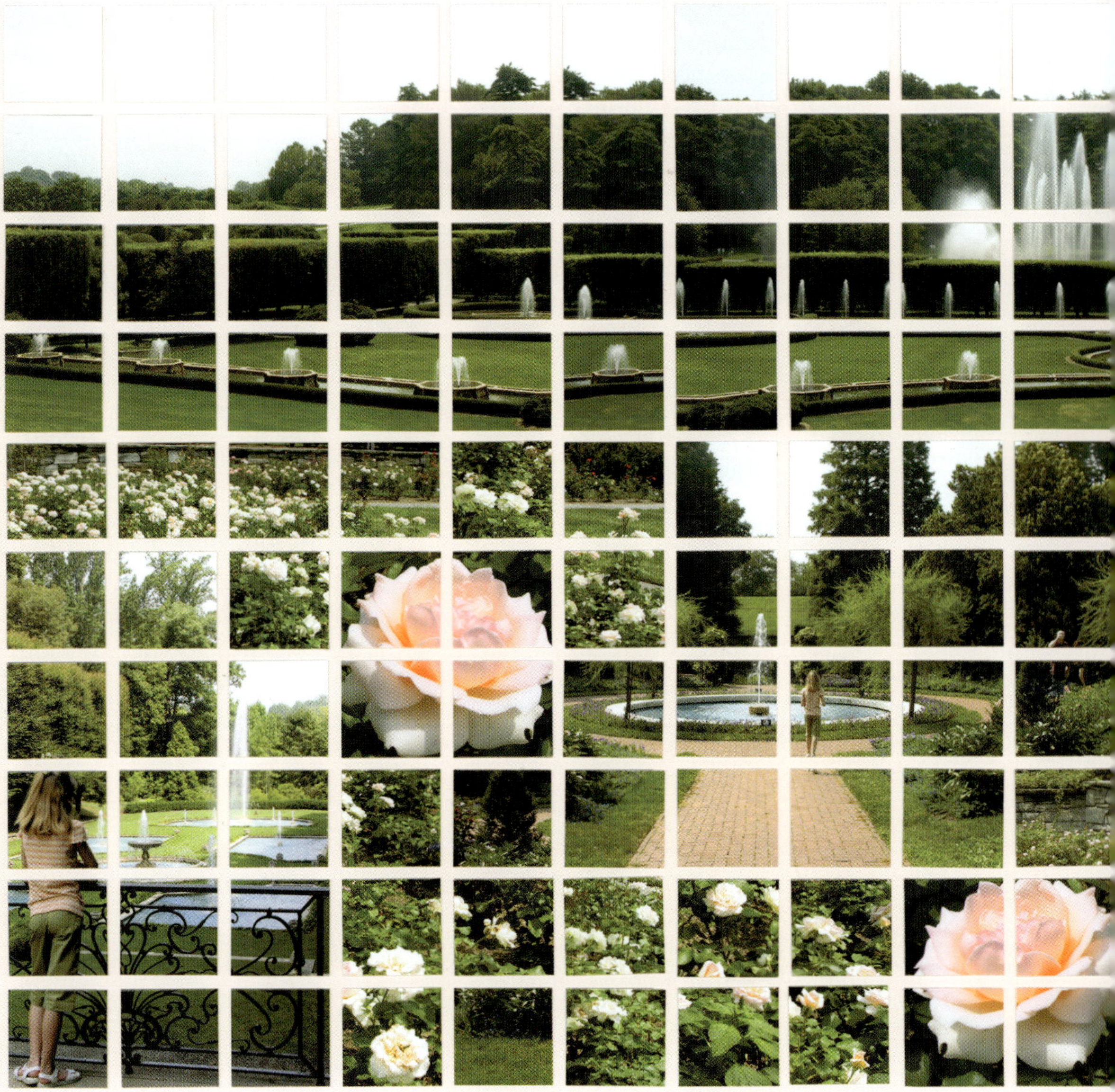

Perfect Anyway

When I took these pictures, I knew that I would make a mosaic out of them. The grand scale of the fountains called out to my mosaic sensibilities. As I gazed upon the endless views of green grass and beautiful blushing roses, in my mind they were already cropped into tiny squares, before I ever snapped the first photo.

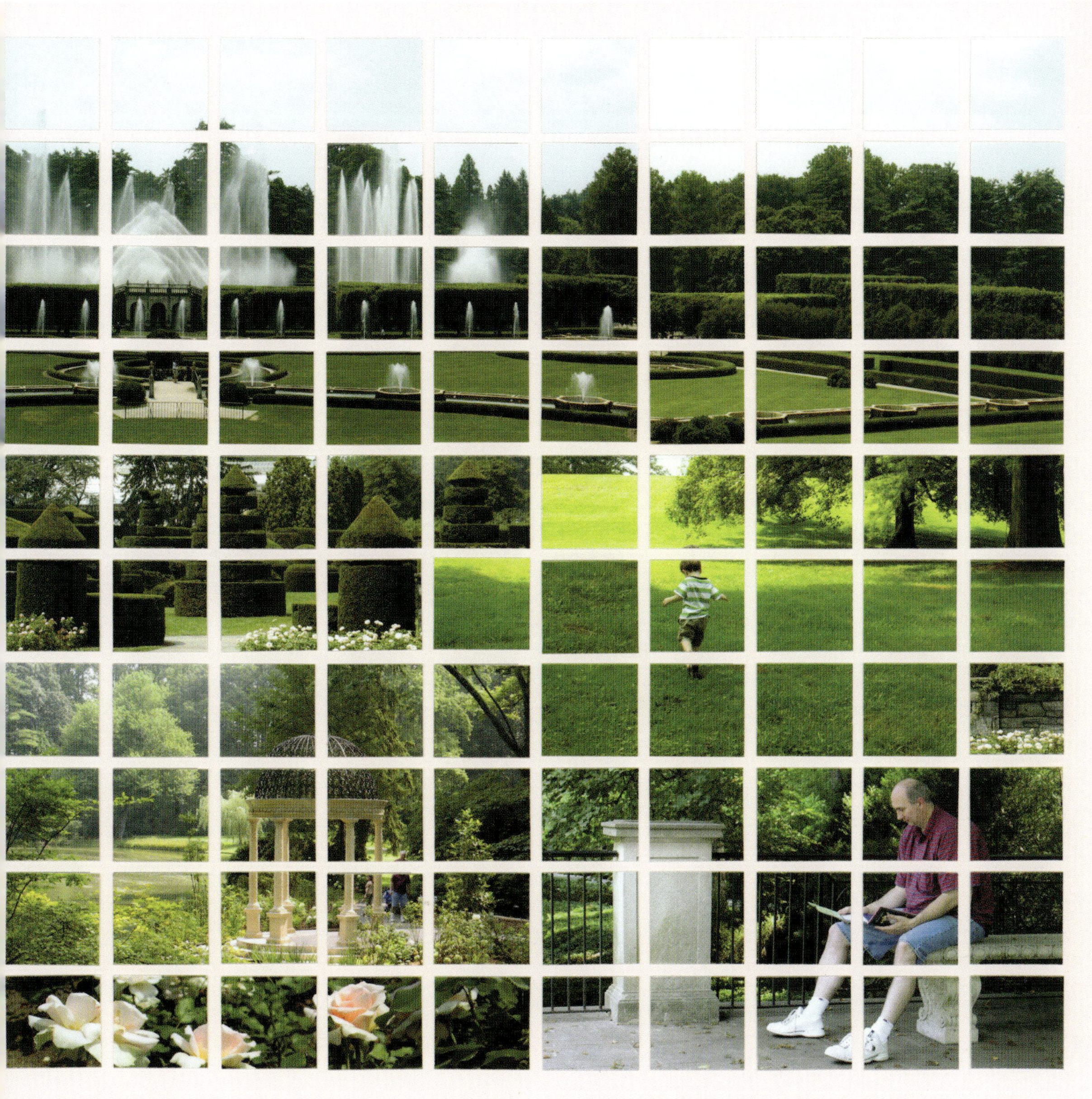

Longwood Gardens: Tami Potter
number of photos: 13

In my mind, everything works out perfectly. My baby boy will fit just right in the squares, the fountains will be centered on the page and I will have room for a little of everything seen in the garden. When I print my photos, I often discover that life isn't always perfect. Even though some elements in the photos are not exactly as I imagined, put together in mosaic form they are perfectly exquisite!

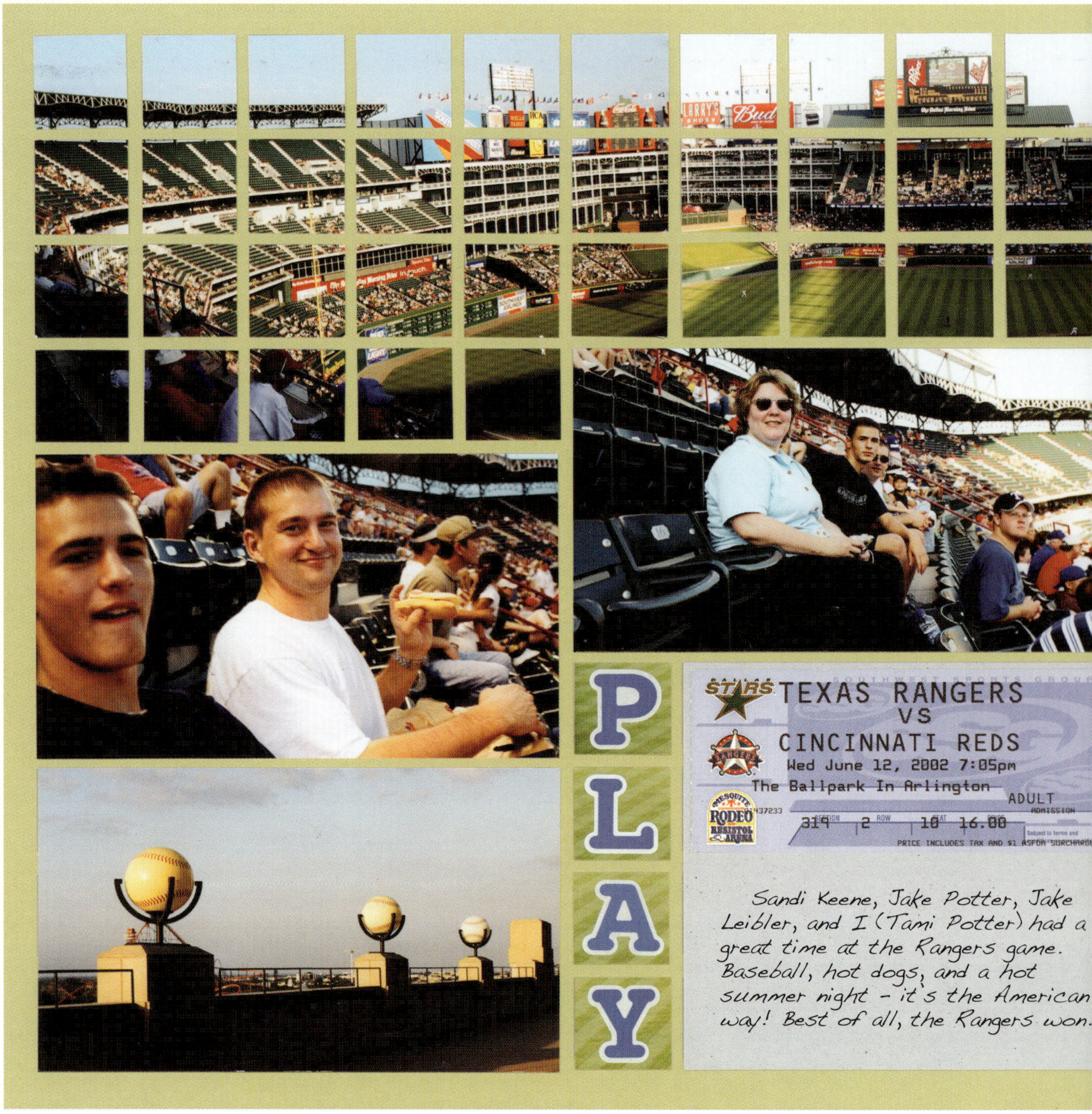

Grand Standing

As exciting as it is to watch a baseball game, capturing the scope of this beautiful stadium on film was on my mind from the minute I sat in my seat. With four consecutive snaps I preserved the grand view.

Excess photo pieces of grass were used to fill the squares behind stickers that spell out P-L-A-Y and B-A-L-L. A photo taken after dark was placed behind the laser cut "Texas Rangers" symbol. A game ticket was saved and placed at the top of a journaling square to offer game information. Additional photos were placed in a

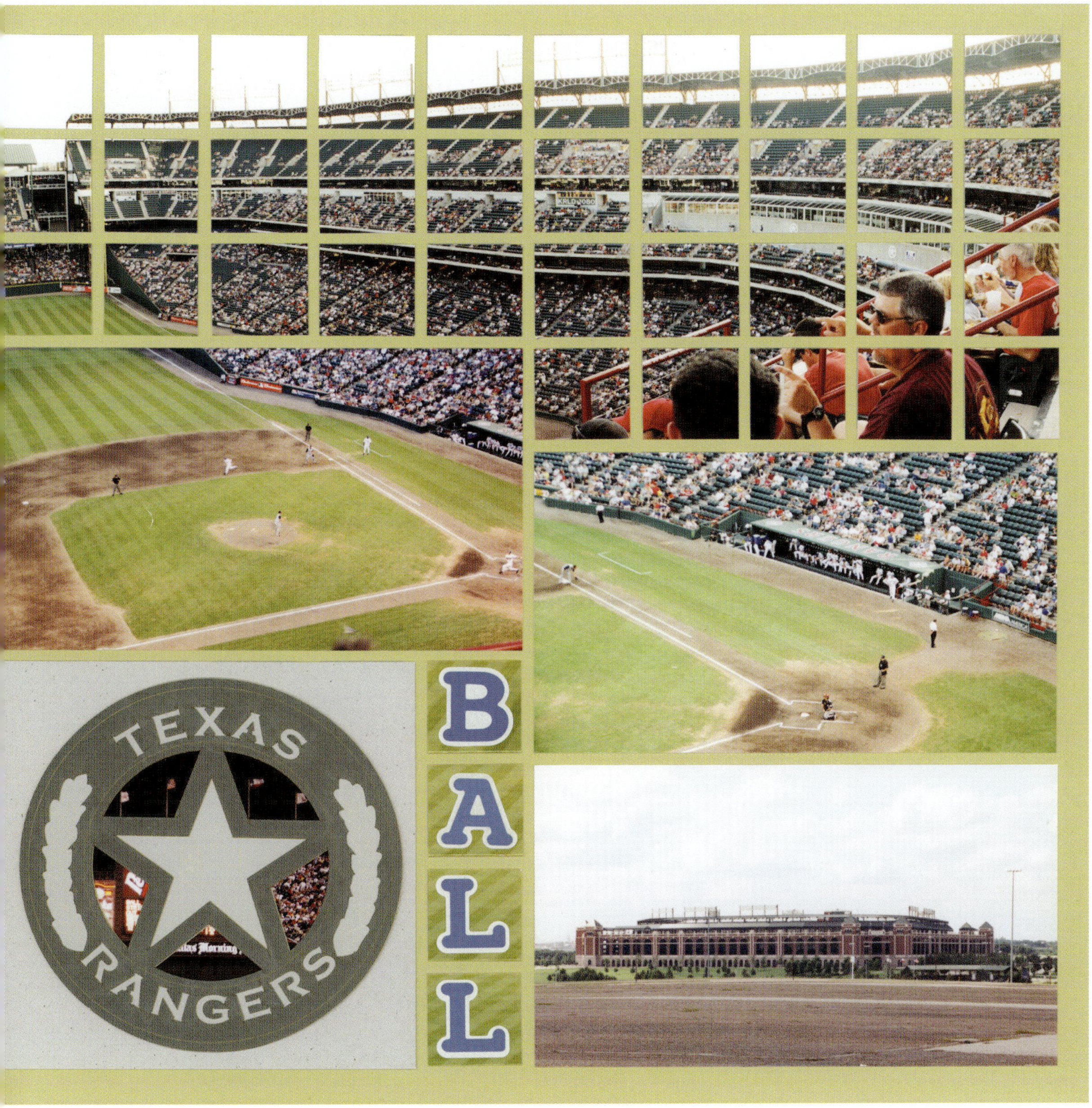

Play Ball: Tami Potter
number of photos: 11

symmetrical pattern below the mosaic border. Remembering the friends who attended, as well as the fantastic architectural details of the stadium (see the baseball shaped light fixtures pictured in the bottom left corner), is as important as remembering the great summer view.

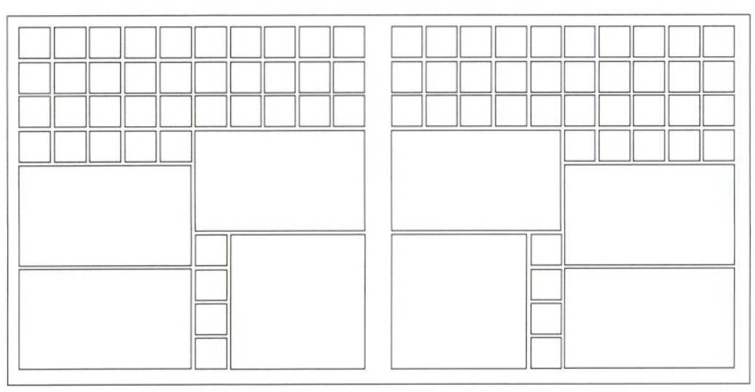

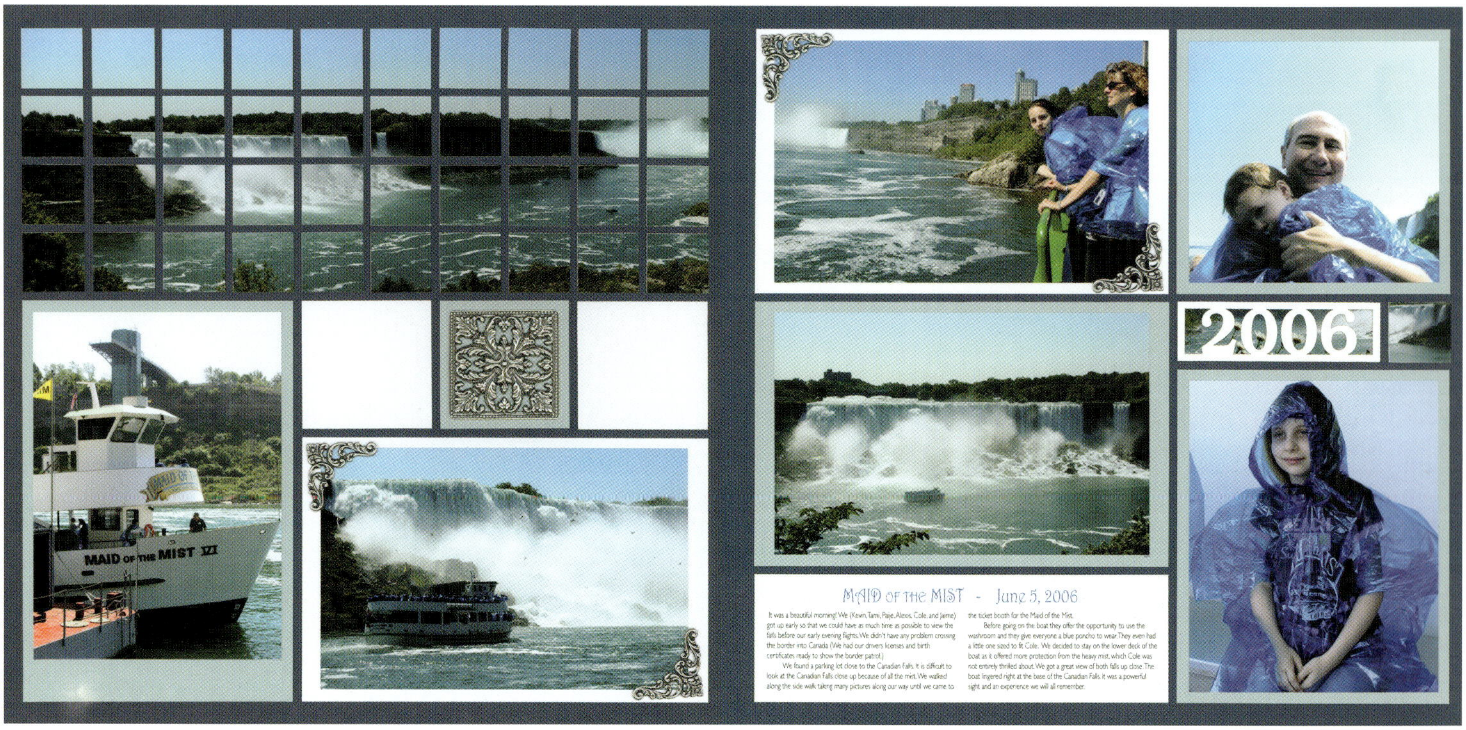

Maid of the Mist: Tami Potter
number of photos: 8

Capturing the View : Niagara

Gazing upon the wonders of nature is a favorite past time of many people throughout the world. I haven't found a better way to capture mother nature's work (via snapshots) than by turning those snapshots into photo mosaics.

I took so many pictures while visiting Niagara Falls, that I decided to focus on one subject at a time. This spread focused on the Maid of the Mist boat ride tour.

The spread above is designed with a mosaic border that leads the viewer across the page margins to a large photo on the opposite page. A tiny photograph of the falls in the distance was mounted behind the laser cut year for a little added interest. A few fancy metal embellishments were added to evoke the romantic nature of the falls and the story of the Maid of the Mist.

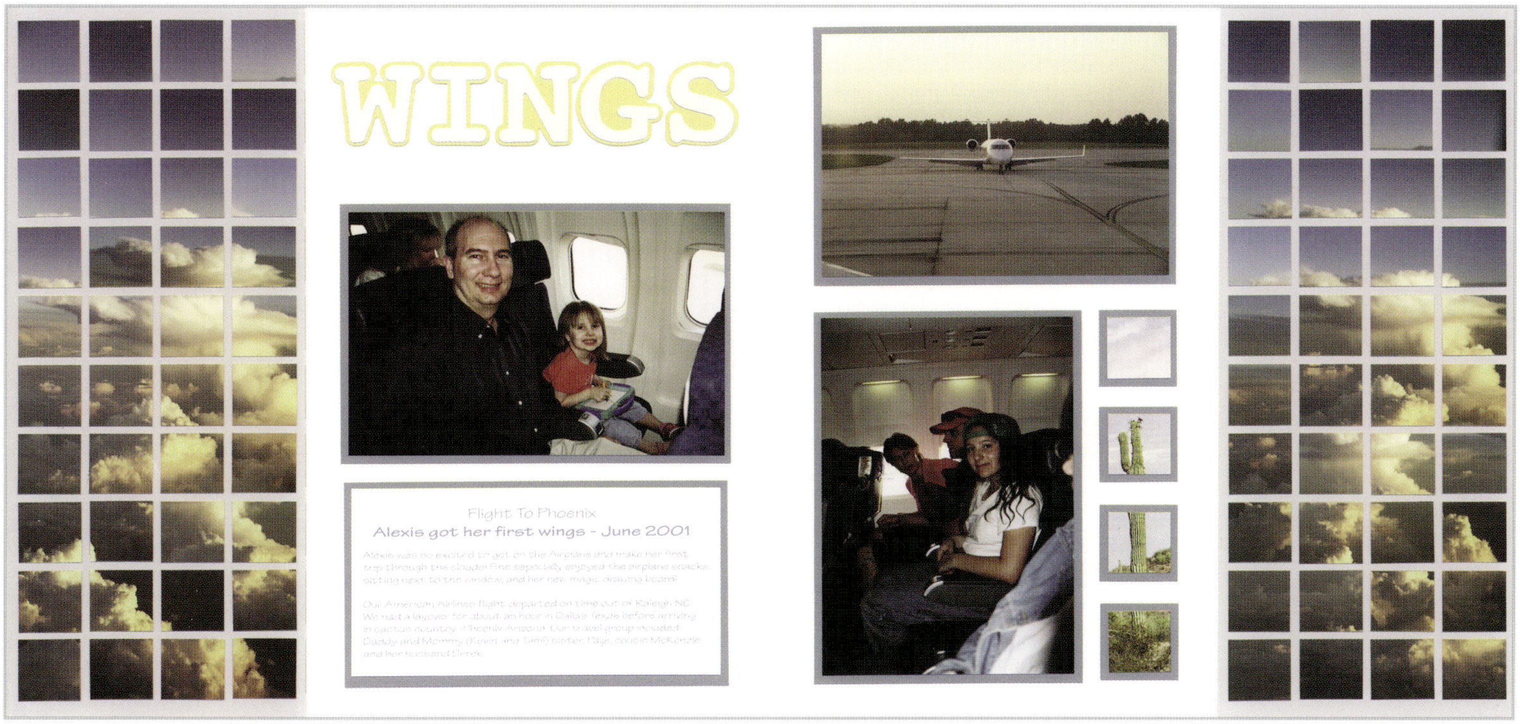

Wings: Tami Potter
photos: Kevin Potter
number of photos: 9-10

Capturing the View : In flight

Have you ever taken a picture of a beautiful sunset and then sighed with disappointment when the dramatic vision you remembered came back from the developer?

By using several photographs to build a border, you can recapture the essence of the view you remember.

Four to six cloud photos were used to create the photo mosaic borders. Photos were cut into one inch squares and placed onto Mosaic Moments™ Grid Paper. The grid paper was trimmed to include a 1/8 inch edge and mounted onto 12x12 cardstock sheets.

1x1 inch "stacked" cactus photo blocks were mounted on cardstock cut with a 1/8 inch border. The blocks filled an awkward gap on the page and added additional information and meaning to the layout.

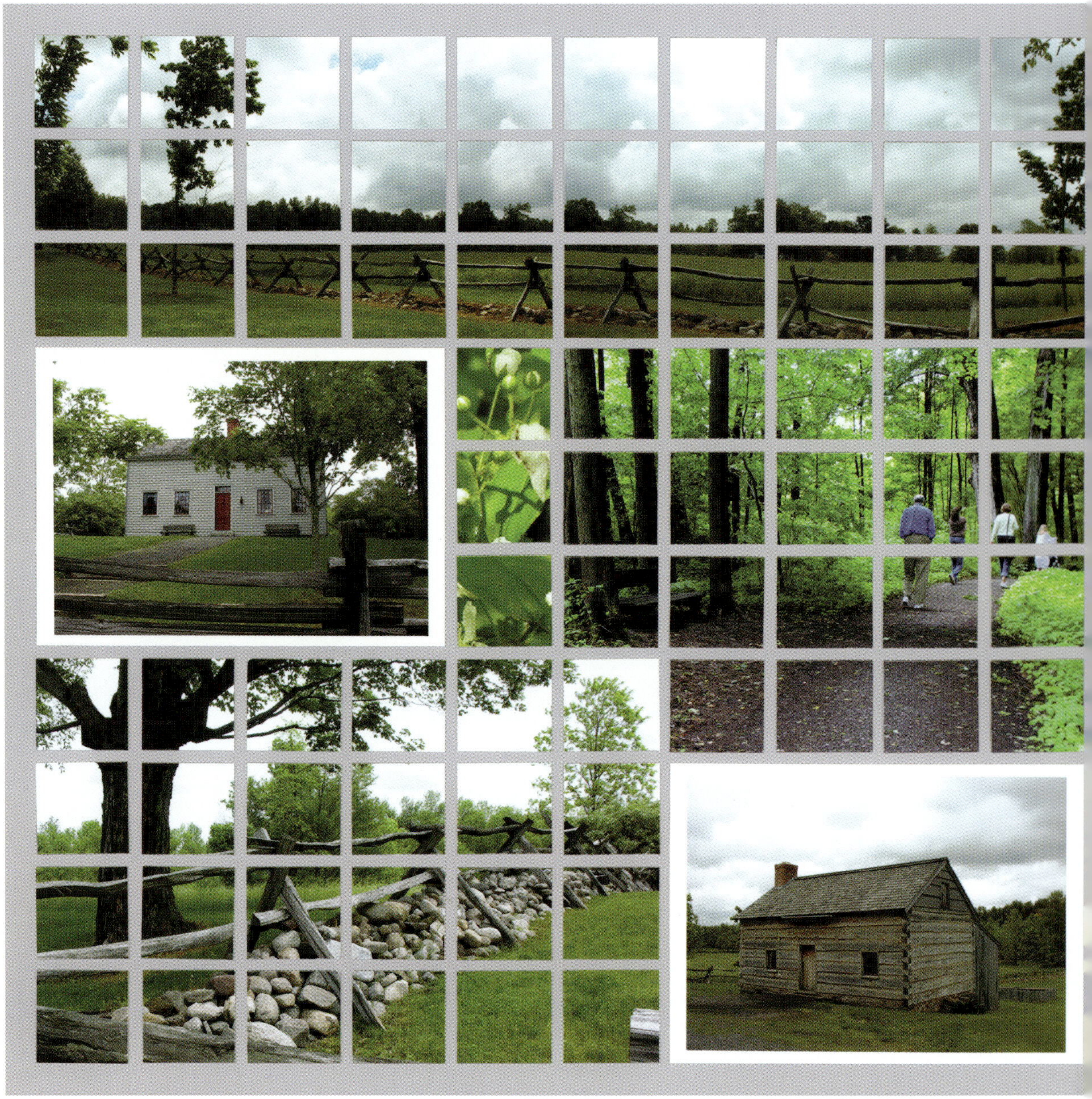

Creating Multiple Areas of Interest

Multiple focal points are established across this two page photo mosaic by leaving specific photos uncut. Matting the photos worked to further emphasize them as points of focus.

A strong angular line is created by the contrast between grass and rocks in the lower left photo which leads the viewer into the center

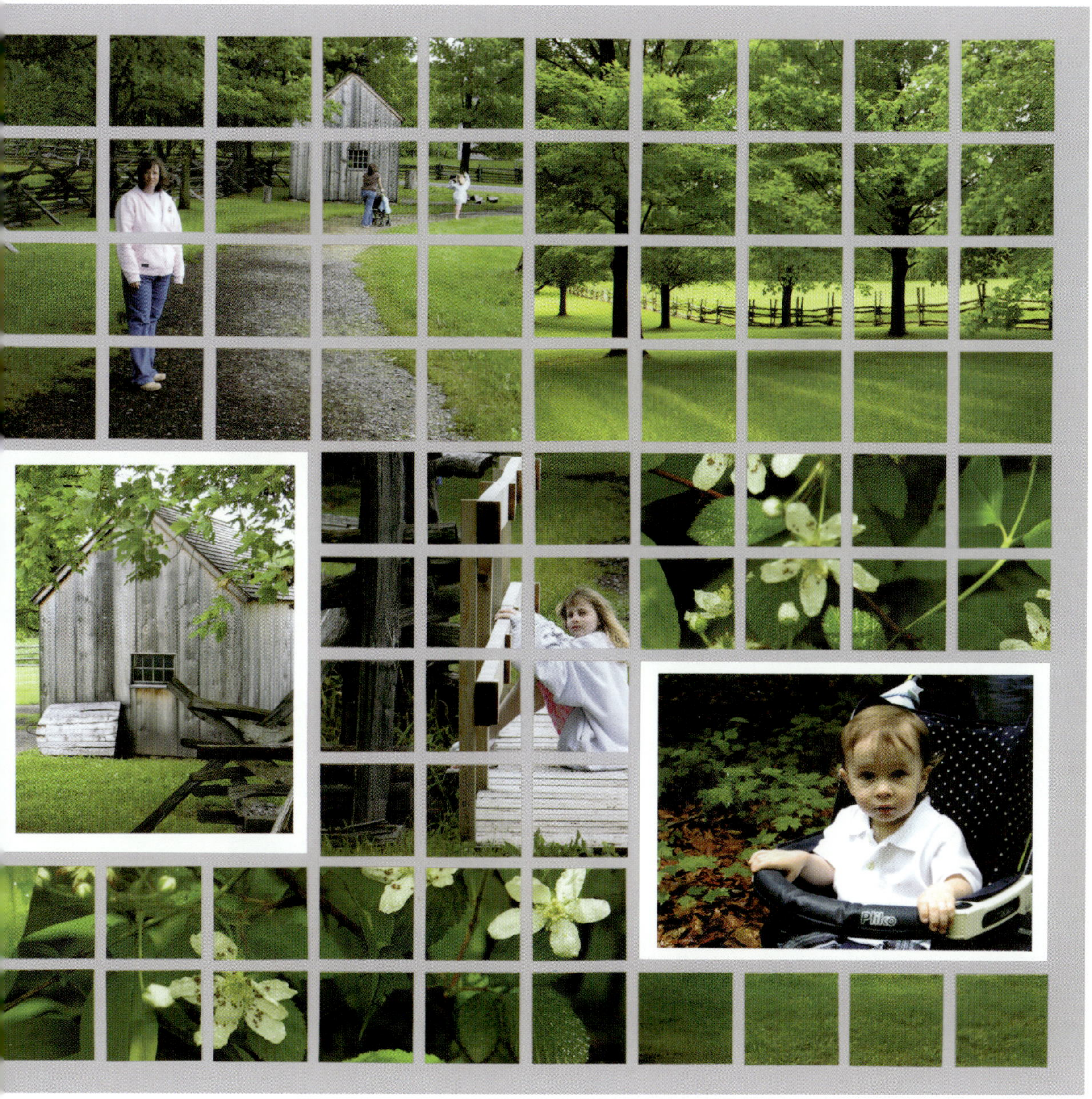

Joseph Smith Farm: Tami Potter
number of photos: 12

of the page. The angle continues in the next photo and onto the next page where a trail leads the viewer further into the distance.

A detail of small white flowers adds interest with its unexpected change in scale. The wild flower photo also acts as a filler for gaps between and around the key photos.

Point of View

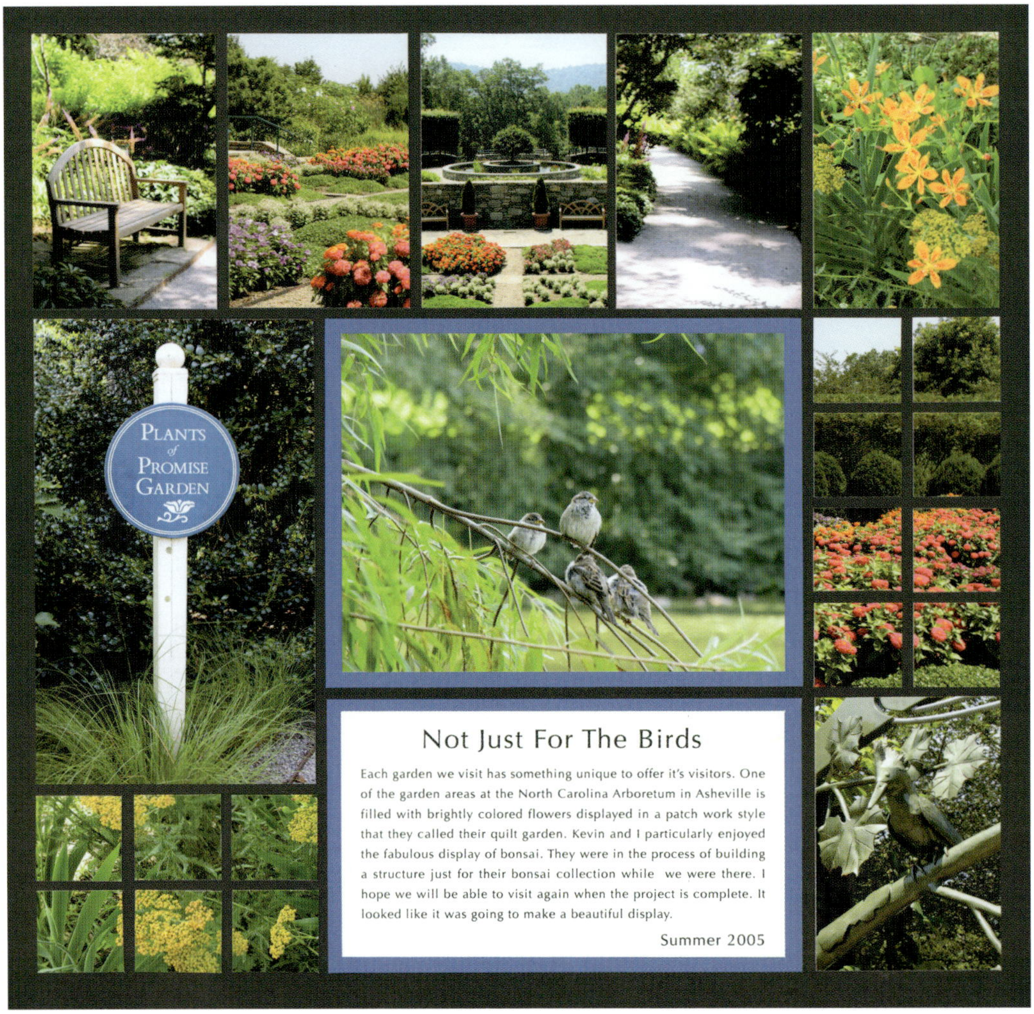

Asheville Arboretum: Tami Potter
number of photos: 9

Detail in a Border

Point of view | This scrapbook page is dedicated to the fabulous garden features found at the North Carolina Arboretum. The birds, who are a clear focal point on the page, actually live in Central Park, New York City, where that photo was taken. Though Central Park is wonderful, I imagine the birds wish, as I do, that they could live in this beautiful and immaculately maintained garden.

Design | Across the top, a row of 2 1/8 x 3 2/8 inch rectangles is a splendid place for adding garden details.

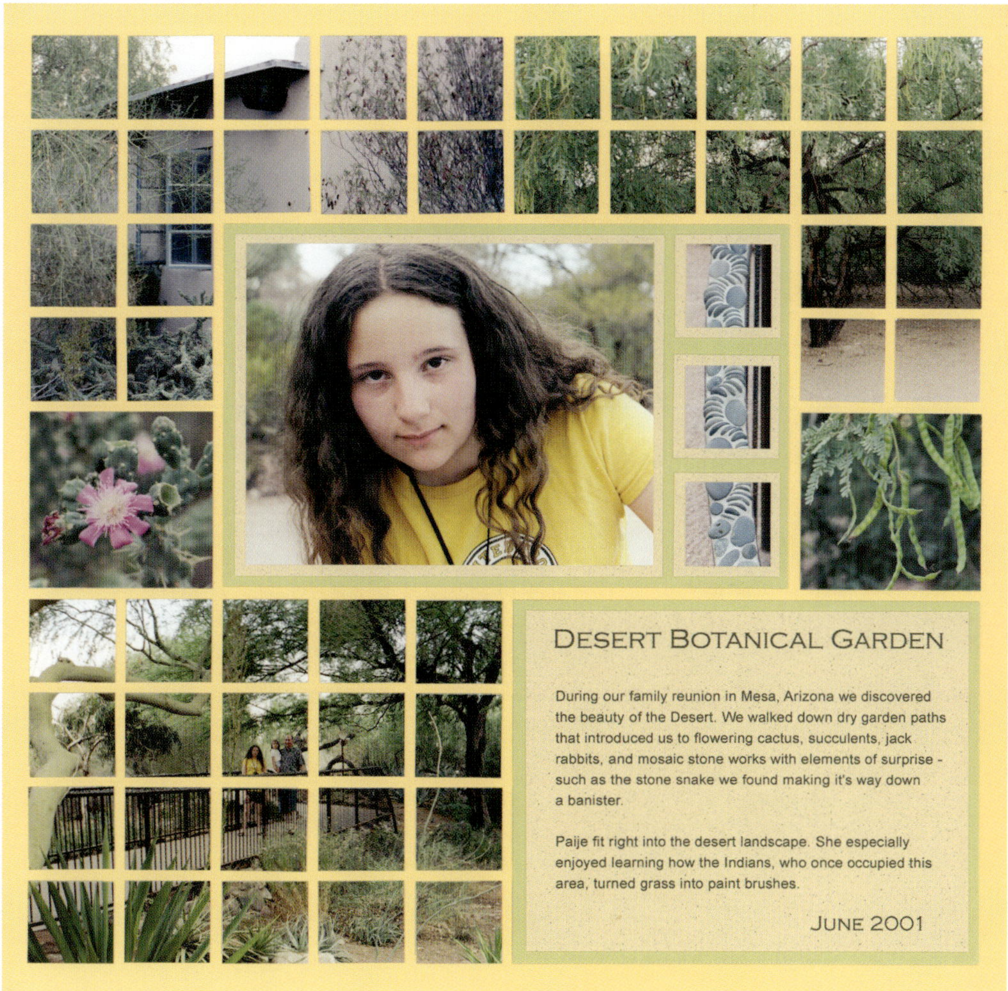

Desert Botanical Garden: Tami Potter
number of photos: 7

Detail in Squares

Point of view | There were so many wonderful little details to be discovered at the Desert Botanical Garden in Phoenix, Arizona. I took photos from a distance and then got in close to capture the details. Both views were of equal importance.

Design | In the page above, the two 2 1/8 x 2 1/8 inch photo squares on each side of the center photo are close up shots of the plants shown in the mosaic photos directly above.

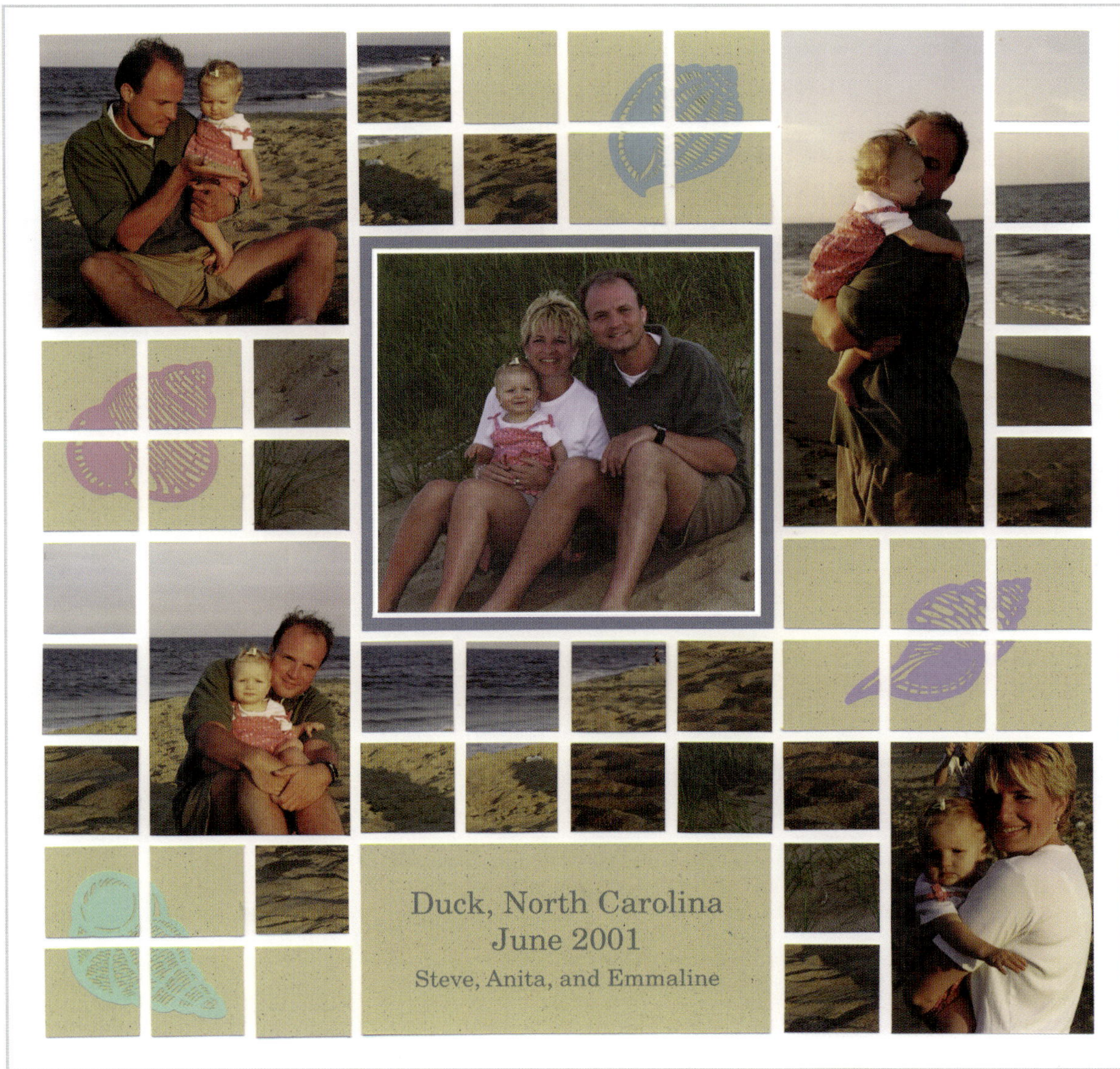

Duck, NC: Tami Potter
photos: Anita Czajkowski
number of photos: 5

Central Focus

Point of view | Precious family moments.

Design | A focus was created by matting and placing a family photo in the center of the page. Supporting photos are cropped tightly to fit the grid. Remnant pieces are made into mosaics and placed to create a sense of the beach area surrounding the subjects. Stickers placed on sand colored cardstock are cut into 1" square pieces to further establish the beach theme and add additional interest.

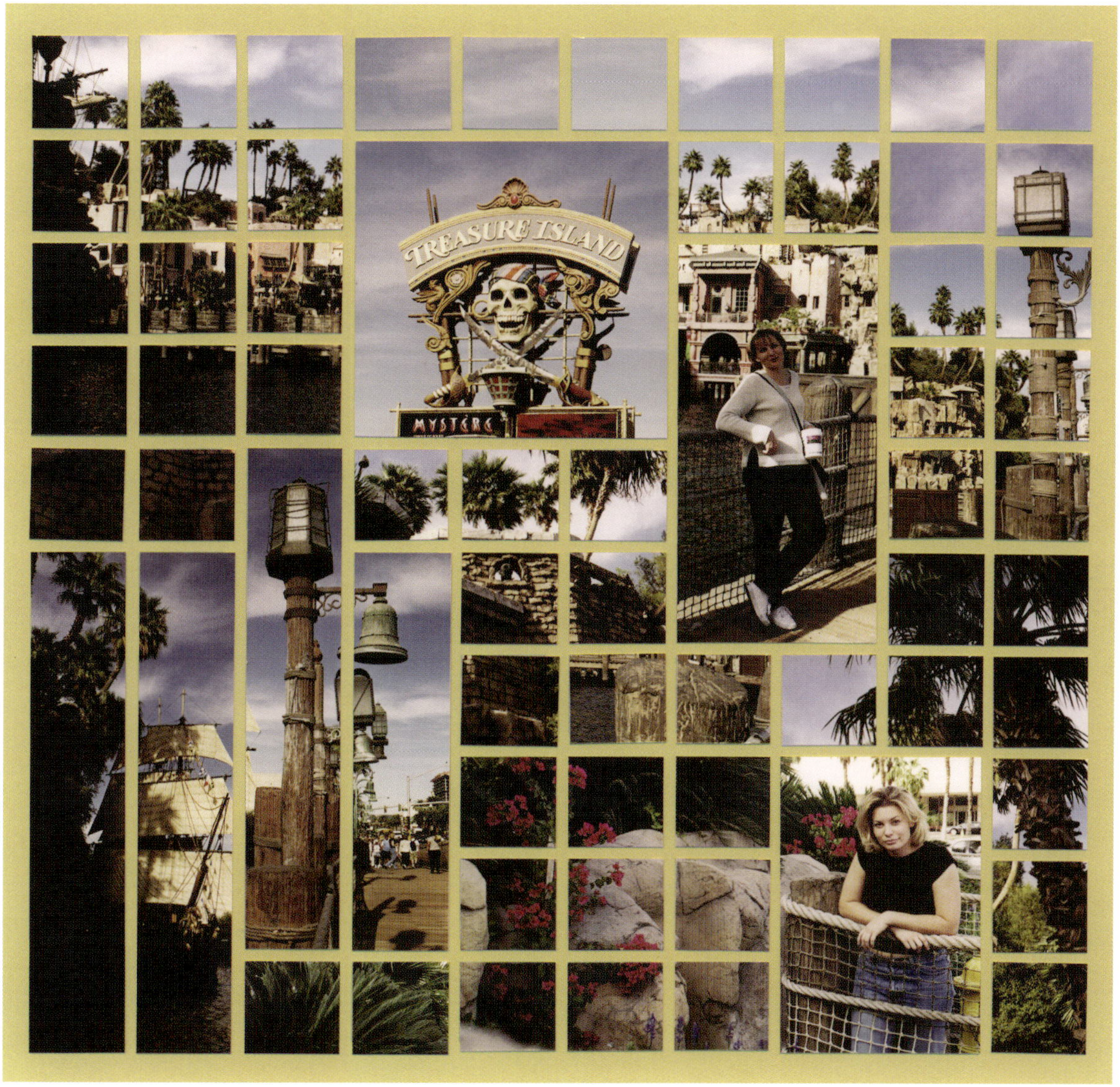

Treasure Island: Tami Potter
number of photos: 8

In Detail

Point of view | The "disney-esque" nature of this Las Vegas hotel was the inspiration behind this page. The fabulously fun sign, seen above, is now only an element of the past, having been replaced. For me, it was a disappointing change, making clear one of the many reasons why I take pictures and make scrapbooks. I want to preserve fond memories.

Design | Mosaics were used to blend many photos together, capturing in a small space some of the details enjoyed during this trip.

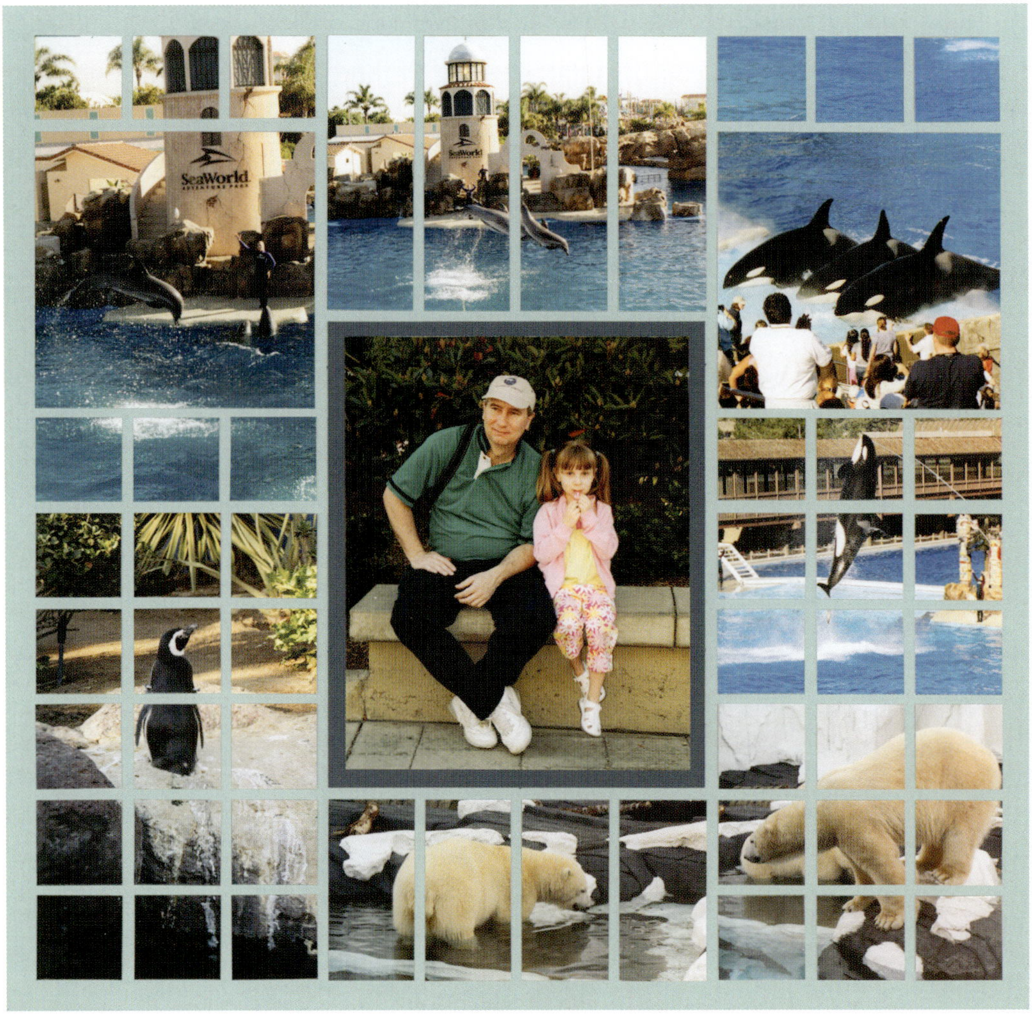

Sea World: Tami Potter
number of photos: 8

Symmetry

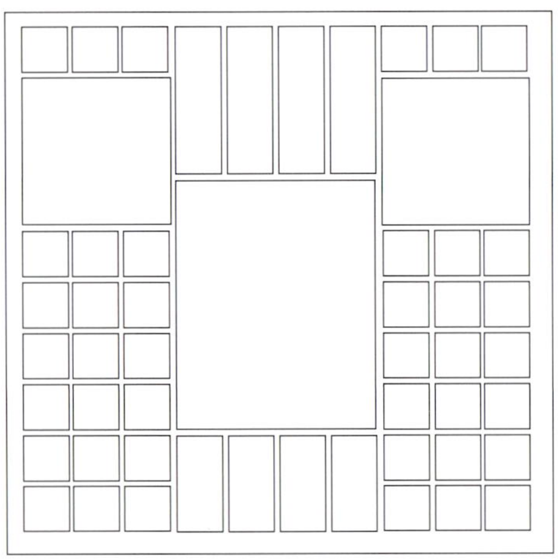

Point of view | This page was inspired by a father and daughter at Sea World. I wanted to feature them and show a glimpse of the things that entertained them at the park.

Design | You just can't miss the main idea when it is centered in the middle of the page. As for the supporting photos, a symmetrical layout is accomplished by making a mirror image design - though the symmetry is not necessarily obvious at first glance, it becomes more apparent when viewing a sketch of the page (see image left.)

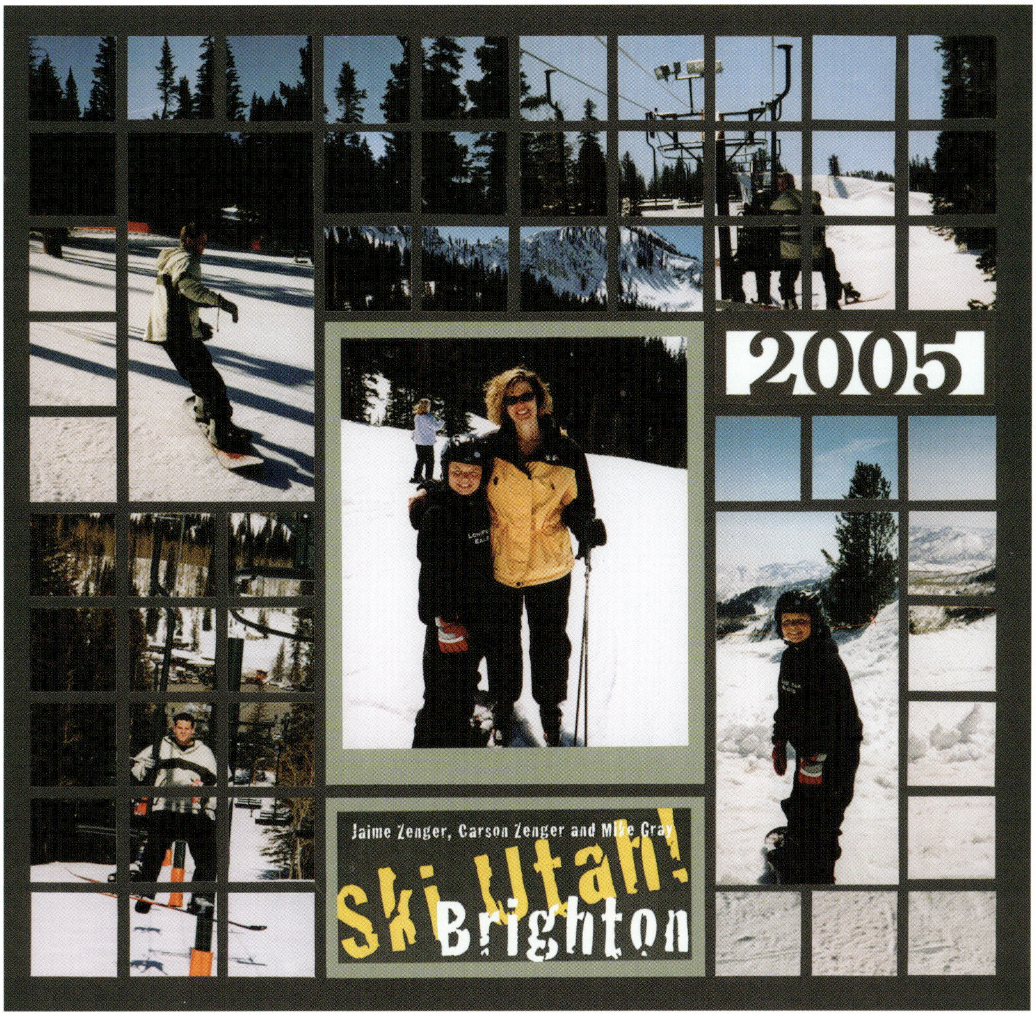

Ski Utah: Tami Potter
photos: Jaime Zenger
number of photos: 5

Asymmetry

Point of view | Sometimes, the goal of a page is pretty straight forward. In this case, it is a day spent enjoying a favorite Utah sport.

Design | The photo of mother and son is the central focal point of this page. The juxtaposition of the two photos on either side of the center photograph gives balance to the asymmetrical design. Additional photos were cut into one inch squares adding interest to the layout while allowing the viewer to maintain focus on the featured photos.

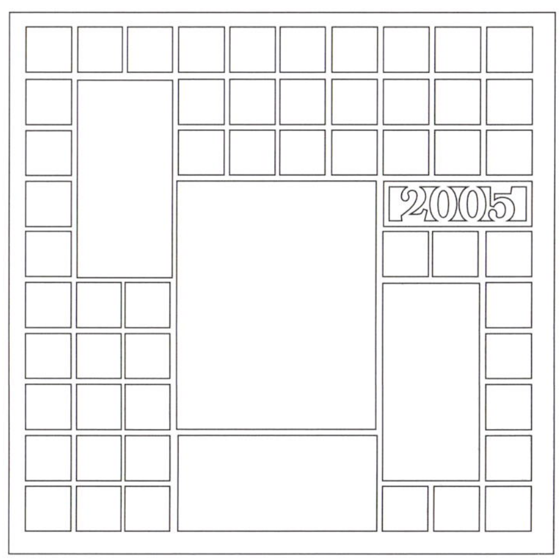

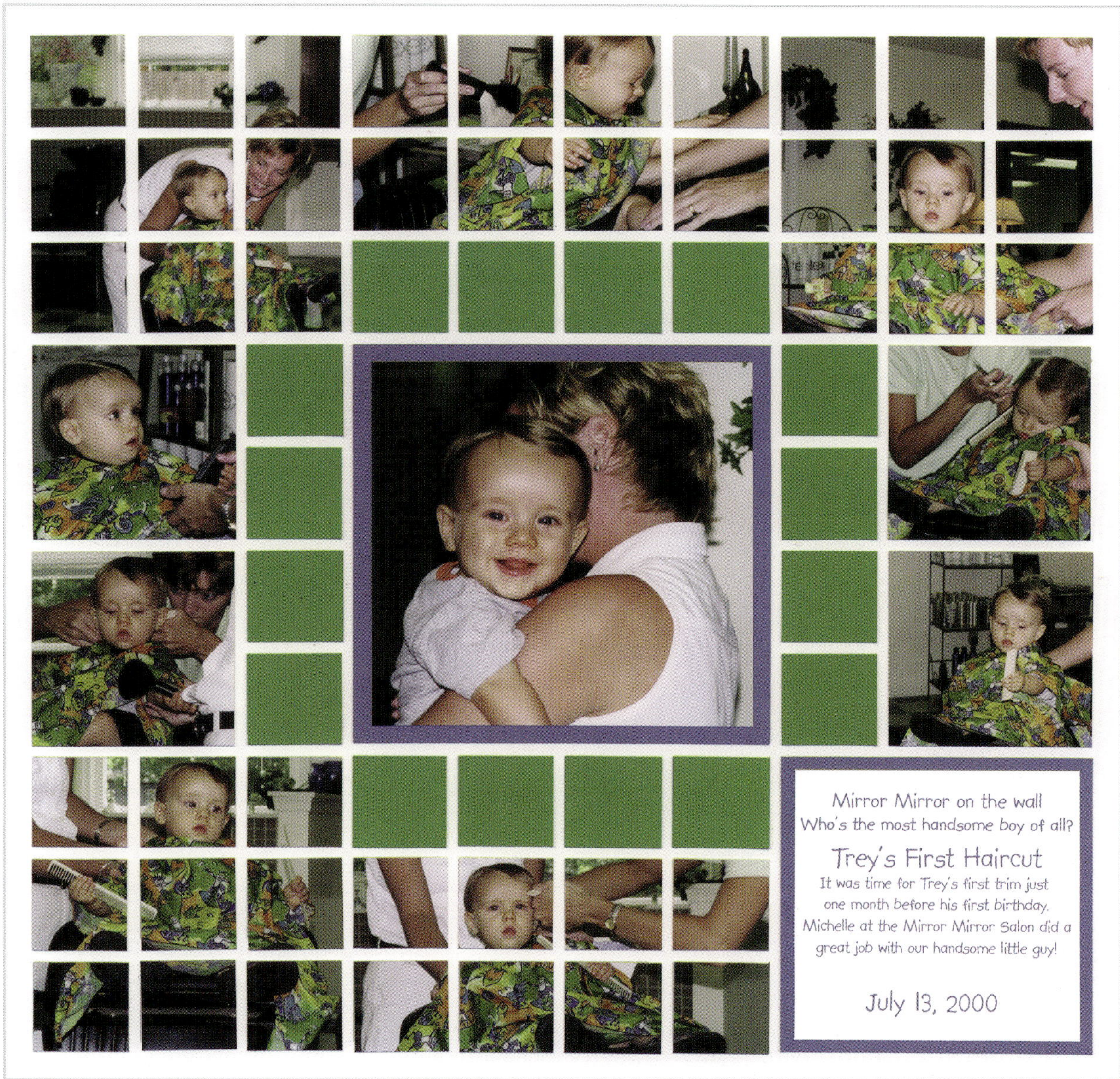

Mirror Mirror: Tami Potter
photos: Keila Underwood
number of photos: 10

Measured in Moments

Point of view | Little ones grow and change so fast! What a grand thing it is to capture their expressions, especially when they are experiencing something for the first time.

Design | Using tightly cropped photos, this page is designed to capture the many expressions of a curious toddler during his first haircut. Green paper cut into one inch square pieces frame the central photo - giving it even more emphasis.

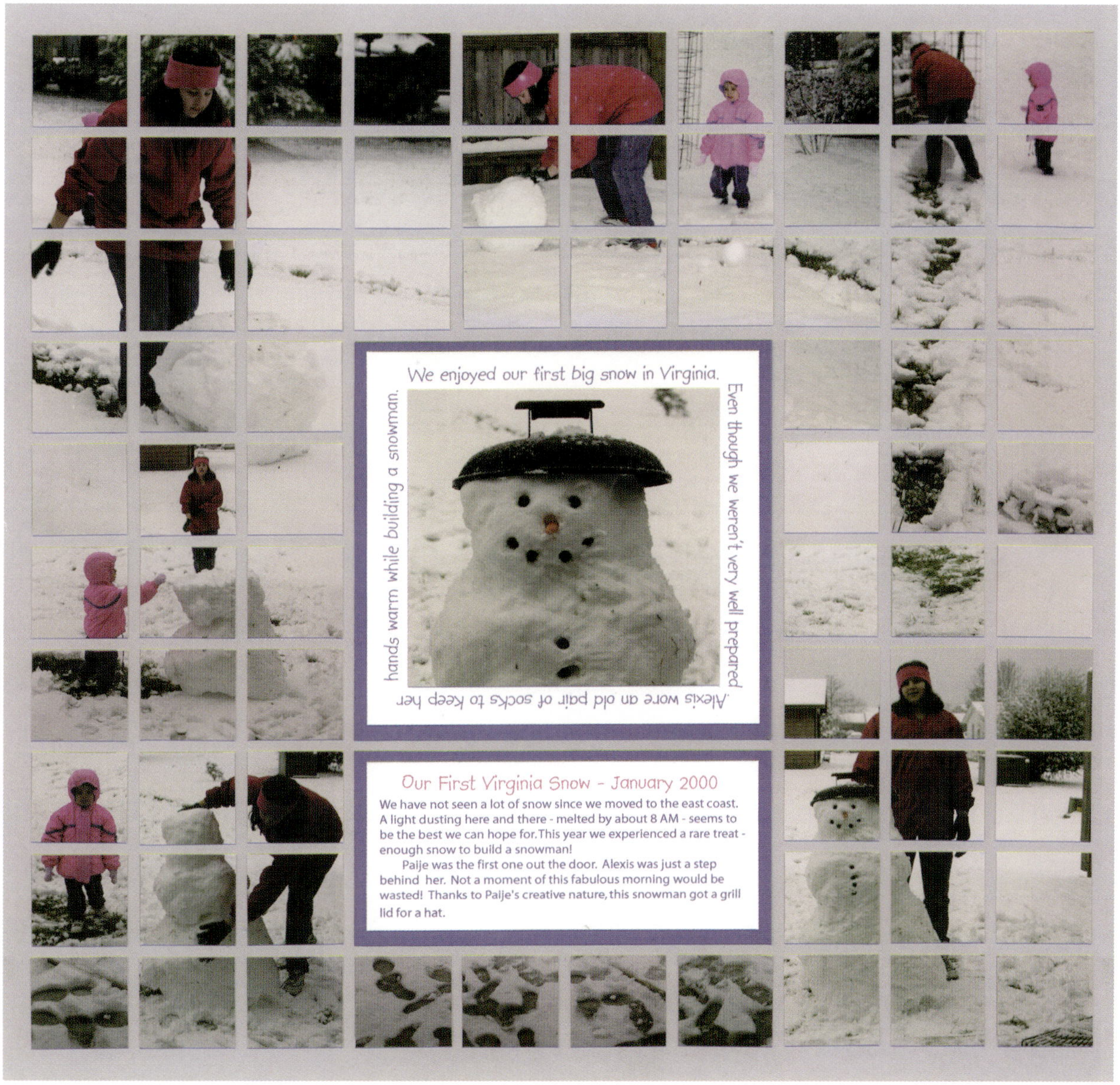

Virginia Snowman: Tami Potter
number of photos: 7

Sequence of Events

Point of view | Building a frosty friend with a unique hat is the central focus of this page.

Design | The six pictures that encircle the central design are placed in sequence from start (top right corner then counter clockwise) to finish (bottom right corner) creating a time lapse effect. Tidbits of information are written around the center photo adding a sense of whimsy that seems befitting of a fun childhood event.

Designing the View

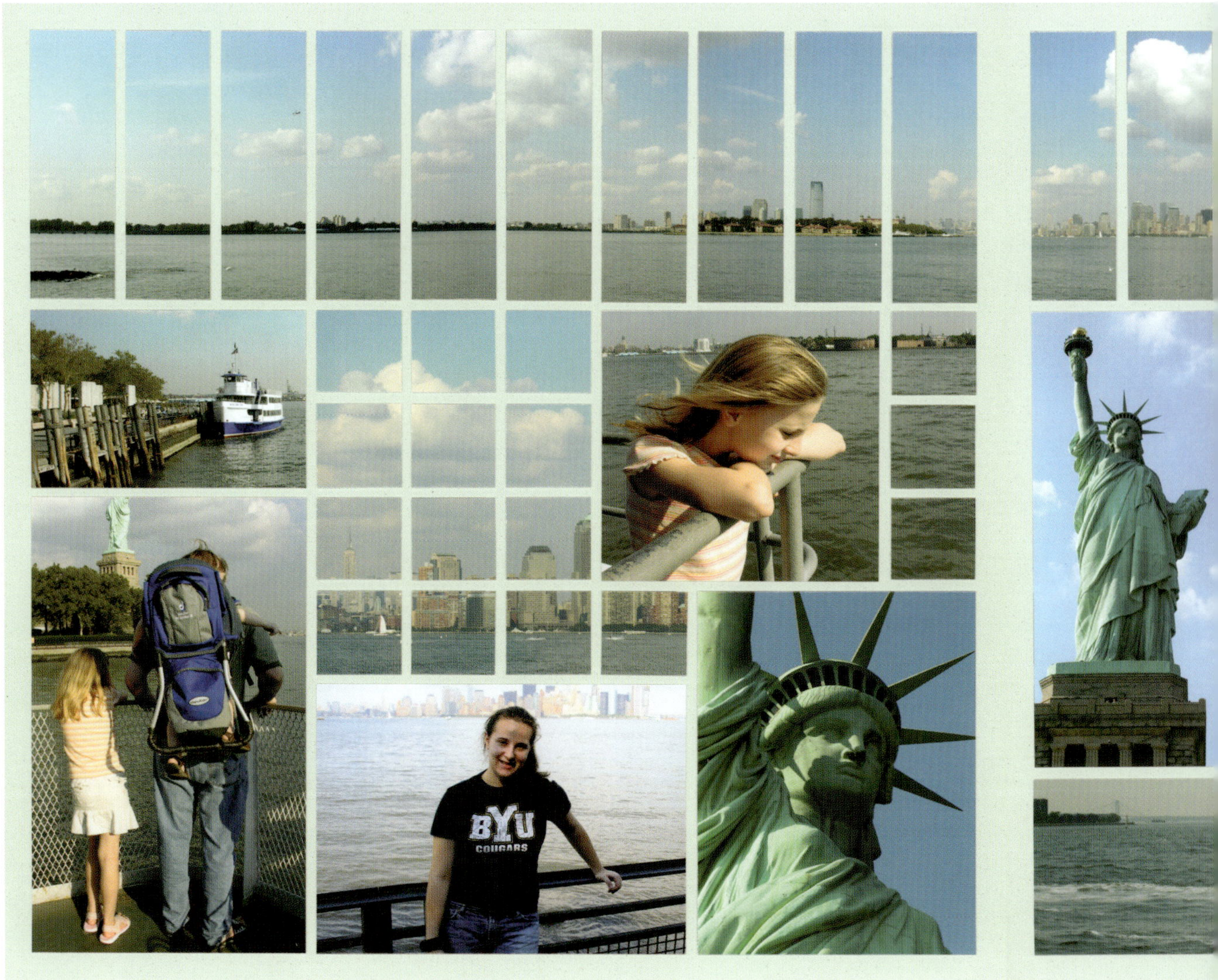

Liberty Island: Tami Potter
number of photos: 15

A Forgiving Nature

One of the best things about the photo mosaic process is its forgiving nature. As hard as I may try, my photos do not always line up properly (see figure A). This problem is easily cured using the Mosaic Moments™ mat with 1/8 inch grid lines. Simply line photos up on the mat (see figure B) and trim off the excess (see figure C) before cutting them into photo squares or strips.

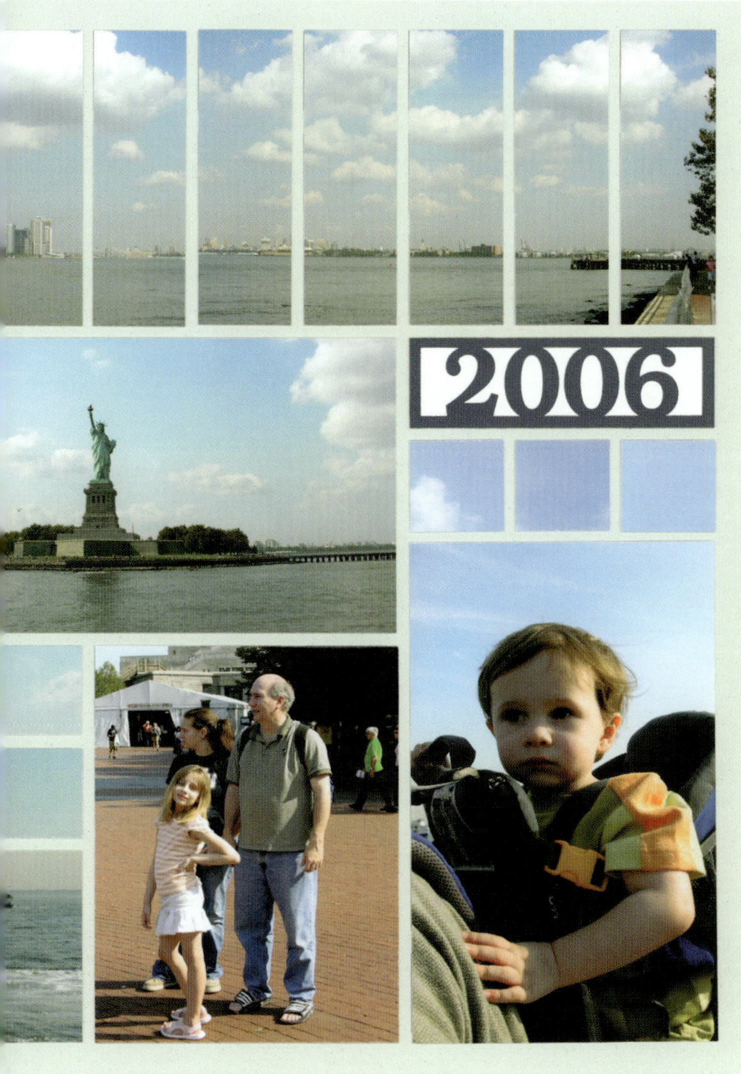

Mending Horizons

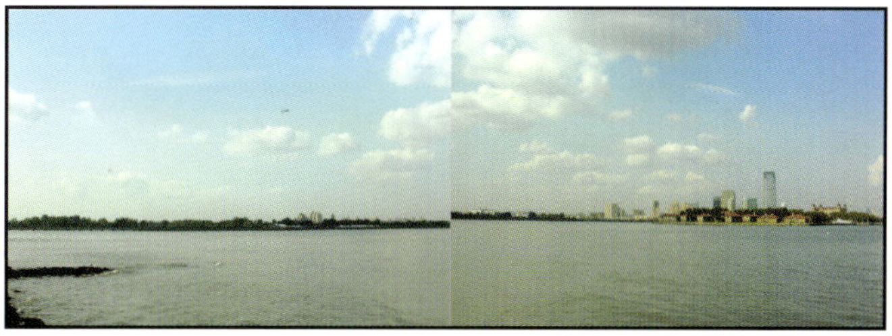

A - Photos taken with a panoramic view in mind may not always line up the way you hoped they would.

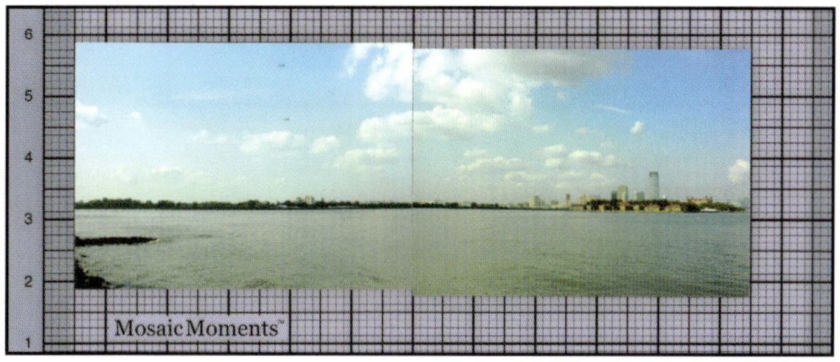

B - Adjust photos so the horizon line is straight

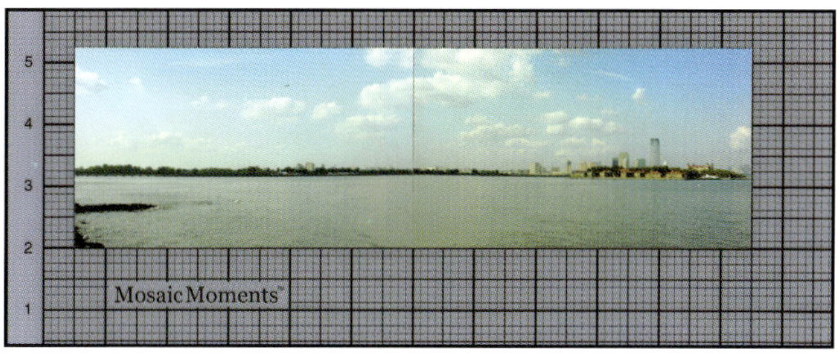

C - Trim uneven area from the top and bottom of photograph while sizing them to fit the grid.

■ Tip

Using 1x1 inch photo squares to fill between larger photo blocks helps to engage the viewer and avoid a chunky looking layout.

The photo in the bottom right corner of the layout above is less cumbersome after a portion of the sky was separated from the main photo block and cut into 1 inch squares.

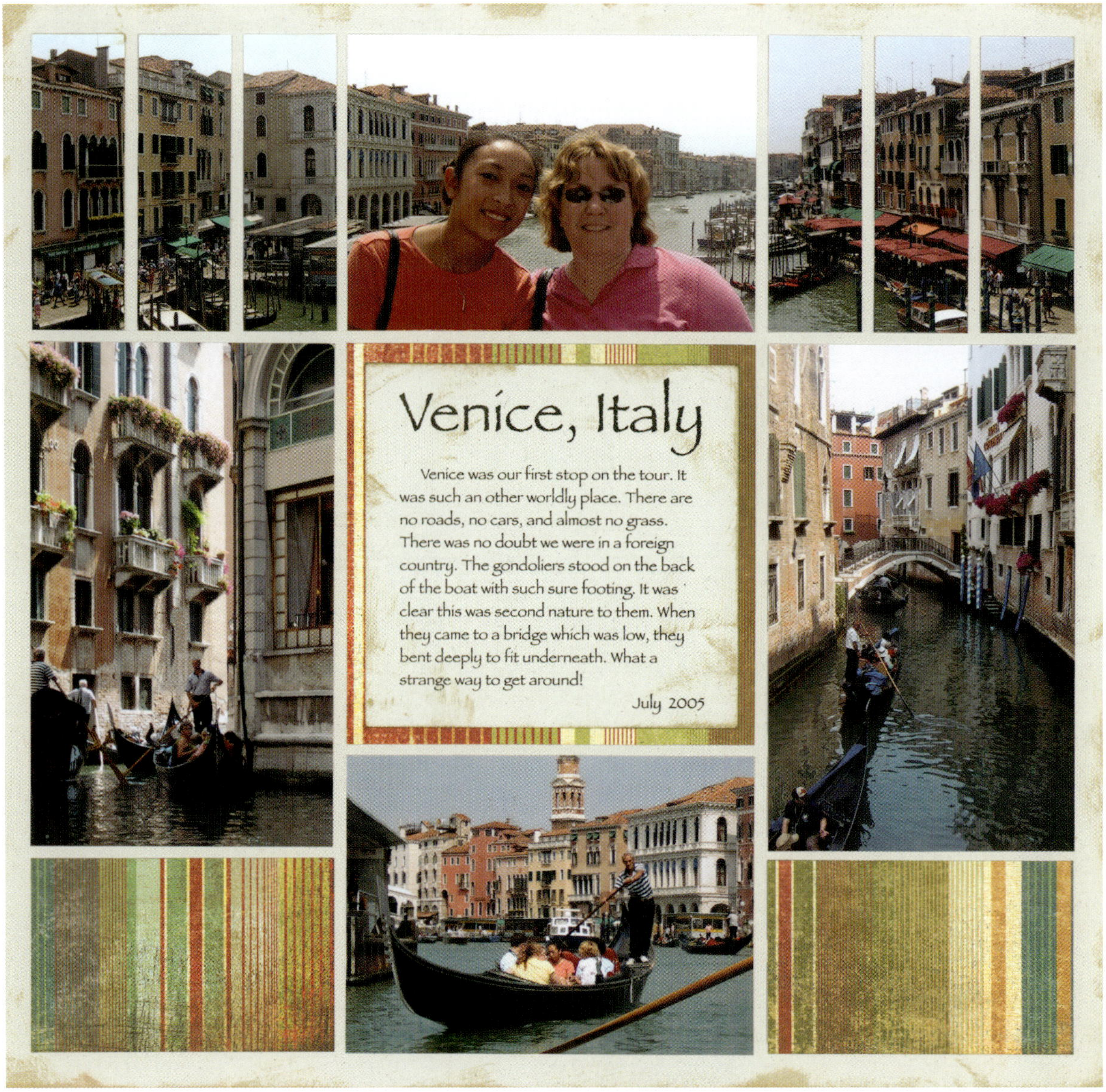

Venice: Tami Potter
photos: Sandi Keene
number of photos: 6

Creating a Broad View

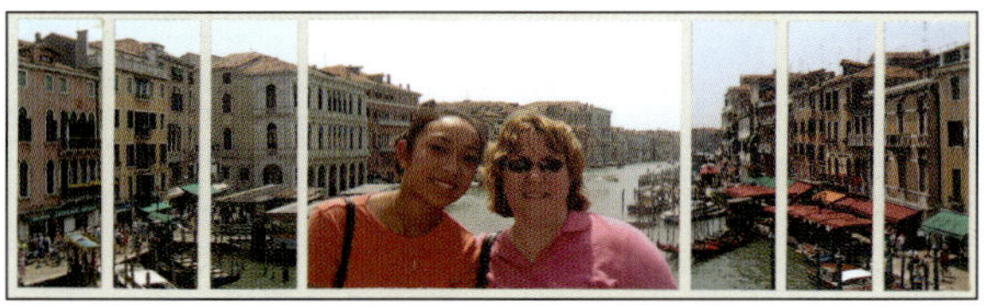

Trying to get a picture that shows both the lovely smiles of loved ones, as well as the great view behind them, can be a bit tricky. Stand back far enough to take in the view and those sweet smiles have become a glint in the distance. Try taking that close up shot up close. Then snap a shot to each side. Put the three photos together using photos strips to break them up and give the illusion that they all came from one click.

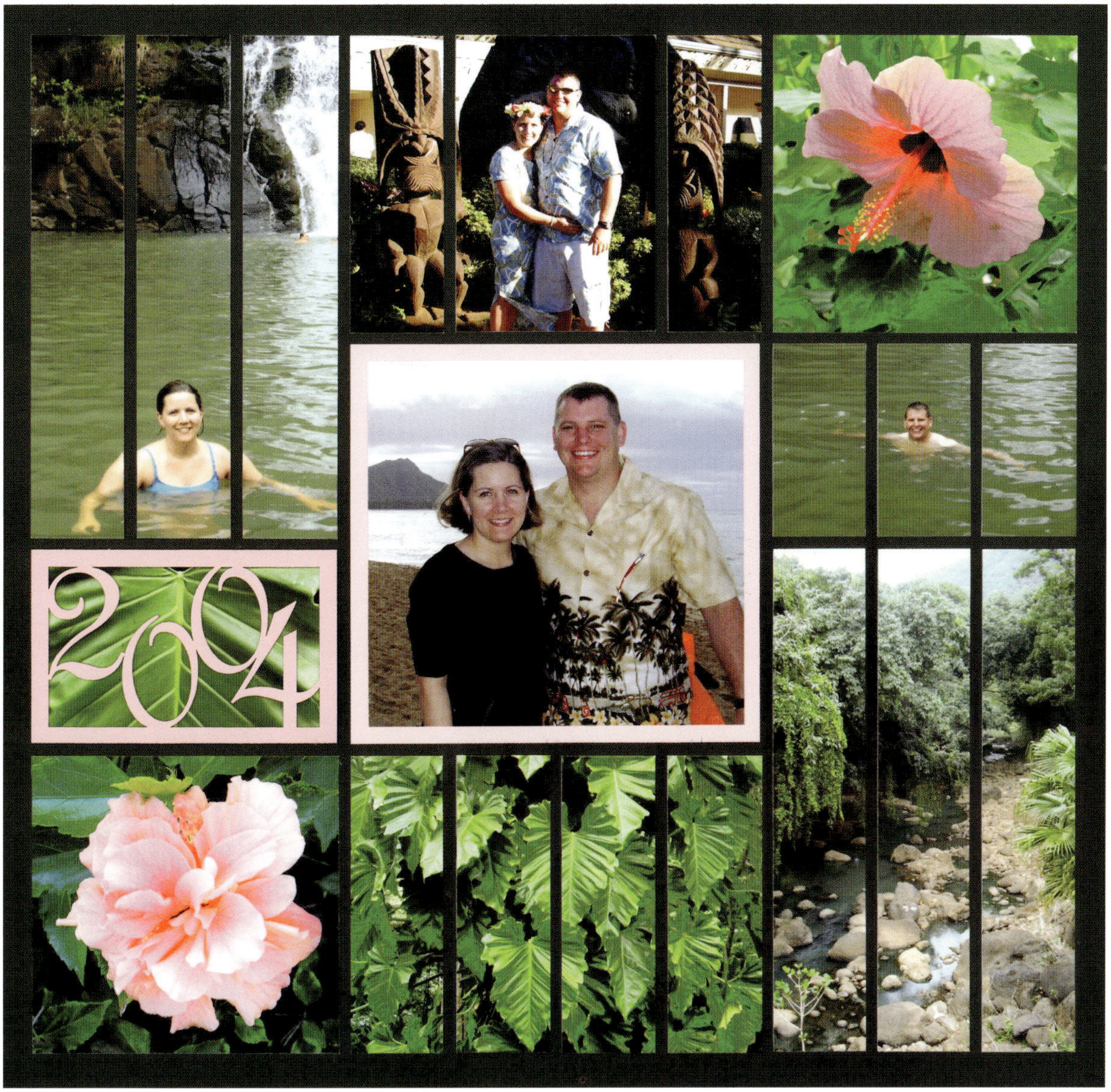

Hawaii: Tami Potter
photos: Paije Abplanalp
number of photos: 9

Changing Perspectives

This Hawaiian delight was created using photo strips on grid paper. It is amazing to see the difference between using 1x1 inch squares and 1 inch strips. Notice how the longer photo strips elongate the photographs and change the perspective.

Another fun tidbit: notice the photo placed behind the laser cut year.

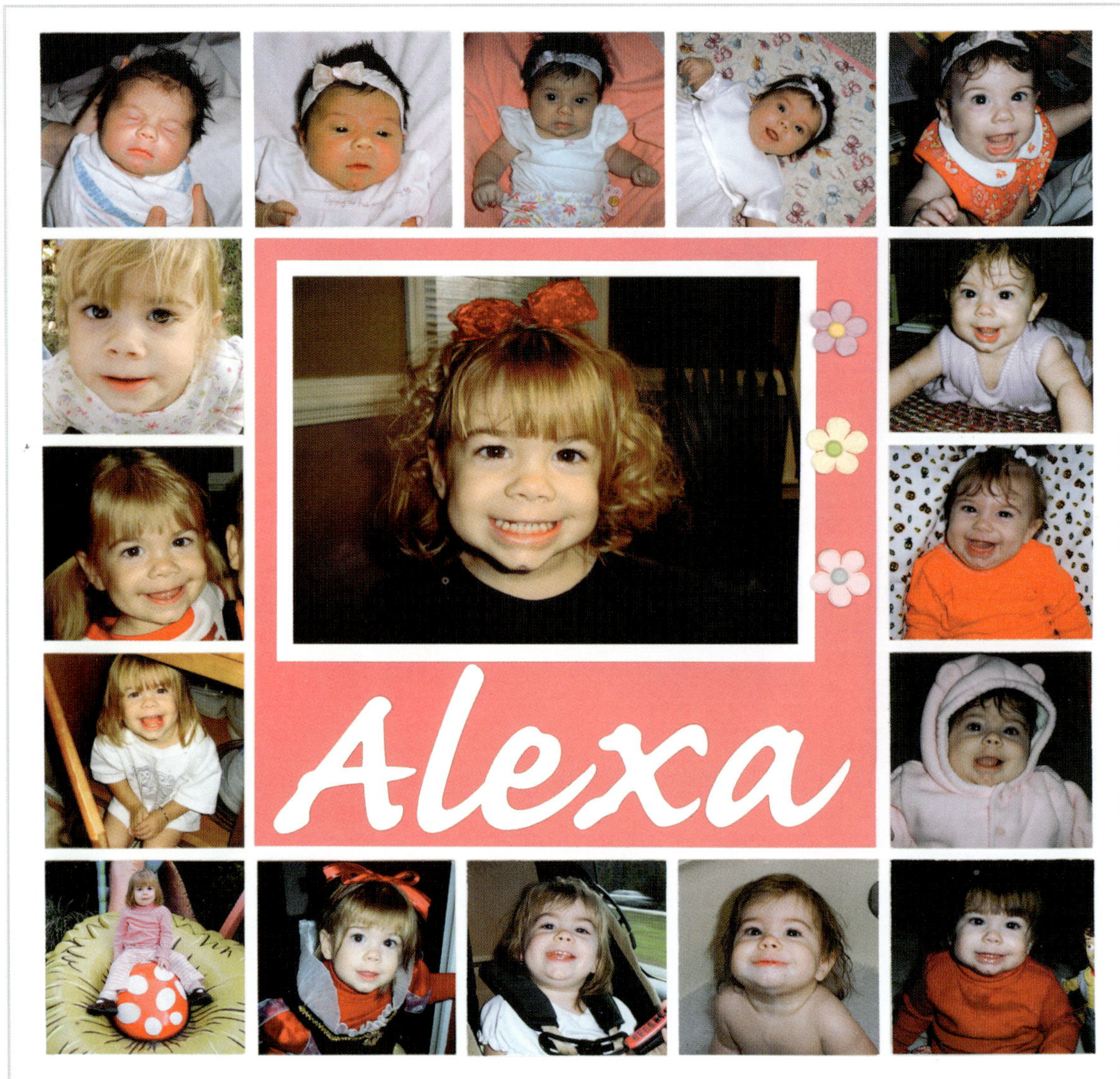

Watch Me Grow: Shannon Johnson
number of photos: 17

Sweet 17

Photo squares cut to 2 1/8 x 2 1/8 inches are perfect for those situations when you wish you could fit it all on one page. The layout above offers 17 smile spots. Alexa is seen growing by months. This would also be a great solution for birth to high school graduation, family faces, expressions at a birthday bash, or the many pebbles in a childhood collection.

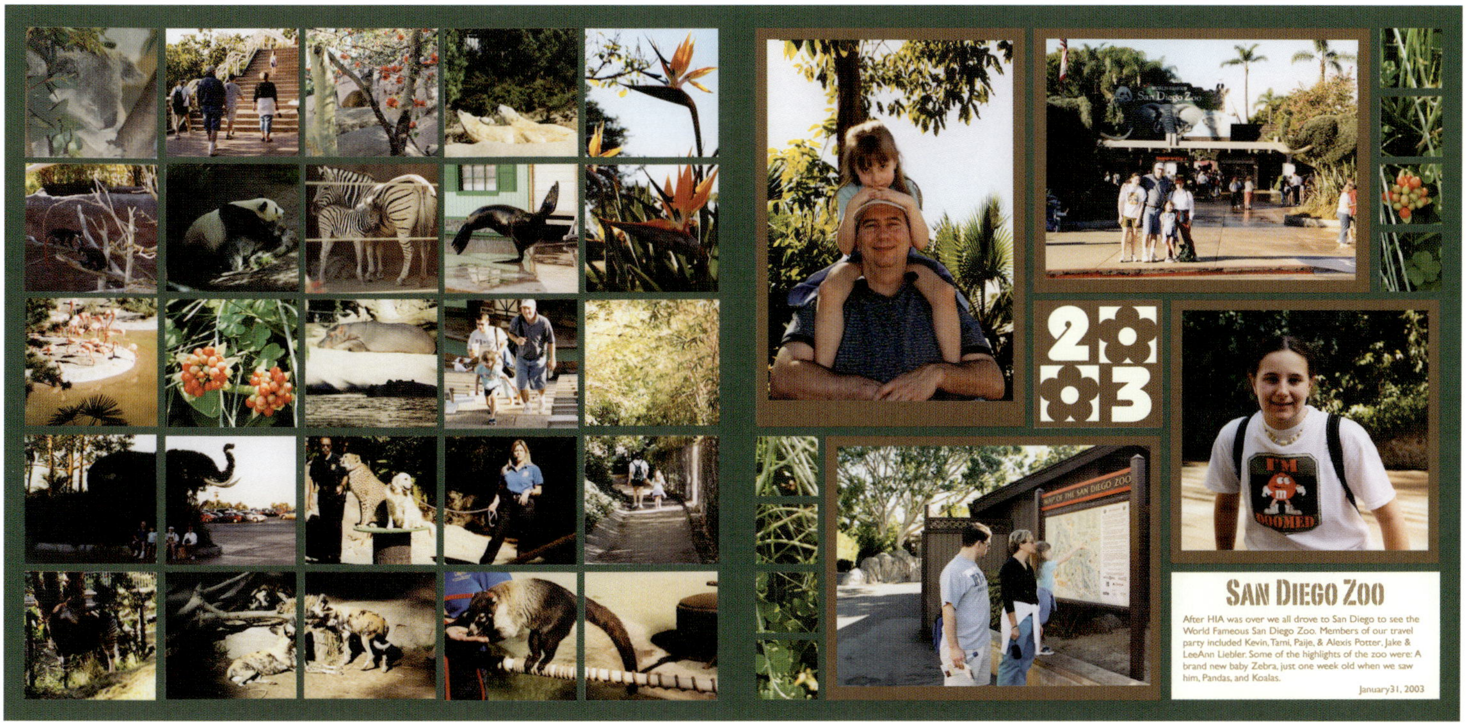

San Diego Zoo: Tami Potter
number of photos: 22

Hip to be Square

I love the zoo. I have been to a lot of them. I always take oodles of pictures which used to get thumbed through once or twice before retiring to "the photo box." I just couldn't see that happening to the photos I took at the San Diego Zoo. I wanted to try a layout using 2 1/8 x 2 1/8 squares. This was my opportunity.

Things to notice:

- Not every square is a different photo. When necessary, I used two 2 1/8 x 2 1/8 inch squares cut from the same photo to either fill space or show more of the photograph.
- I used 1x1 inch remnant photo pieces to fill a little space on the right hand page.

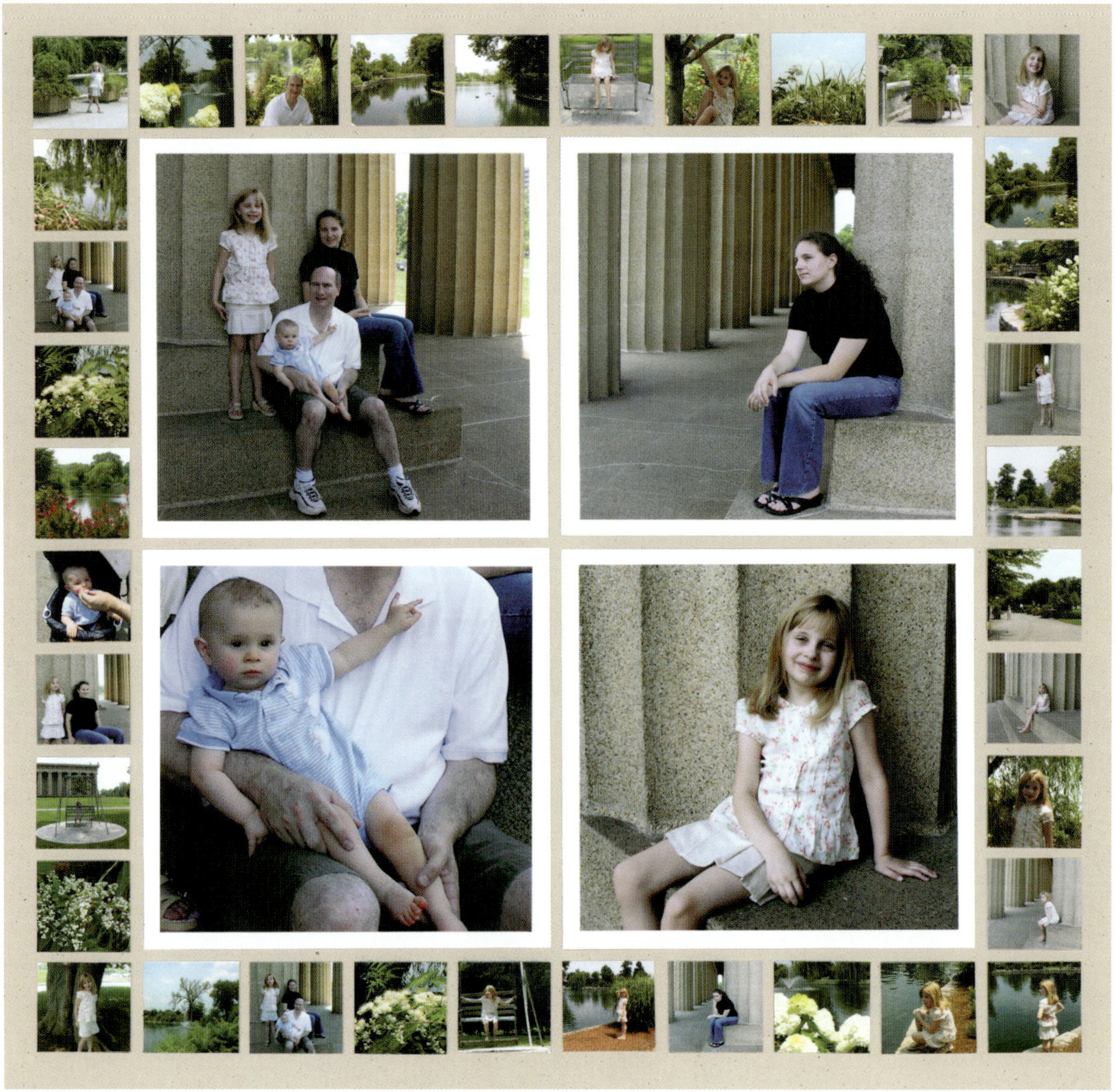

Nashville's Parthenon: Tami Potter
number of photos: 40

Forty Photos

I got 40 photos on one page! I bet that is something you don't see everyday. So, maybe you don't want to put 40 photos on every page, but I have to say, I think the time I put into this tedious process was worth the effort. I love both of these pages. I would never use all of these pictures at full size. I just don't have the time to make that many scrapbook pages. However, I like how the colors

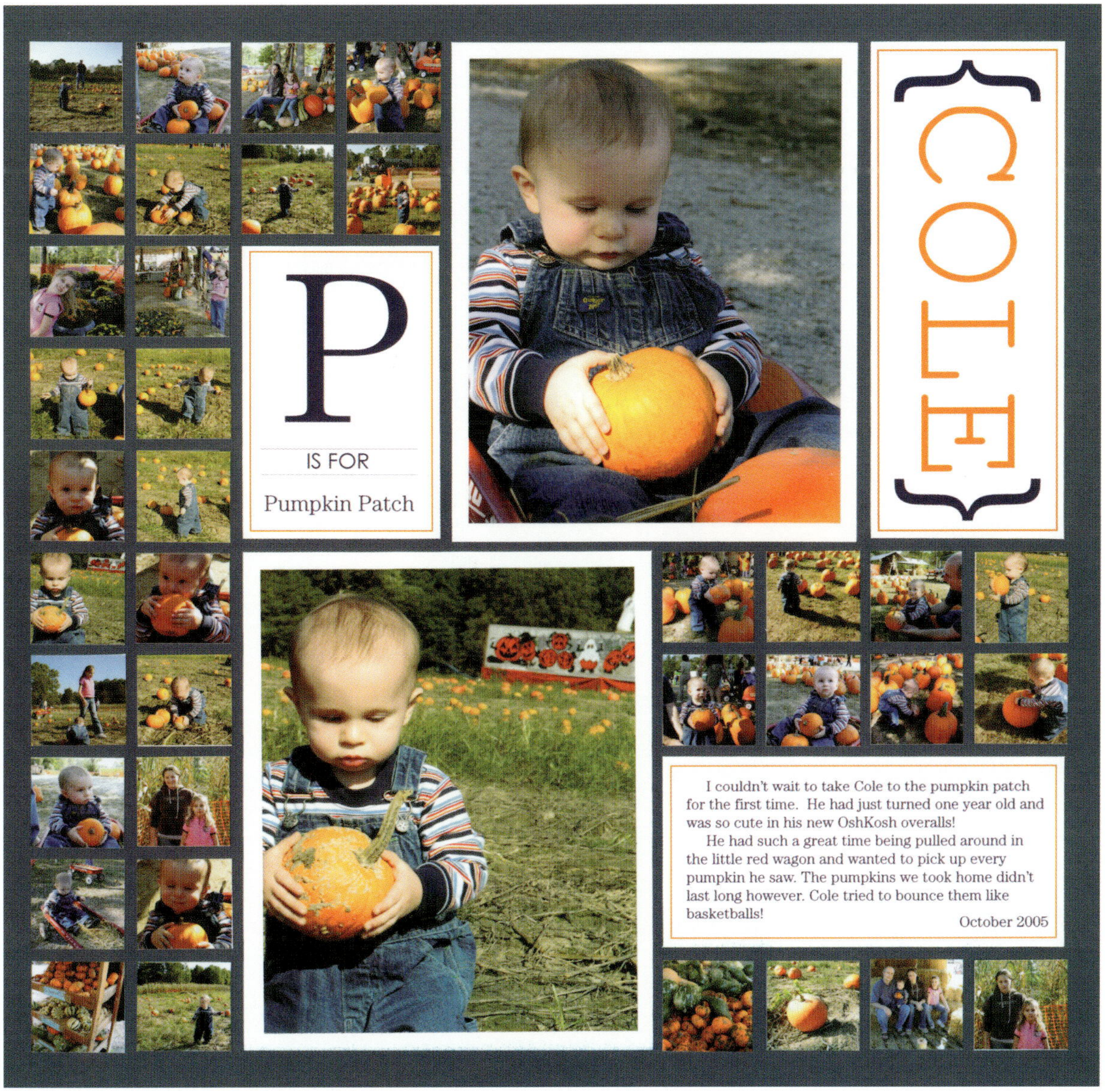

P is for Pumpkin: Tami Potter
number of photos: 38

Thirty-Eight Photos

of the tiny photos blend with the big pictures. It is sort of like they are the ultimate coordinating paper!

To get the tiny photos, just print a contact or thumbnail sheet. I printed 6 up on 4x6 photo paper. Then cut them into one inch squares.

Designing on Grid

You may have begun using grid paper to design a 1x1 inch photo mosaic page similar to the one pictured to the right; so, did you stop there?

The most time consuming part of designing a scrapbook page is the decision making process. There are no rules, it is up to you to define each new project from scratch. Wouldn't it be nice to know that there was something you could count on? Something that would work every time?

Grid paper works. It establishes rules for the shapes and sizes of design elements used on the page. (See Mosaic Moments™ quick grid guide on page 64.) All you have to do is cut your photos or paper into pre-determined sizes and position them on the grid paper.

You might think – "if all my pages are designed using grid paper, my book will be limited or boring." However, along with its natural ability to guide and organize, grid paper offers a huge amount of flexibility.

There are 10 columns and 10 rows to play with. Multiply that by unlimited photographs. When you add color and texture as well as your favorite embellishments and techniques, the possibilities are endless. Every page in this book was designed using the same grid paper; each has its own unique look.

The pages you've seen so far have focused mainly on photo mosaic techniques with a little photo blocking and paper blocking thrown in. Now it is time to tell you exactly what photo blocking and paper blocking are and how you can use these techniques to make *fabulous* pages *fast!*

Strap in!

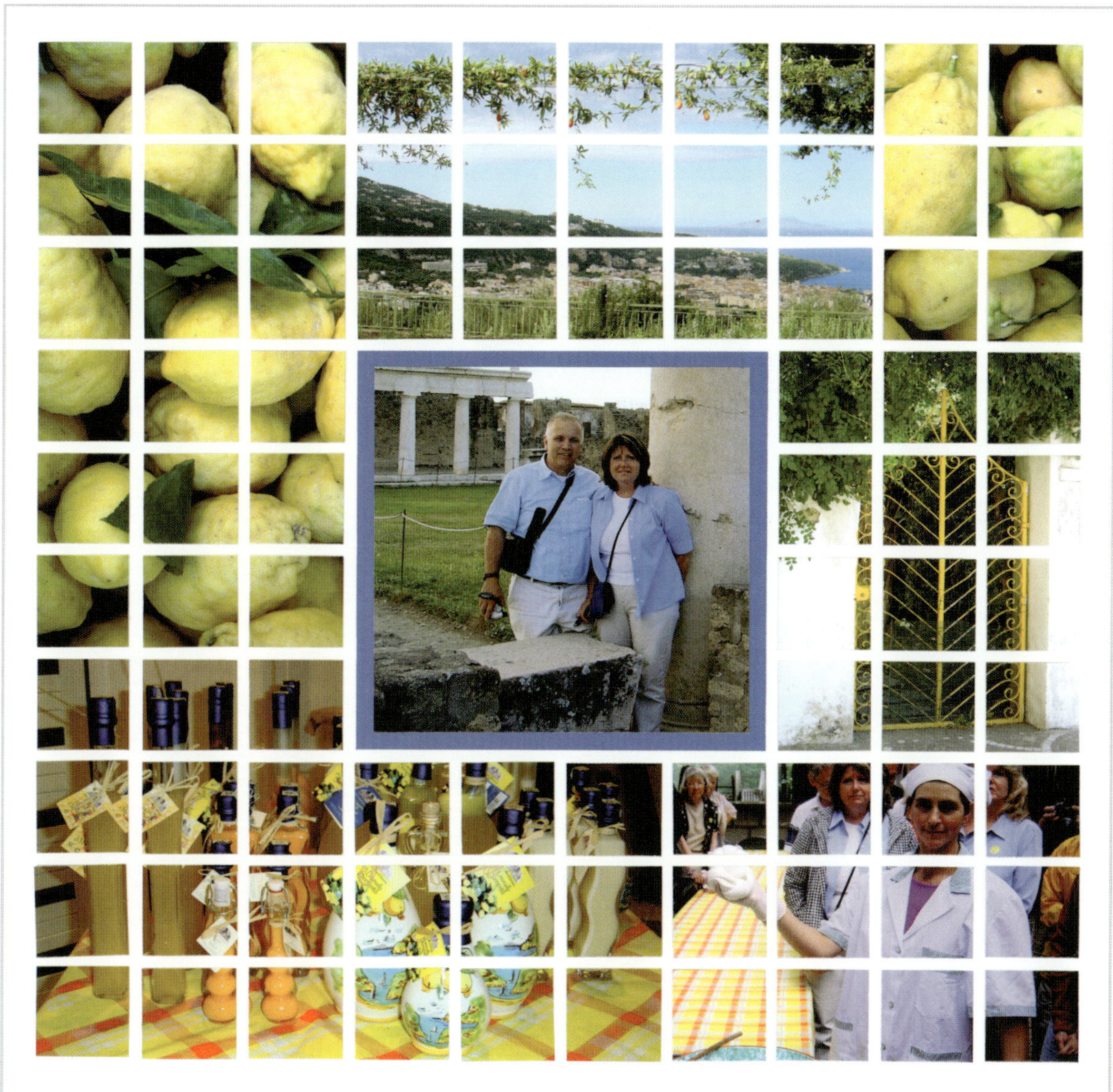

When Life Offers Lemons: Tami Potter
photos: Stan Palmer
number of photos: 6

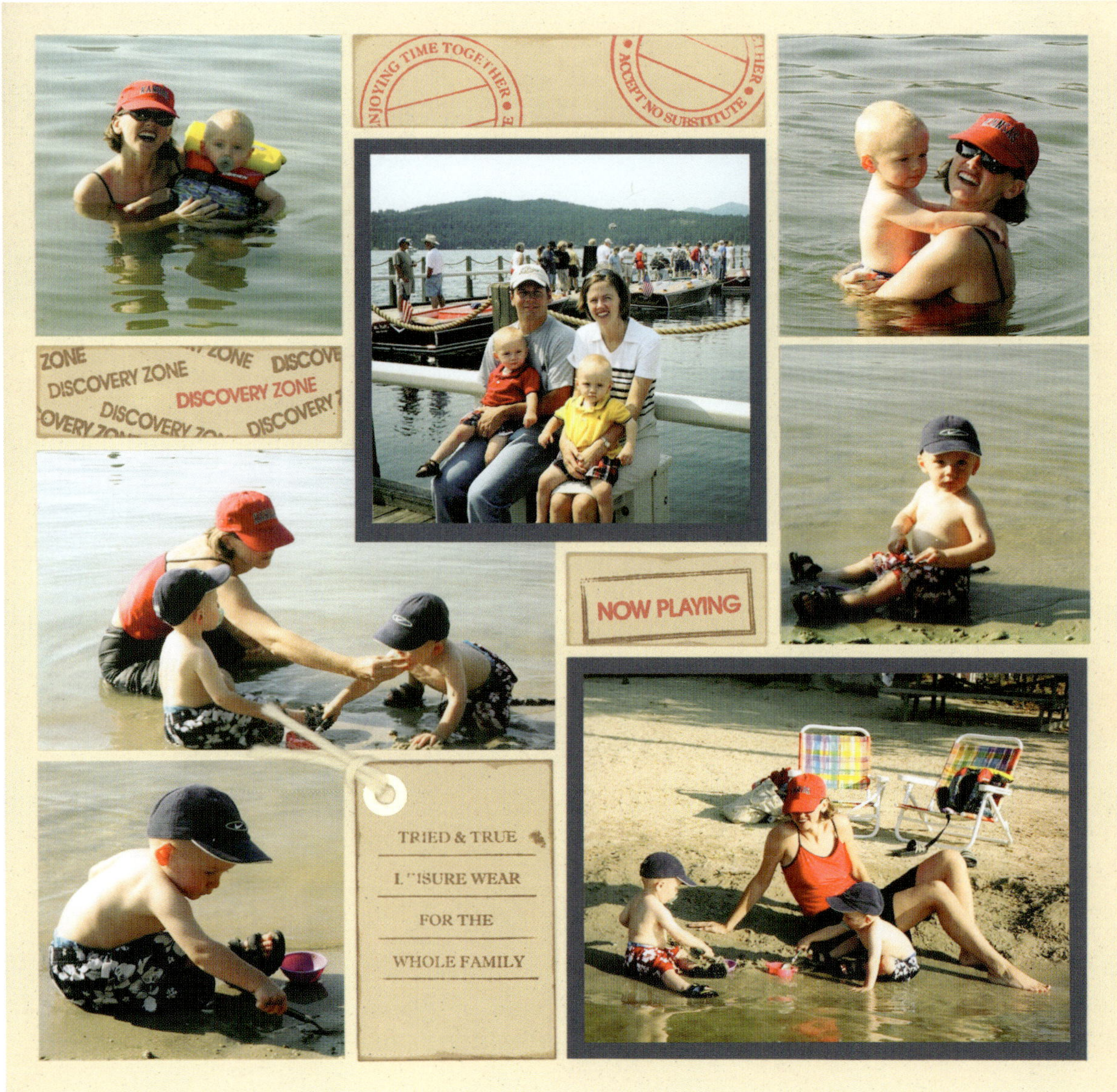

Now Playing: Tami Potter
photos: Carla Palmer
number of photos: 7

Page Blocking

Covering multiple squares on the grid paper with photos, journaling, or embellished space is called **page blocking**. Okay, so I just made that up - but go with me on this! There are two types of "page blocking" I will refer to: photo blocking and paper blocking.

- Photo blocking is defined as cutting photographs to fit directly on the grid - in other words, photos are not matted.

Paper blocking is defined as a process where paper is cut to fit the grid. The paper could be plain cardstock or patterned paper. Paper blocks can be used as photo mats, space for journaling, adding embellishments, or left unchanged.

The lake-side page on the left shows photo blocking (photos cut to fit directly on the grid paper) and paper blocking (paper cut to fit the grid.)

In the Old Point Loma Lighthouse spread below, the entire page is paper blocked. Larger blocks are used for photo and journaling placement. Smaller blocks create a decorative pattern. Laser cut designs are strategically placed to add color and textural interest.

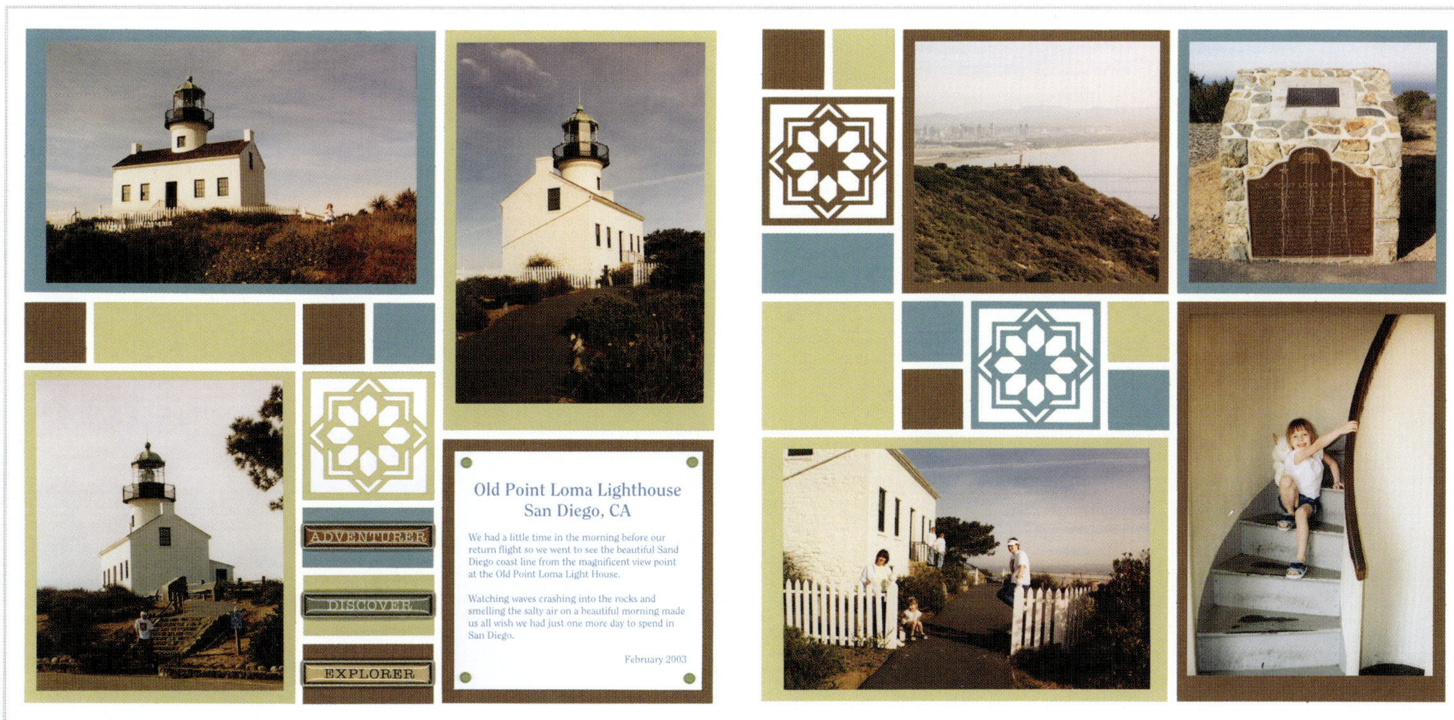

Old Point Loma Lighthouse: Tami Potter
number of photos: 7

Definitions:

page block•ing / covering multiple squares on grid paper.
pho•to block•ing / cutting photographs to fit directly on the grid paper.
pa•per block•ing / cutting paper to fit directly on the grid paper.

Cutting to Fit the Grid

Mosaic Moments™ Quick Grid Guide

Grid Paper	Fraction	Decimal
1 Square	1 in	1.00 in
2 Squares	2 1/8 in	2.125 in
3 Squares	3 2/8 in	3.25 in
4 Squares	4 3/8 in	4.375 in
5 Squares	5 4/8 in	5.50 in
6 Squares	6 5/8 in	6.625 in
7 Squares	7 6/8 in	7.75 in
8 Squares	8 7/8 in	8.875 in
9 Squares	10 in	10.00 in
10 Squares	11 1/8 in	11.125 in

Mosaic Moments™ grid paper is designed with one inch columns and 1/8 inch gutters (gaps between columns.) See detail image right,

Working with Mosaic Moments™ grid paper does not mean you must cut all of your photos into 1x1 inch squares. You can add interest and emphasize focal points by varying the height or width of your photo and paper blocks.

The cutting process can be easily achieved using your Mosaic Moments™ mat with 1/8 inch grid lines. (Additional information page 12.)

- When using Mosaic Moments™ grid paper, the rule is: add 1-1/8 inch for every additional square to be covered. (See Mosaic Moments™ quick grid guide to left.)
- Simply line up your photographs on the Mosaic Moments™ mat using the 1/8 inch guides. Make cuts based on the number of squares you wish to cover.
- Don't forget to use your **Mosaic Moments™ Quick Glance Cutting Guide™** (see template on page 93) to help you make your cutting/cropping decisions.
- Use the decimal point conversion on the Mosaic Moments™ Quick Grid Guide (pictured left) when creating a title or journaling block in your word processing program.

one inch square one-eighth inch gap

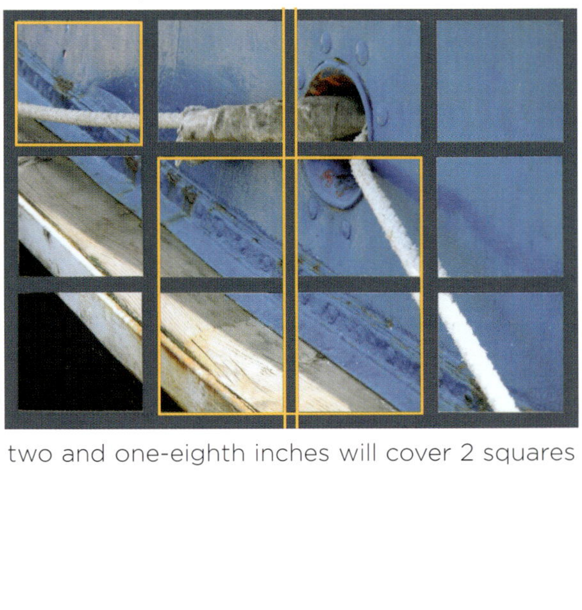

two and one-eighth inches will cover 2 squares

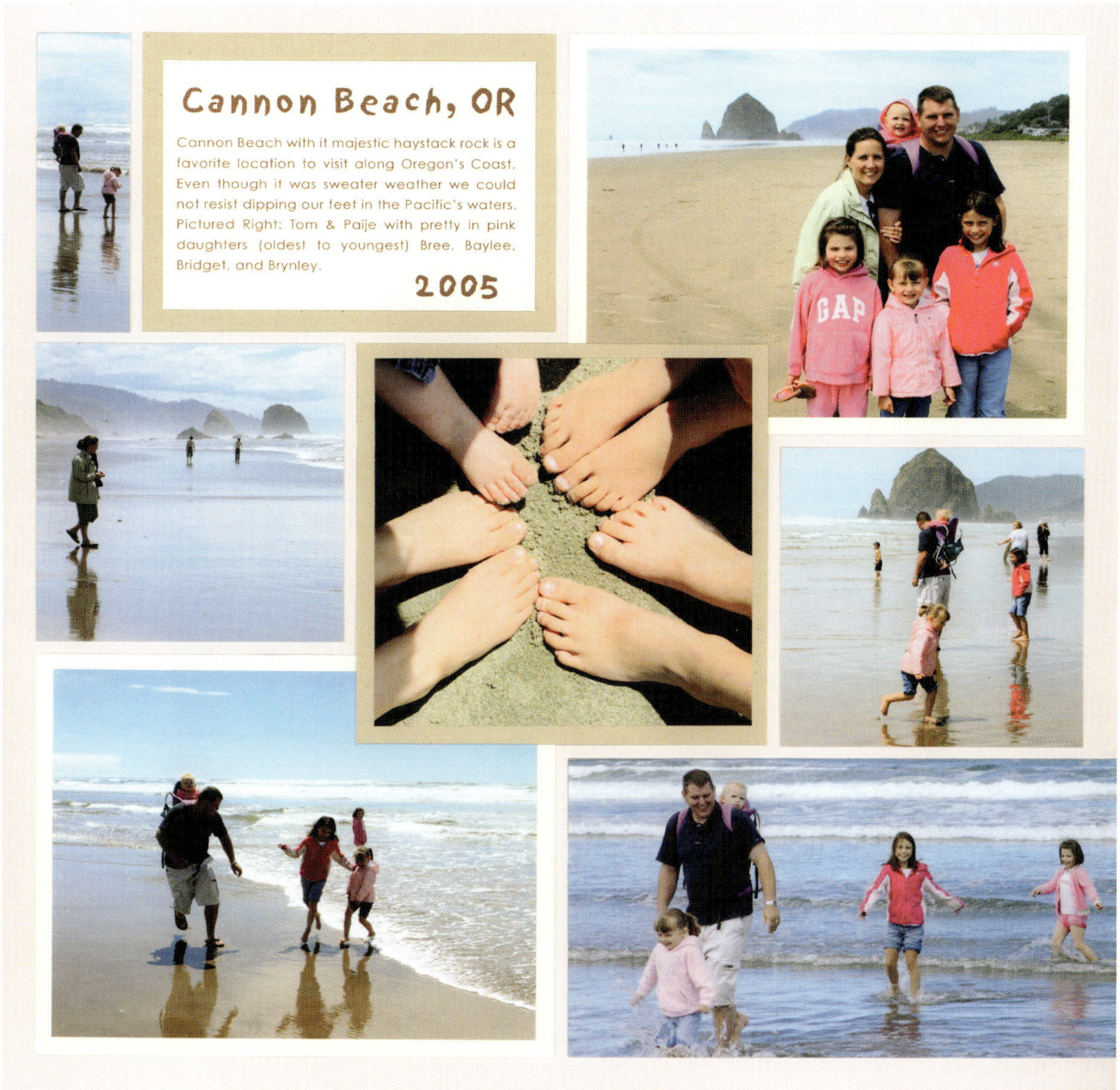

Oregon Coast: Tami Potter
photos: Carla Palmer
number of photos: 6

The Cannon Beach page (pictured above) uses a combination of photo blocks and paper blocks to cover the grid paper. The center photo is matted and overlaps with the two corner photos which are also mounted on paper blocks. The bottom right photo is cut to bleed (extend to the edge of the page.) Bleeding is a good option for this photo because it saves the child near the edge from being cut off. Bleeding can also add interest to the page by breaking out of the margins.

Creating a bleed

- Measure and cut the photo to fit the grid paper in one direction.
- Place the photo on your grid paper letting the excess hang over the edge.
- Trim photo by lining a metal ruler up with the edge of your page. Cut off the excess using a craft knife.

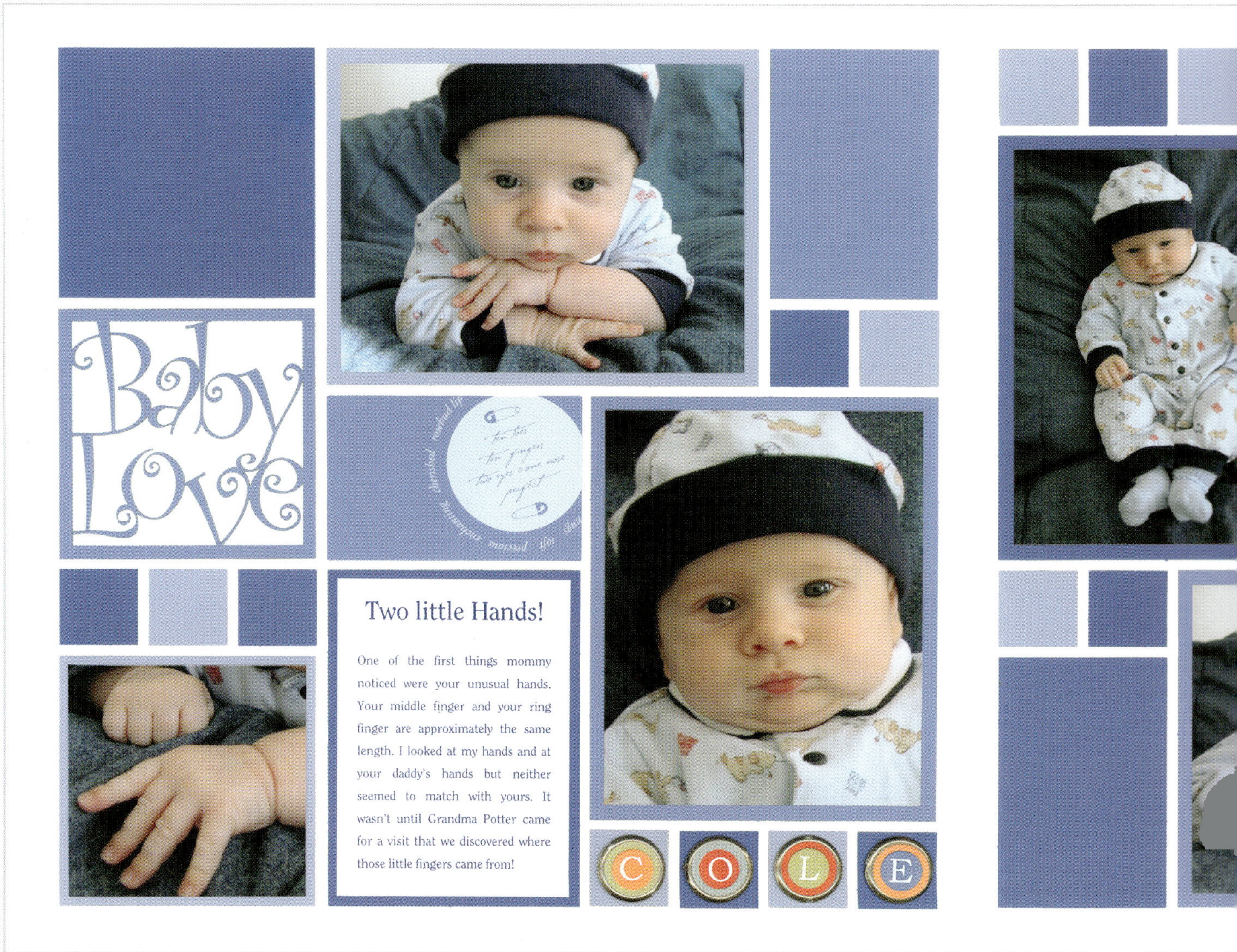

Paper Blocking: Step by Step

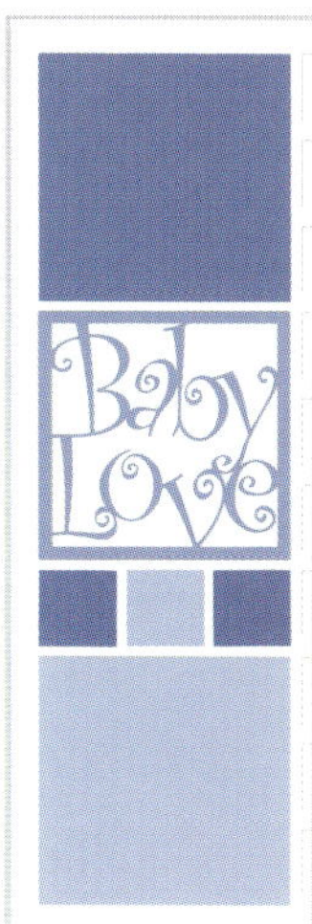

Step One ■ Make a border (or skip to step two). Borders can be placed vertically or horizontally on the top, middle, bottom, or sides of a page. The above layout has vertical borders on the outside edges. (See image left.)

Step Two ■ Begin by arranging the largest paper blocks. Usually these will be the mats for your photos. Try different placements until you find a balance that works well.

Step Three ■ Add "story support" (secondary or supporting elements.) This could be smaller photos or journaling blocks as shown.

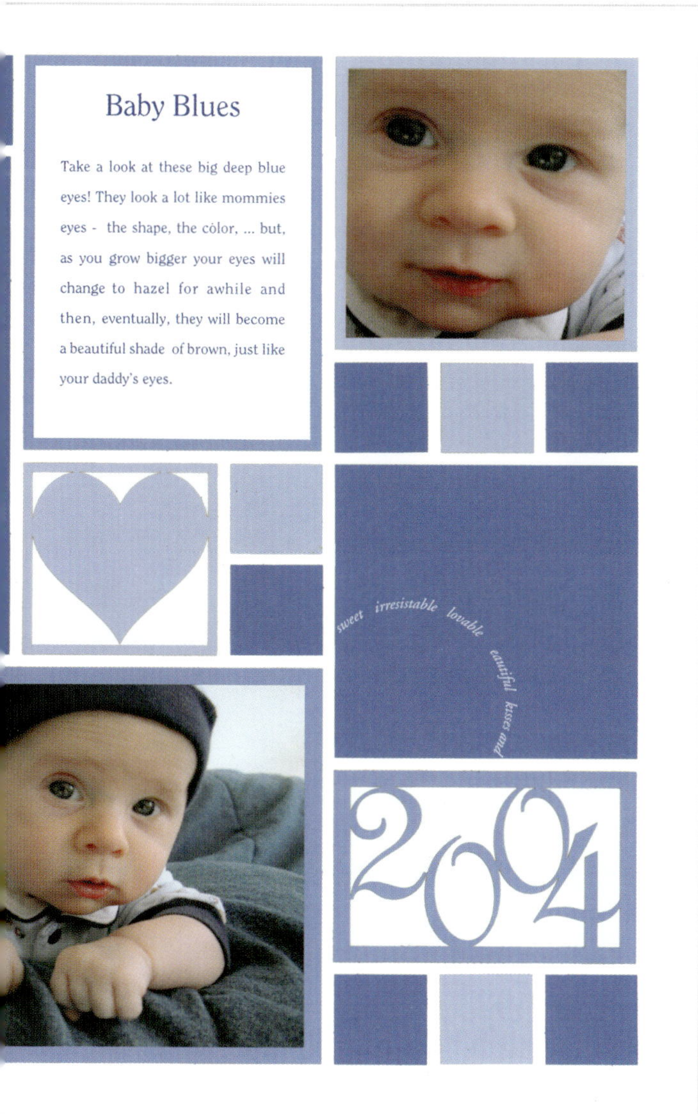

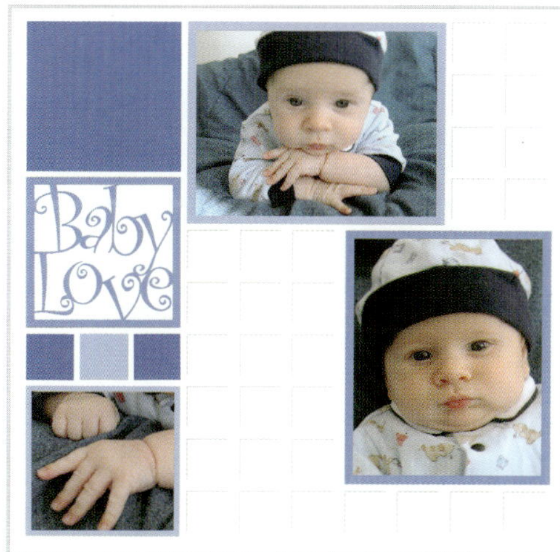

Step One & Two

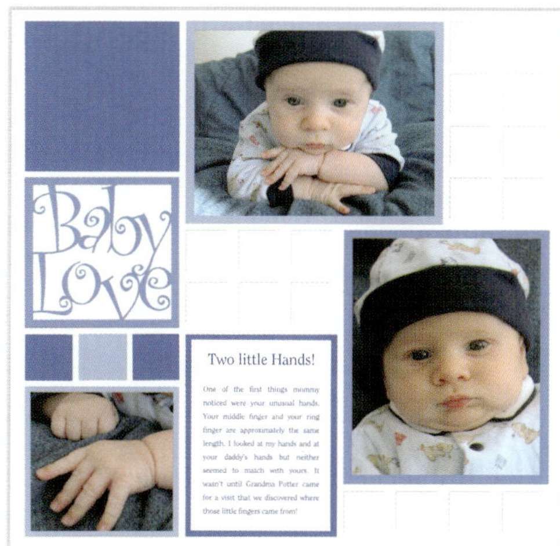

Step Three

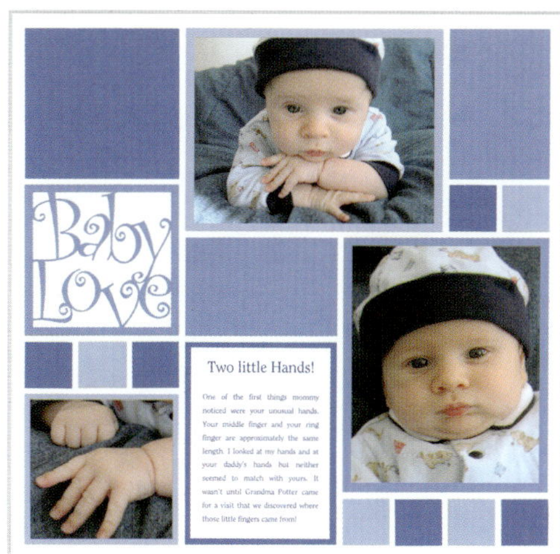

Step Four

Step Four ■ Fill in the gaps. Use various sizes of squares and rectangles to fill in the remaining areas of the grid. You can use monochromatic cardstock as shown above or choose your favorite patterned paper.

Step Five ■ Add embellishments. After you have filled in all of the grid space, try adding embellishments. Anything goes here: stickers, paper, metal, rub-ons, stamps.

> **■ Tip**
>
> Don't overlook placing embellishments off the edge of a block.

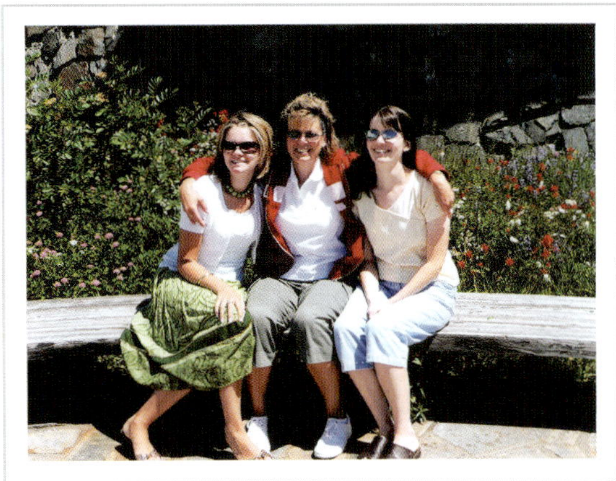

Cutting Photos to Fit Paper Blocks

Step One ■ Place paper block and photograph on mat (lining them up with grid lines) to determine where to make cuts. (See figure A)

Step Two ■ Cut photo using a metal ruler with cork backing and a craft knife or rotary blade.

Step Three ■ After photo is cut, place it centered horizontally and vertically on your paper block.

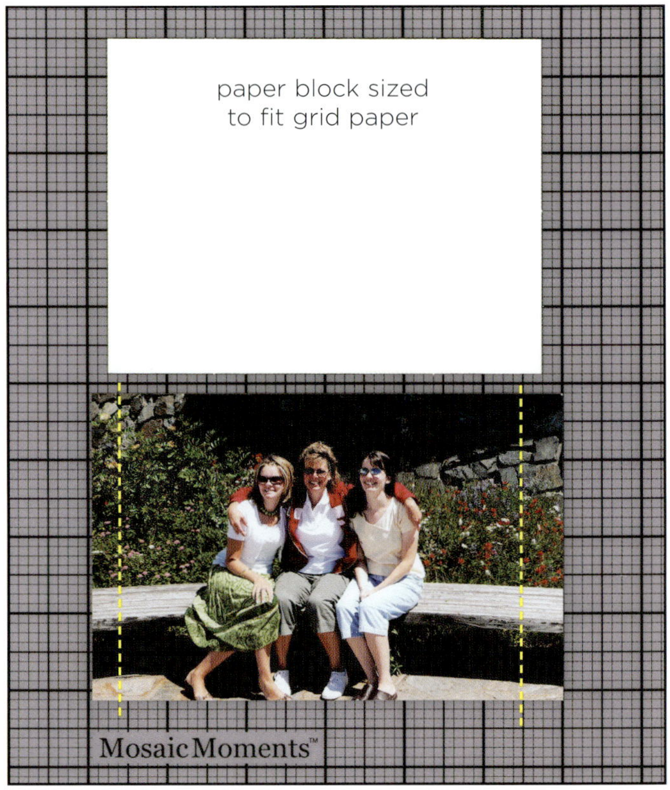

Figure A. Yellow lines show where photo will be cut.

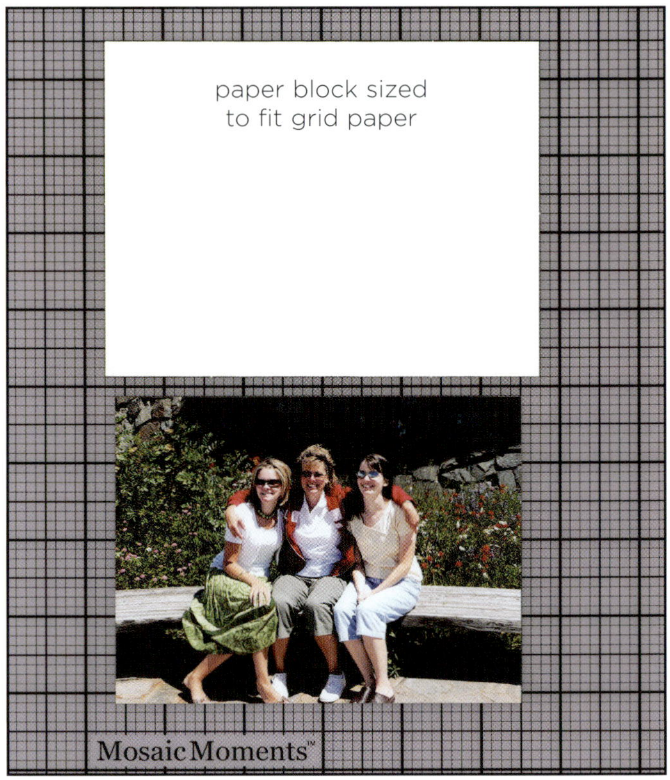

Figure B - Photo is trimmed to 3/8 of an inch smaller than paper block.

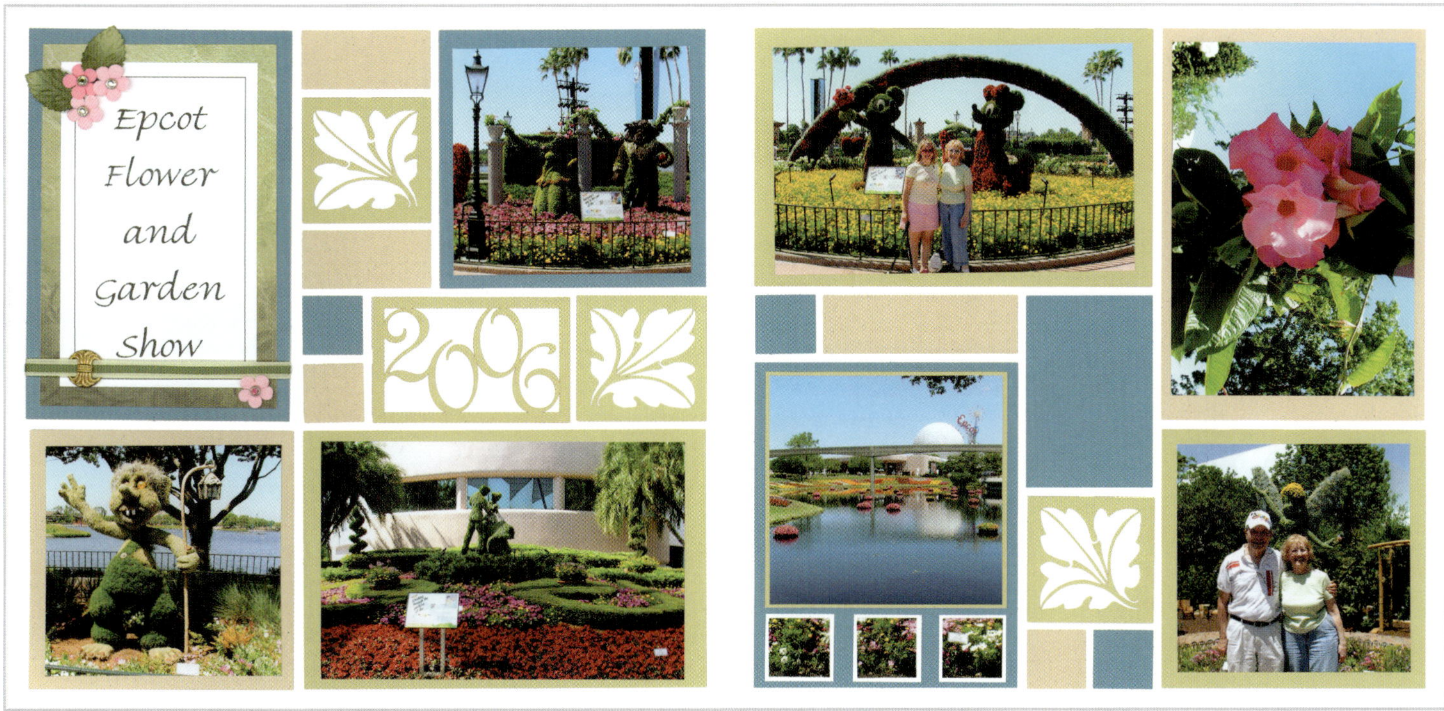

Garden Show: Sandi Keene
photos: Joan Hess
number of photos: 8

Design Solutions

Create Interest on Paper Blocks

Sometimes, when using a paper block that fits your grid space, your photo just doesn't quite match up. This is a great opportunity to design a solution!

Excess block space can be used for many creative applications! Add photo details, as shown in the bottom center of the *Epcot Flower and Garden Show* page shown above. Use a stamped design (right), ribbon (page 71), or a touch of patterned paper (page 70) to fill the space. One of my favorite solutions is to use the excess space for journaling. It provides me the opportunity to write the name of the person pictured, date the photo was taken or whatever tidbit I think is important.

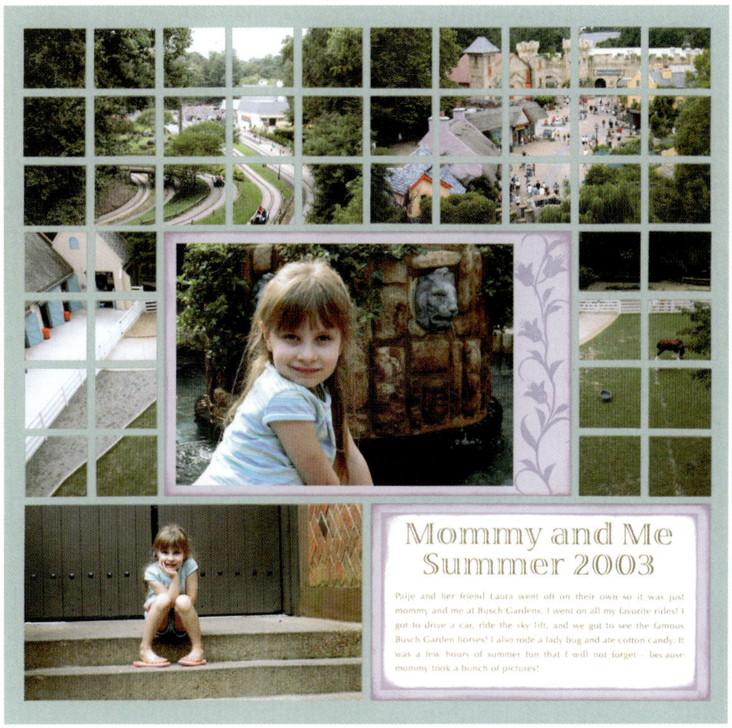

Mommy and Me: Tami Potter
number of photos: 5

Create Interest on Paper Blocks

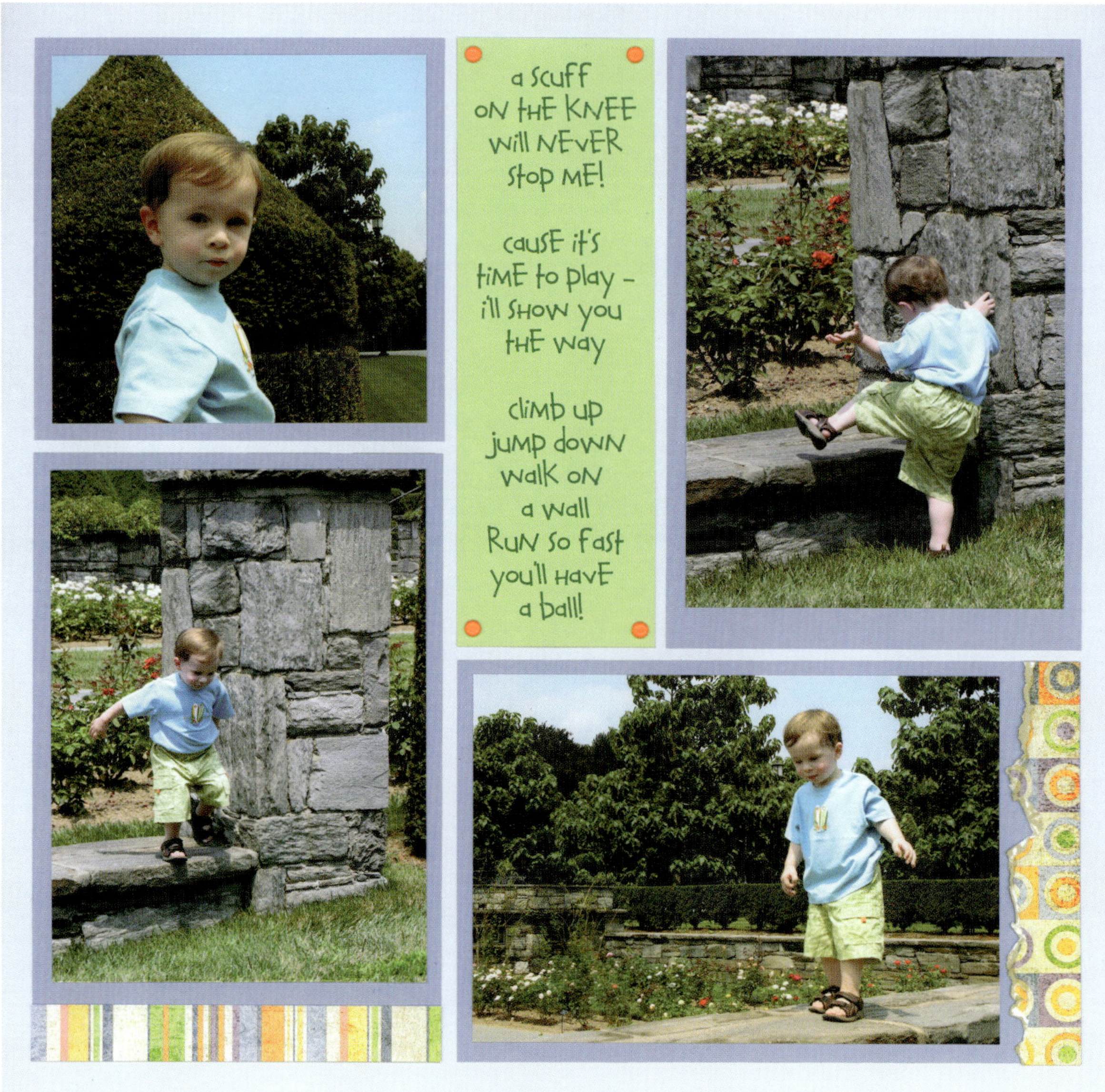

All Boy: by Tami Potter
number of photos: 4

This is Cole, he is my "all boy" boy. I love how these photos catch him in action and how these patterned papers added just a little splash of vibrant color to this page.

When using patterned paper, sometimes a little bit can go a long way. A few strips, as shown above, added a lot of character to the paper blocks.

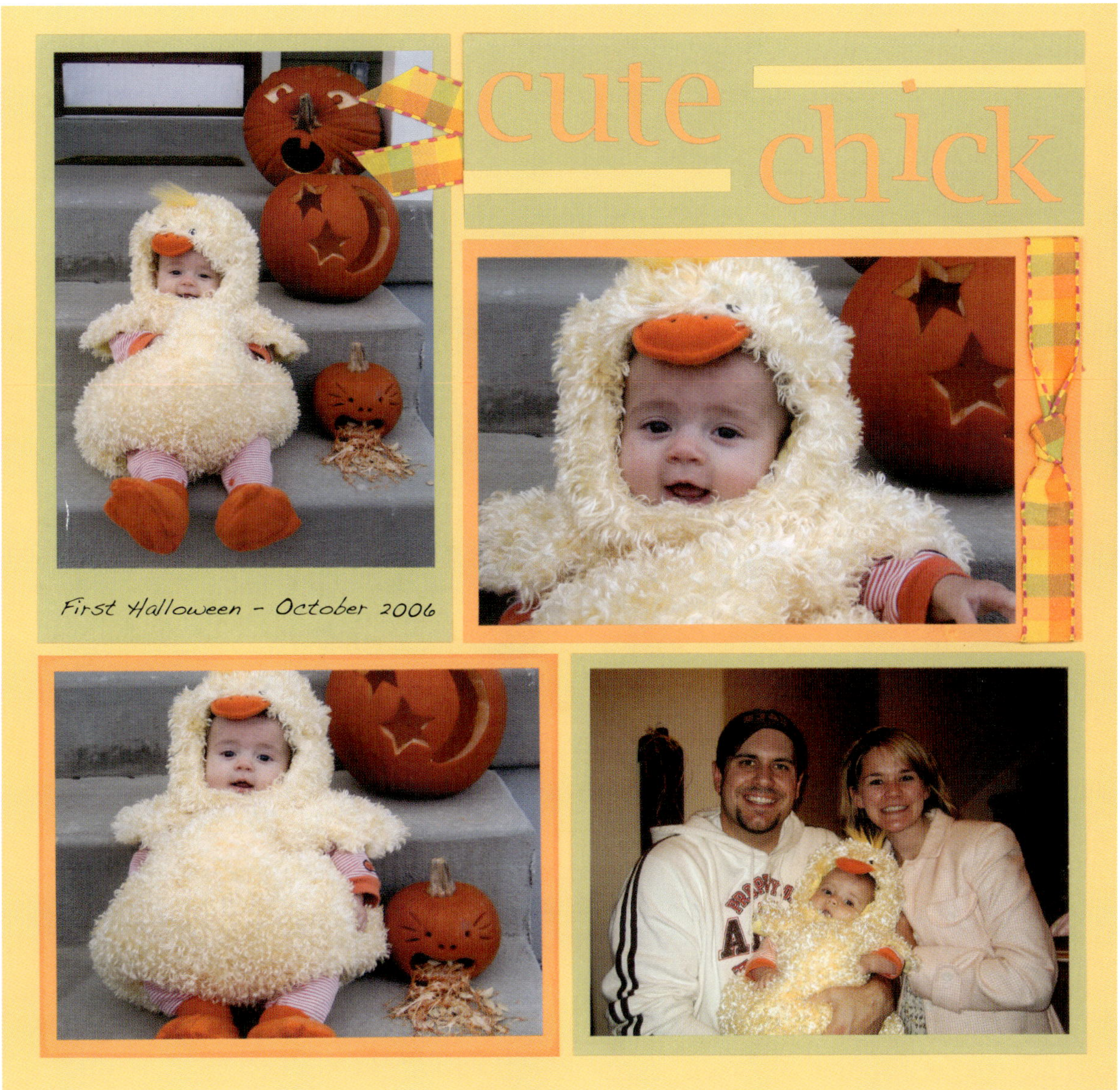

Cute Chick: by Tami Potter
photos by Jaime Zenger
number of photos: 4

Way too cute, isn't she? I needed a paper block solution that could live up to her cute factor. If you run into this problem, try tying a knot or a bow in a length of ribbon and wrapping it around the end of your block.

And let's not forget that paper blocks are an awesome spot for tidbits of journaling!

Three Solutions

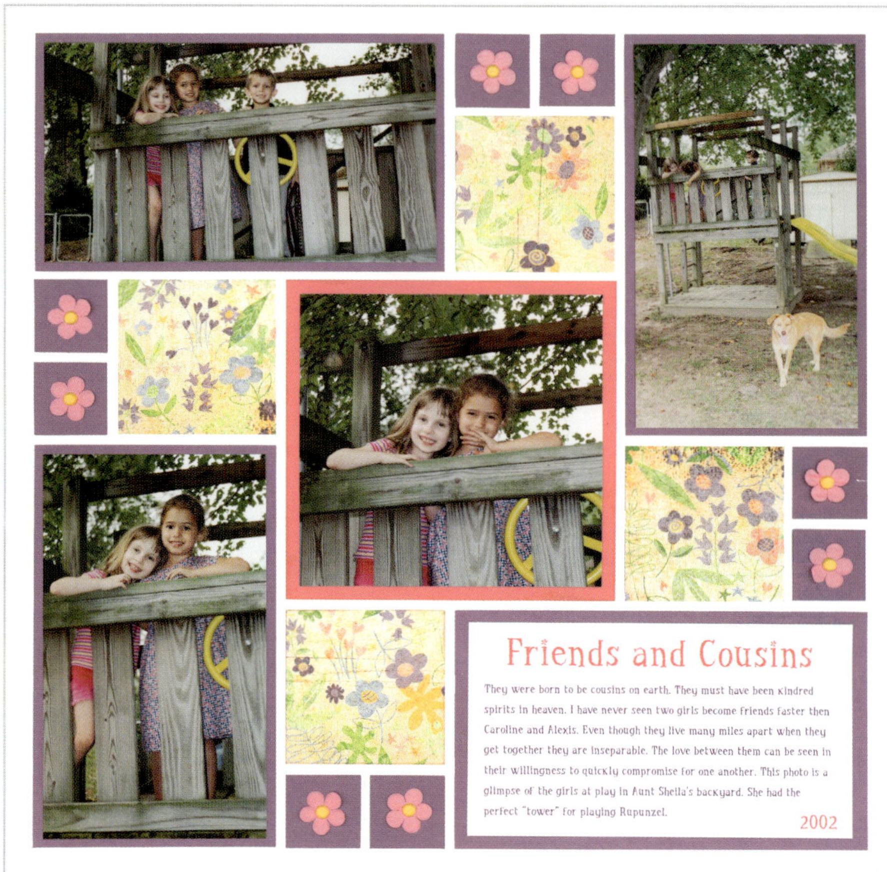

Friends and Cousins: Tami Potter
number of photos 4

Treasure Island: Tami Potter
number of photos: 4

Right page -
San Diego Coast: Tami Potter
number of photos: 9

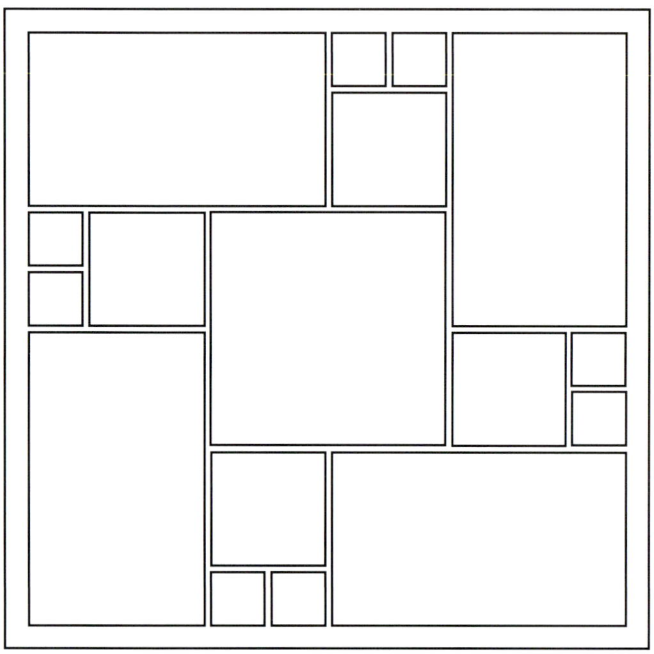

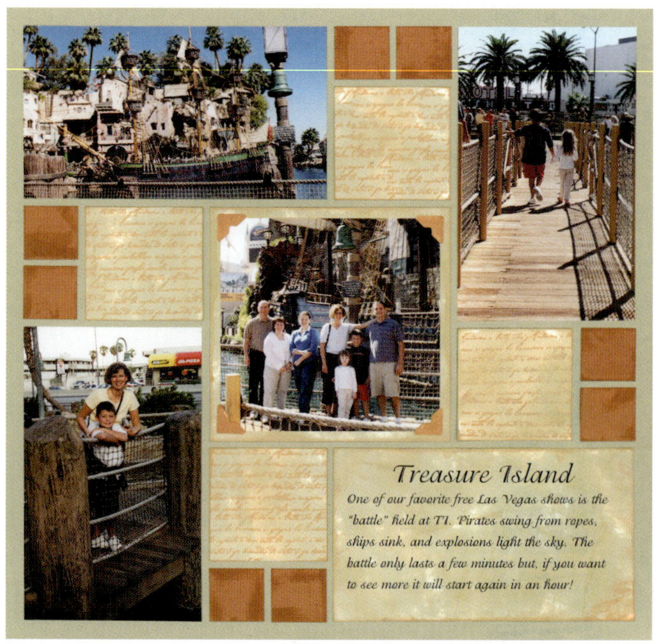

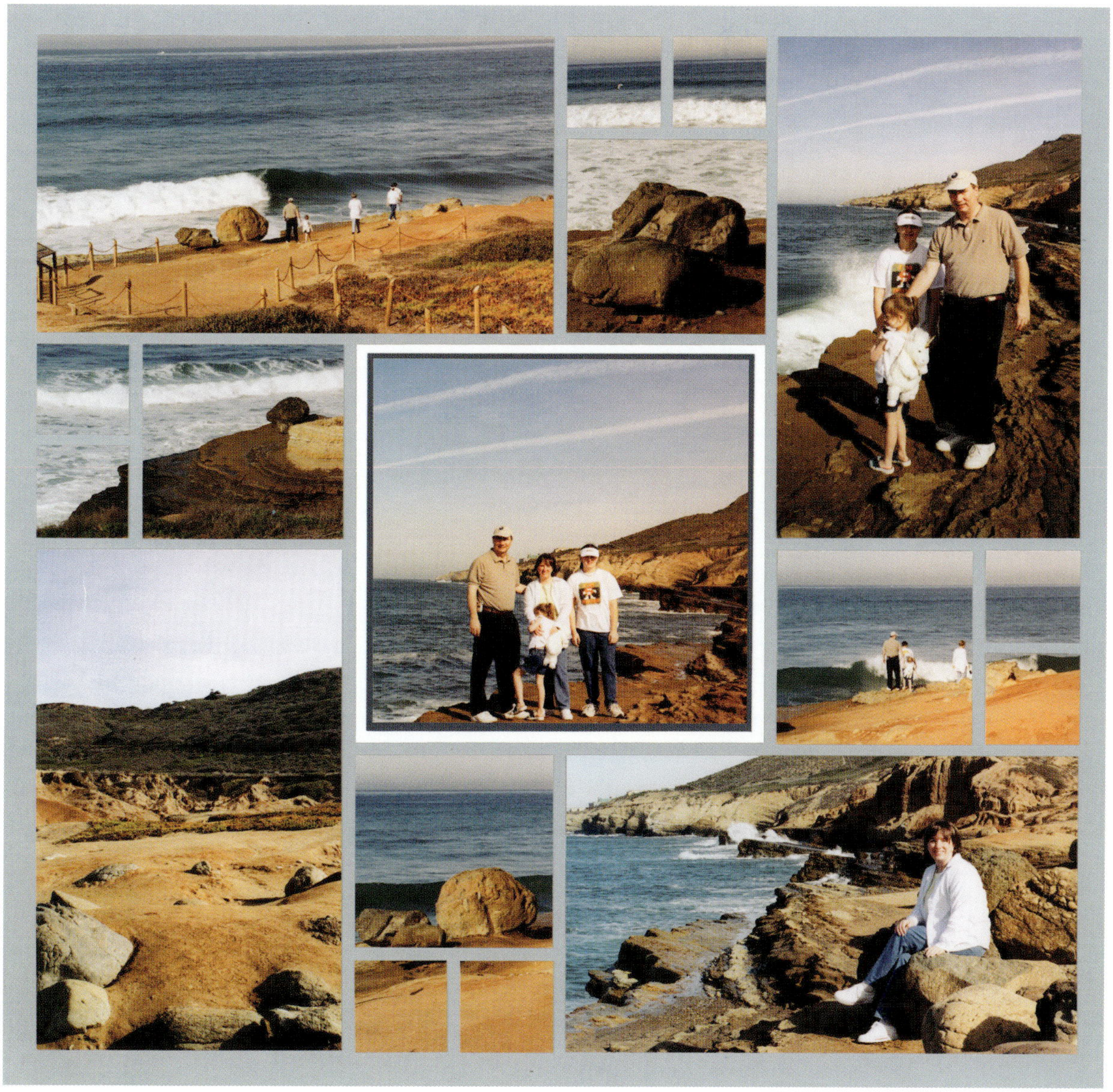

If you have ever sewn a dress, you know how different one pattern can look depending on the choice of fabrics and notions used. Each of the pages shown here uses the same "pinwheel" design; however, the results offer 3 different looks.

Friends and Cousins ■ pretty patterned paper & flowers create a page befitting two young girls.

Treasure Island ■ stamping and distressing techniques are used to create an old and weathered effect.

San Diego Coast ■ Photo details offer multiple perspectives of the unique Pacific coastline.

12x12 Page Patterns

Get your **GRID** on with these page possibilities!

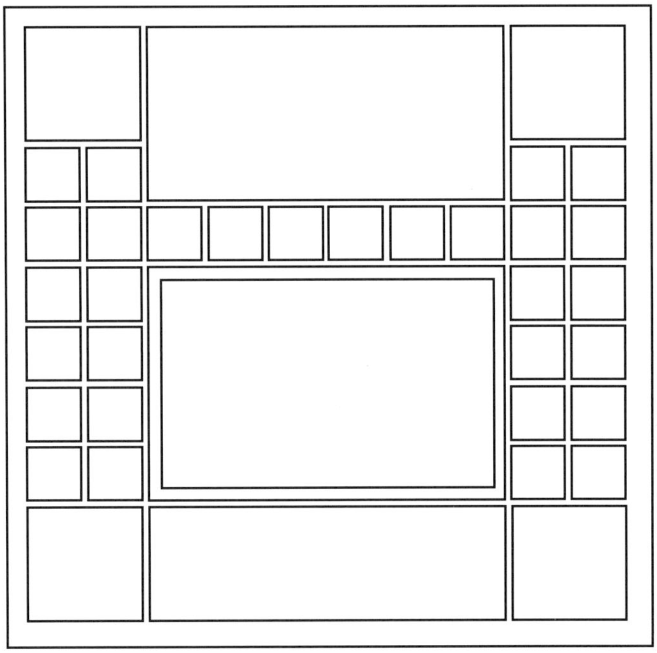

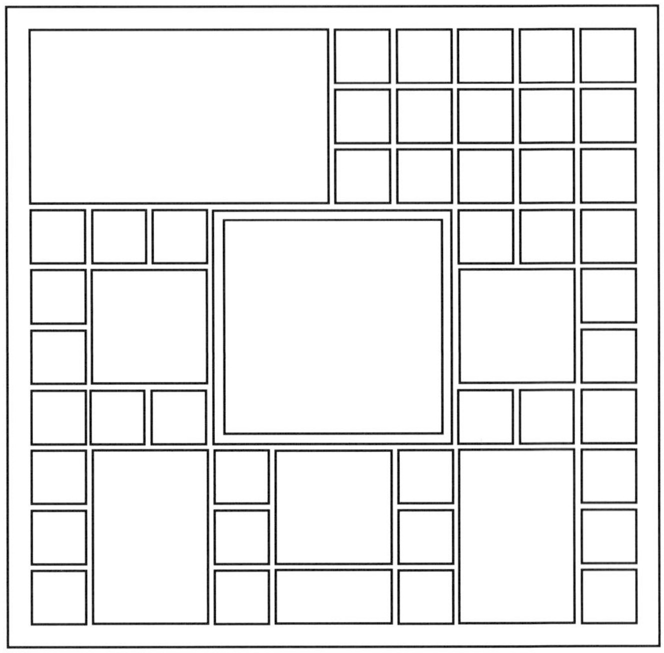

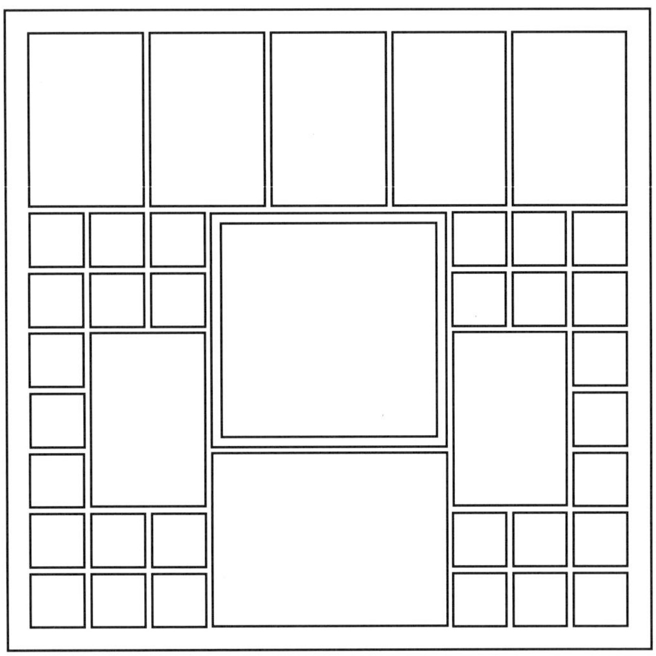

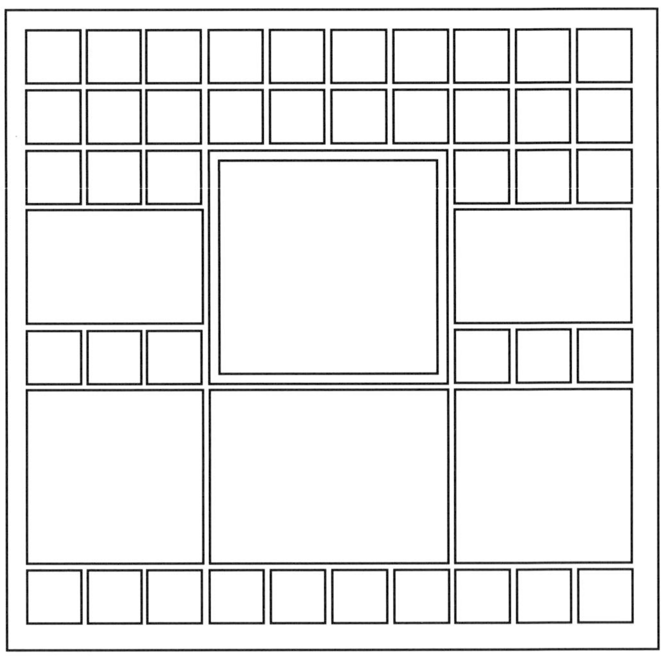

12x12 Page Patterns

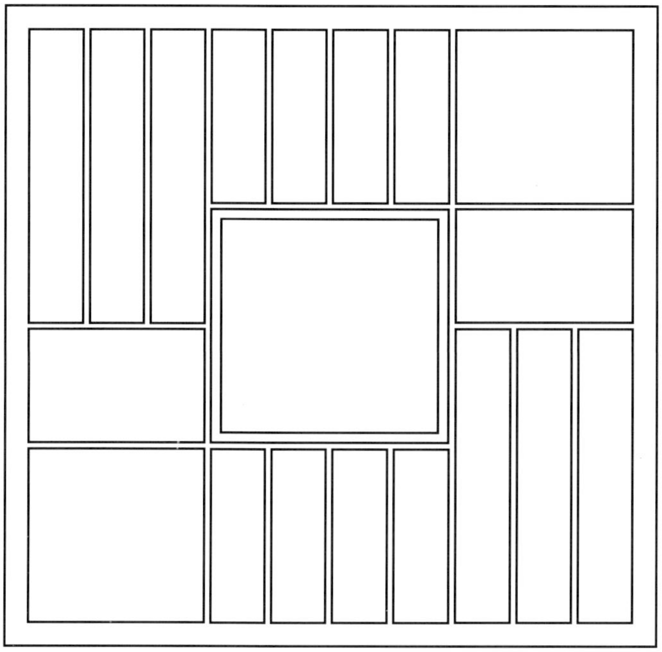

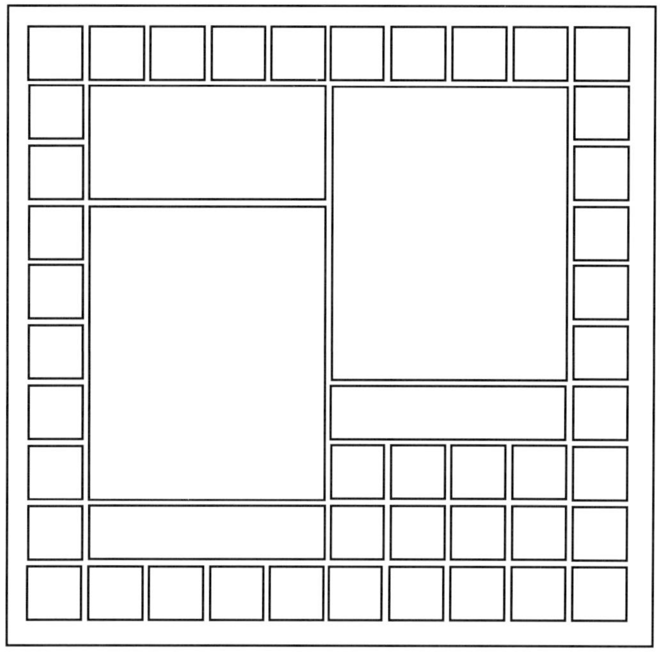

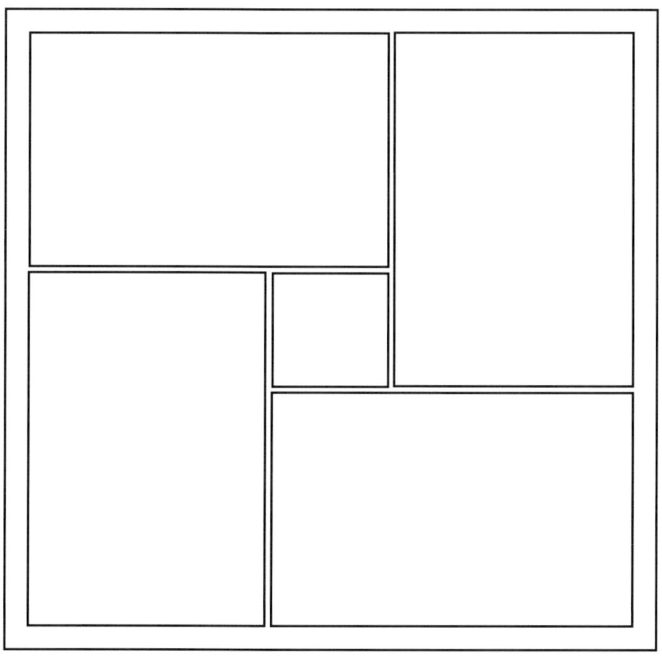

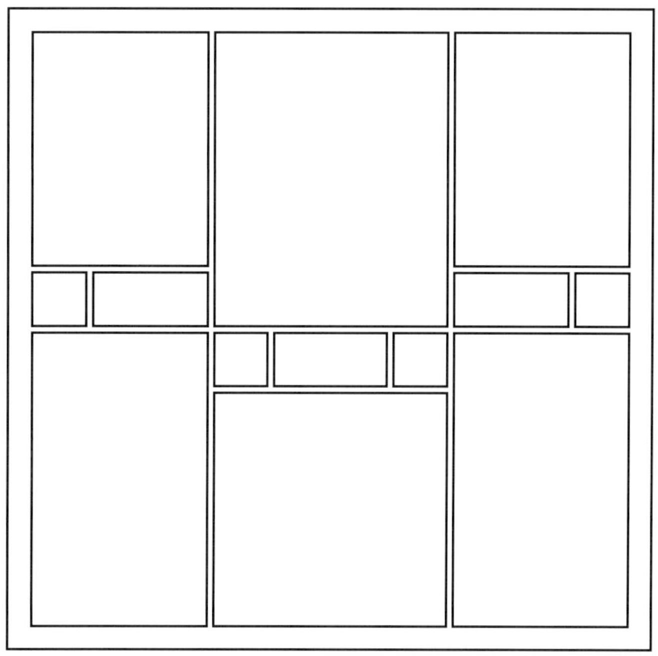

12x12 Page Patterns

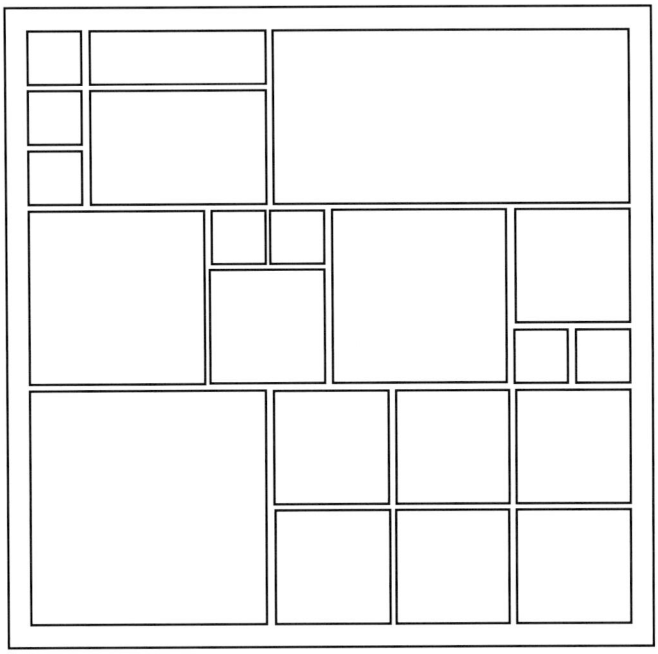

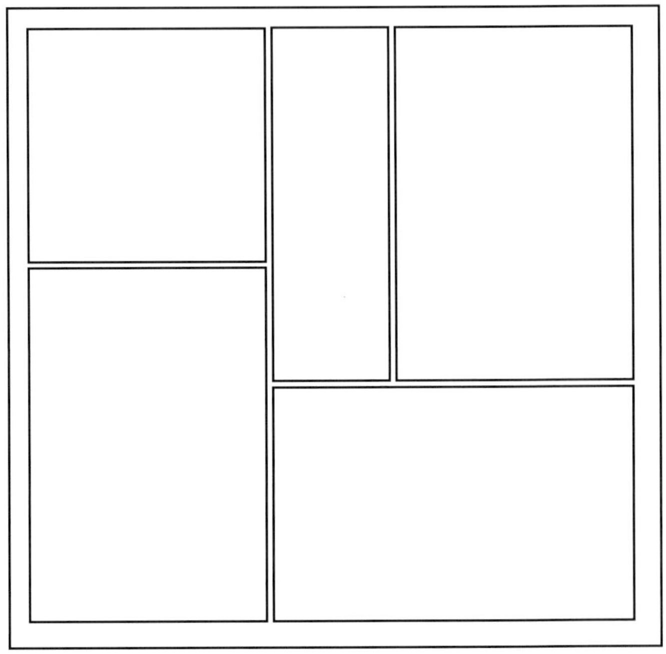

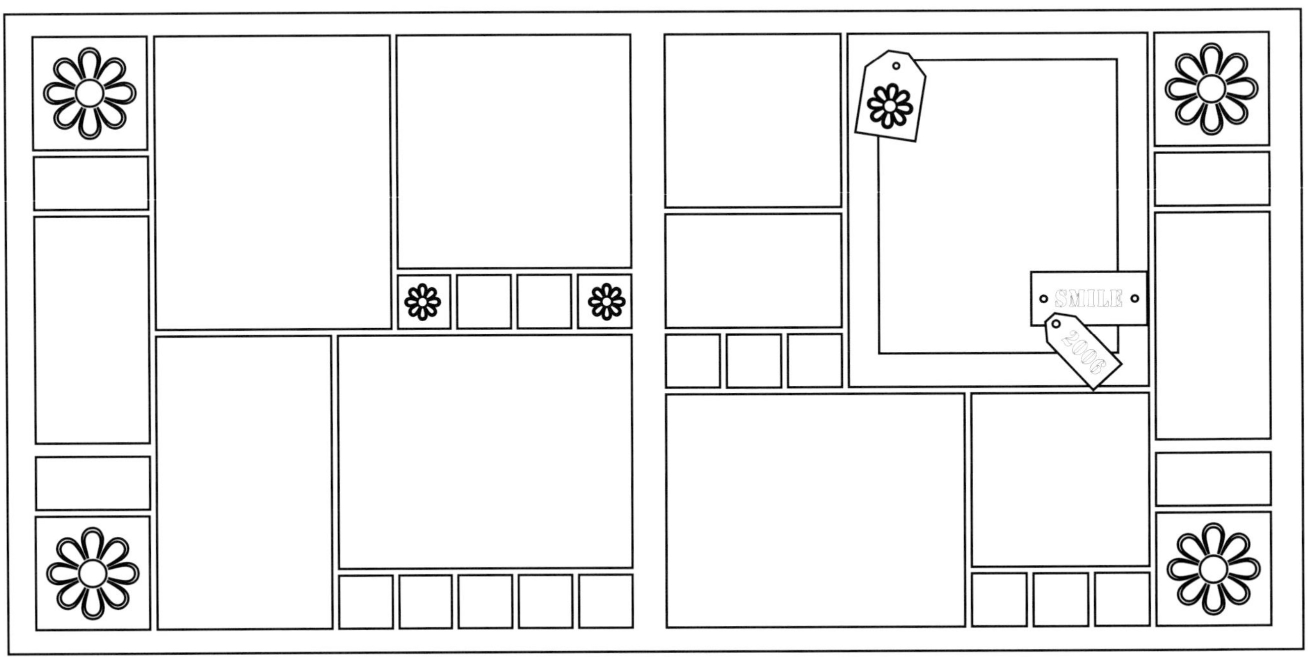

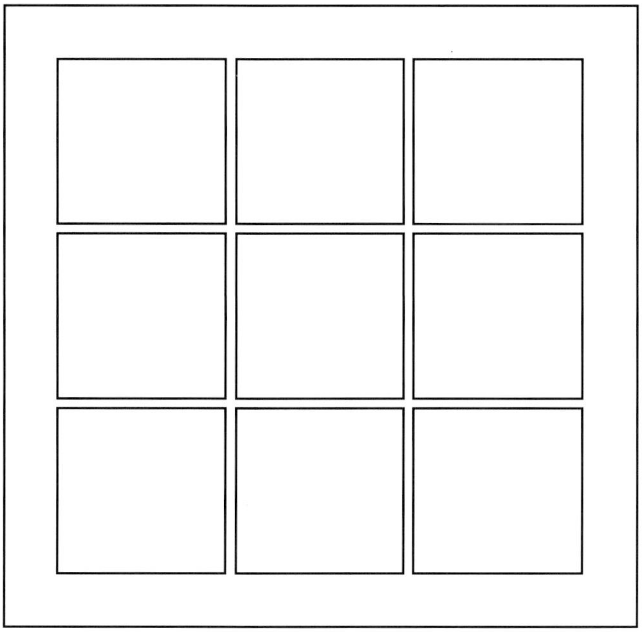

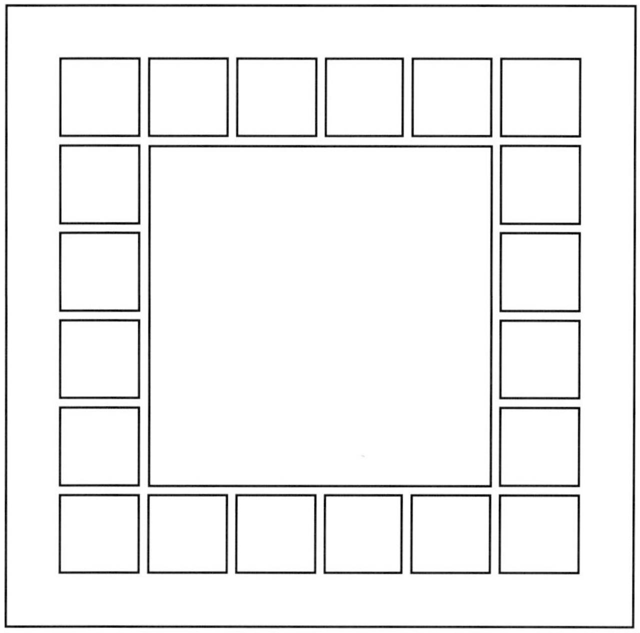

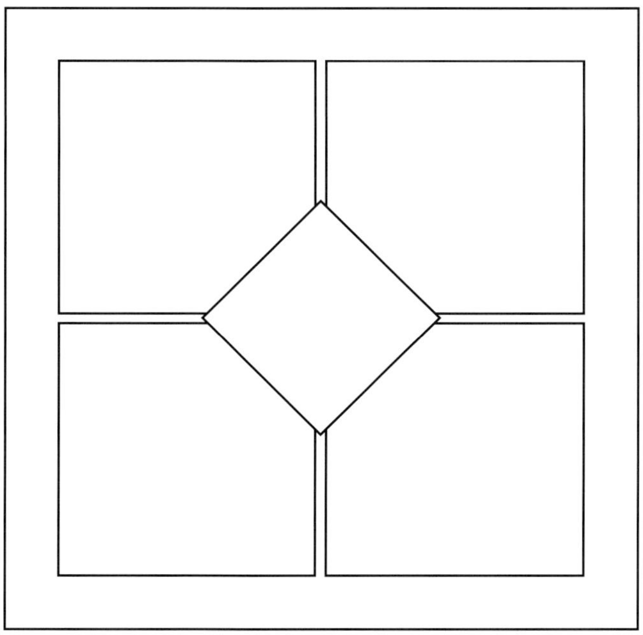

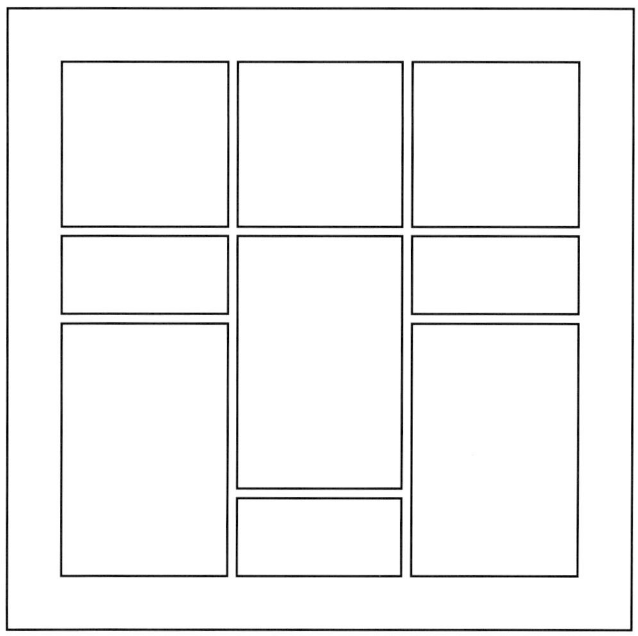

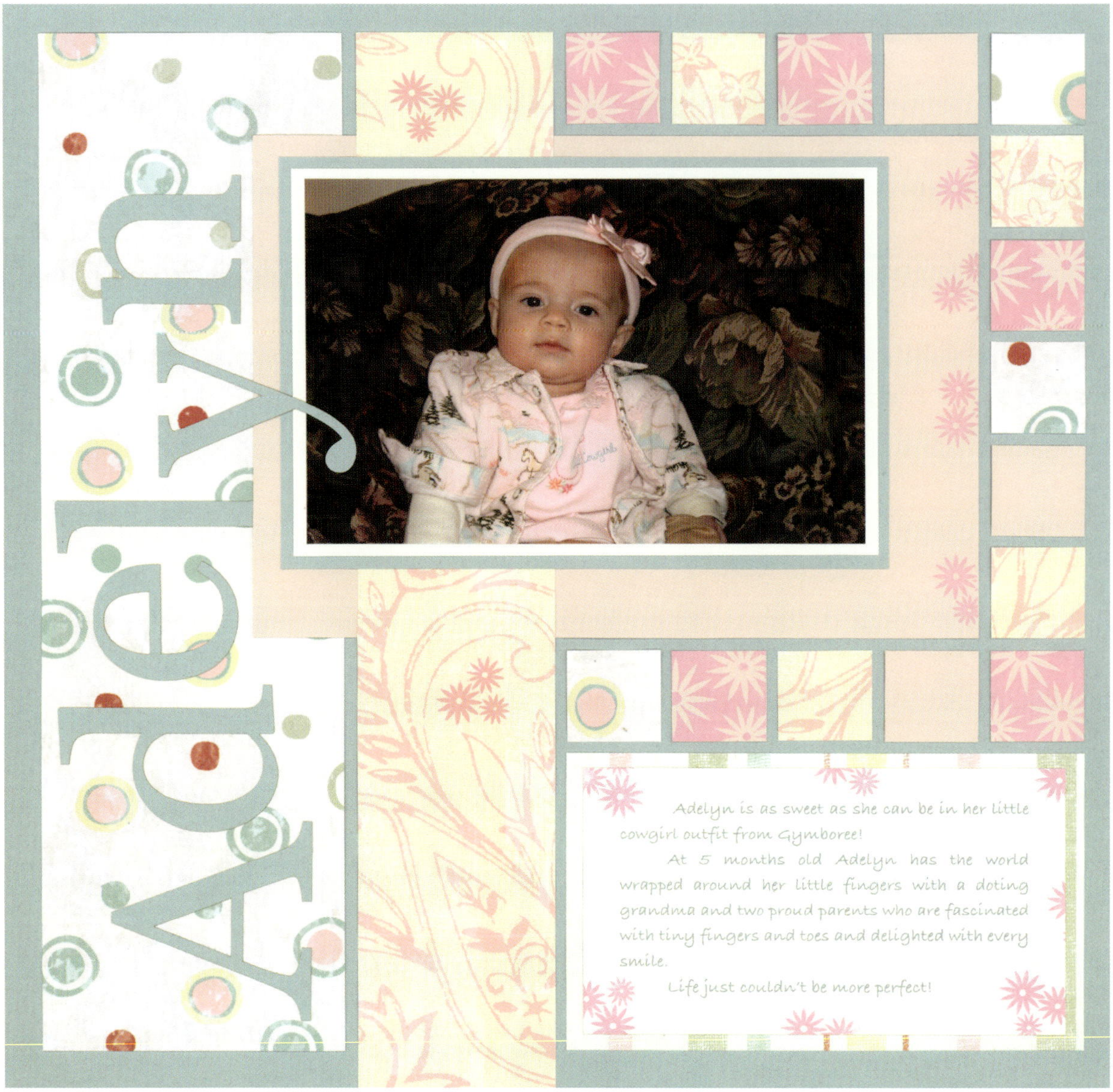

Adelyn: Tami Potter
photo: Jaime Zenger
number of photos: 1

Patterned Paper

There is an abundance of fabulous papers available and it would be a shame not to include some of them on your scrapbook pages. Whether you want to fill a lot of your design with pattern or just add a touch, don't be afraid to cut and highlight the areas of the paper that you most enjoy.

In the sample above, patterned papers are mixed with stamping to create a soft palette for an adorable little miss.

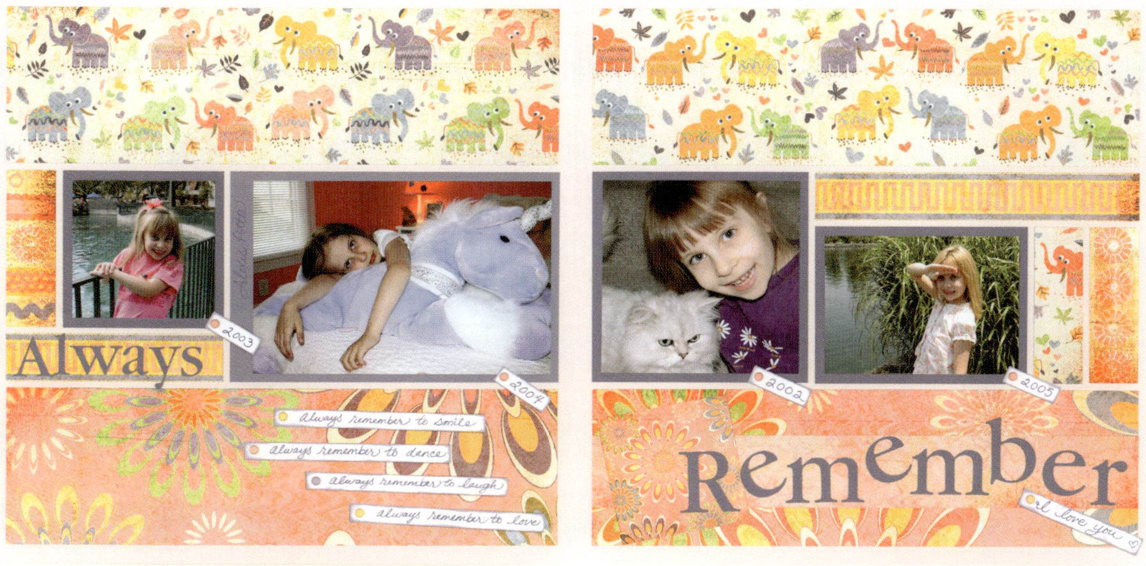

Always Remember: Tami Potter
number of photos: 4

Sometimes a patterned paper can be the inspiration for a page. When I saw these Basic Grey™ elephants I knew they would never let Alexis forget that she is loved.

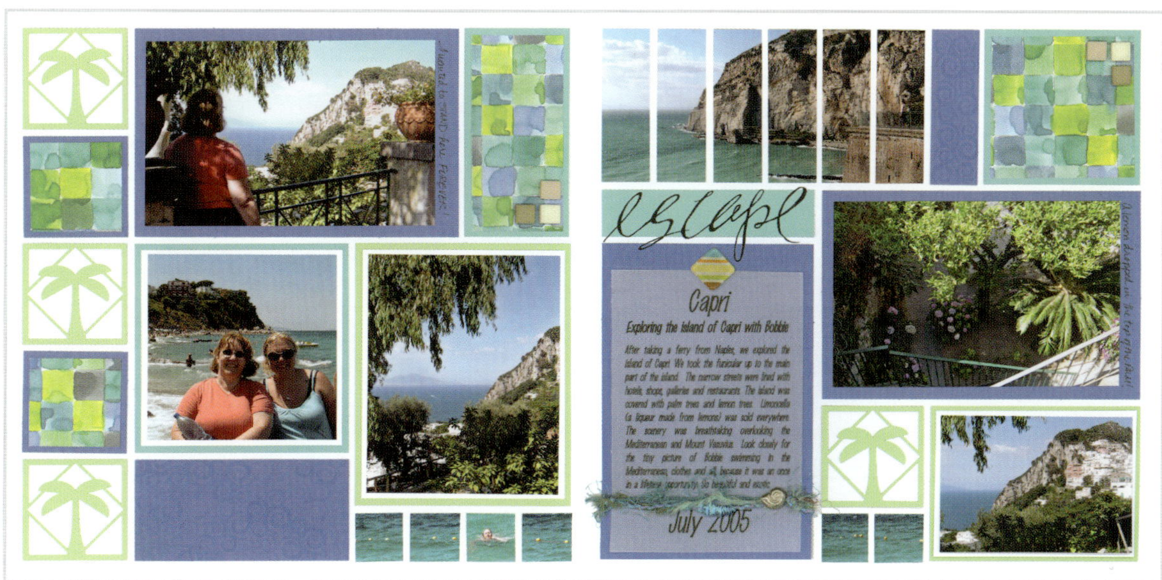

Capri: Sandi Keene
number of photos: 7

Even though she has an extensive collection of patterned papers, Sandi has come back to this "watercolor block" paper again and again. Sometimes a paper just works!

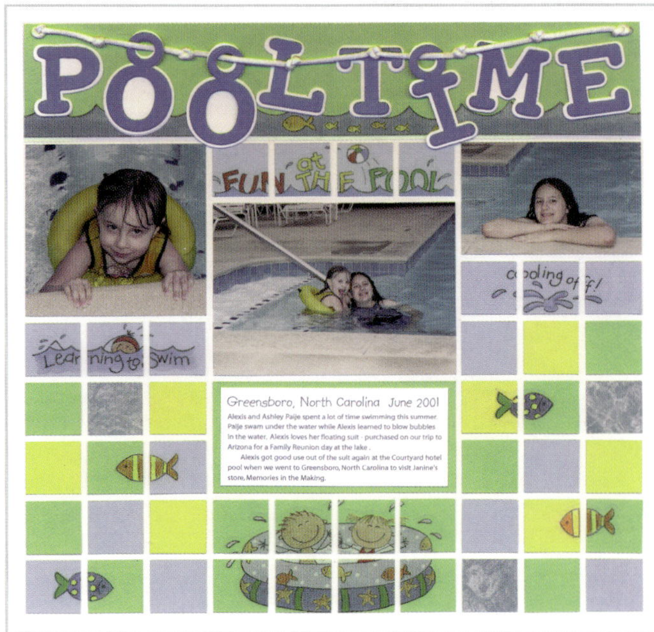

Pool Time: Tami Potter
number of photos: 3

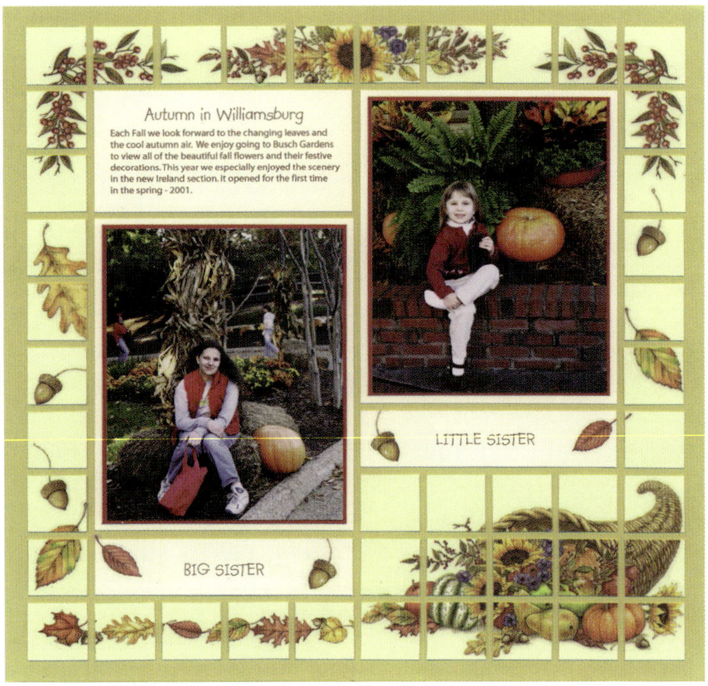

Autumn in Williamsburg: Tami Potter
number of photos: 2

Stickers

Incorporate that great ceramic tile look into your scrapbook pages! Pool side photos are enhanced with stickers mounted onto colored cardstock and then cut into one inch squares.

In *Pool Time*, a few random paper blocks were replaced with 1x1 inch photo squares - extra pieces of "water" that were cropped from the original photographs.

On the *Autumn in Williamsburg* page shown to the left, stickers were mounted on cardstock and cut into 1x1 inch squares before mounting them on the grid paper.

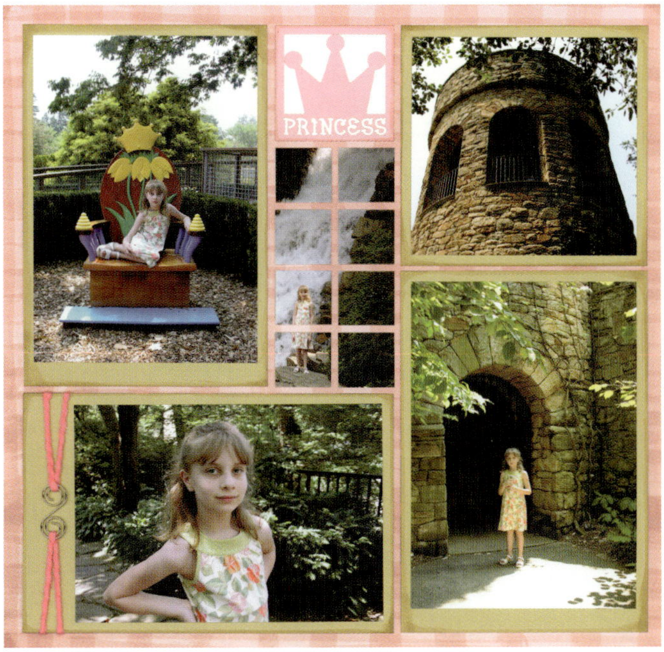

Paper Coloring

Create your own unique grid paper. Many types of inks, stains, chalks, and paints can be used to personalize your grid.

The two pages shown on this page were colored using liquid paper stain.

Princess Alexis: Tami Potter
number of photos: 5

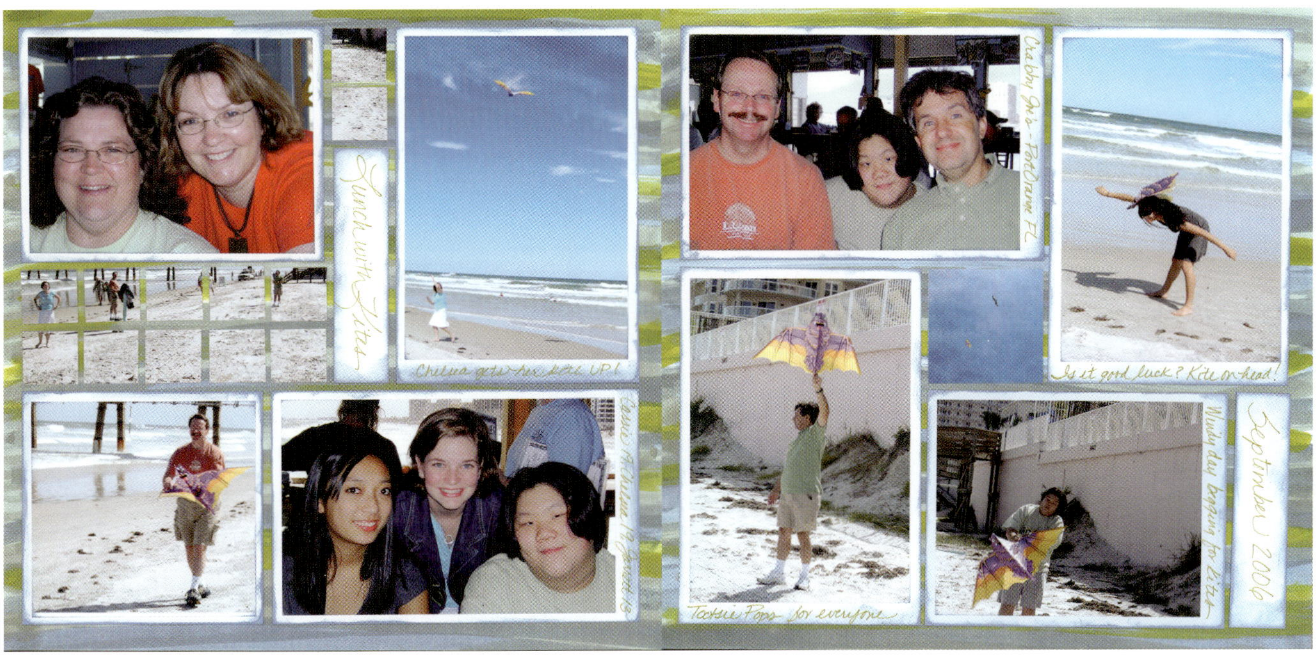

Kite Flying: Sandi Keene
number of photos: 9

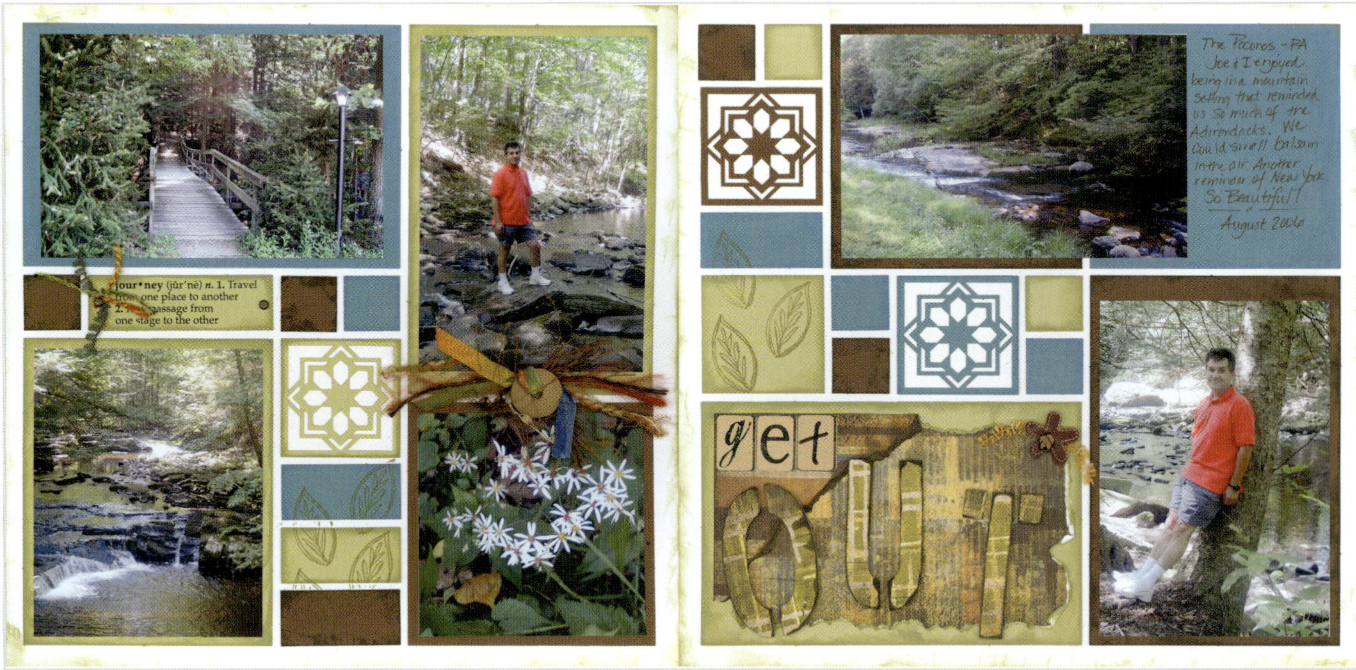

Get Out: Sandi Keene
number of photos: 6

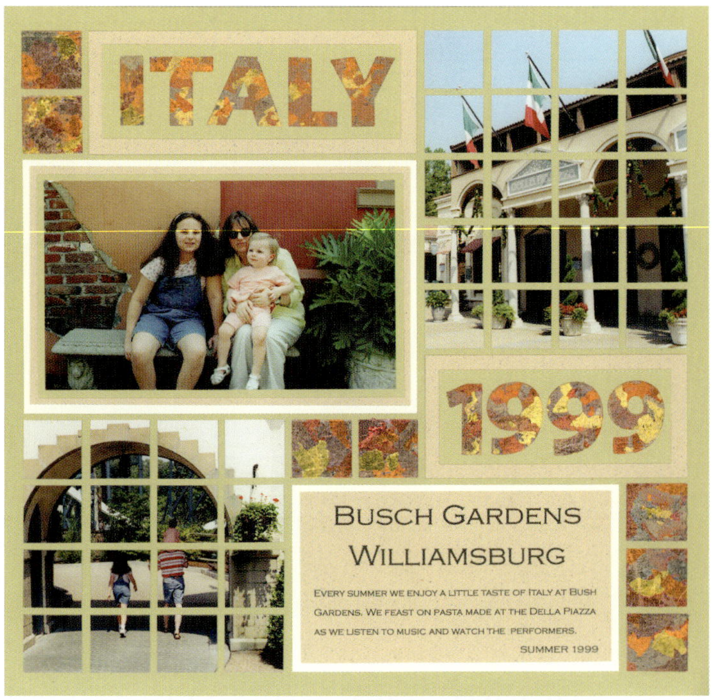

Busch Gardens-Italy: Tami Potter
number of photos: 3

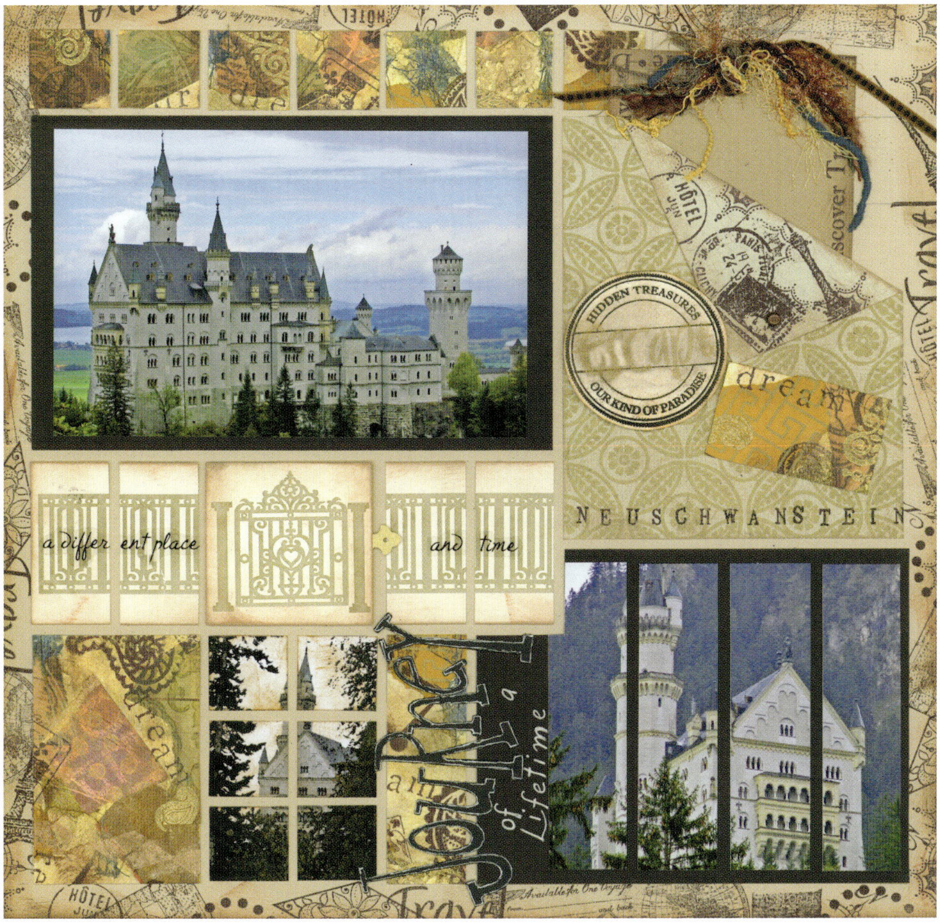

Castle: Angela Andrews
number of photos: 3

Whatever You Bring

There is really no reason, besides your own preferences, to limit yourself when using grid paper. It can be used as your entire background or cut up and used as a border. You can add brads, buttons, ribbons, and fibers. You can layer on it, stamp on it, put pockets on it, tear it, cut it, and stain it. You can alter it until it is hardly recognized, or you can simply add photos. You are the designer. It is all up to you.

- stamping
- fibers
- inking
- staining
- torn paper
- chipboard
- foiling
- layering
- pockets
- everything

but the

kitchen sink

Gallery

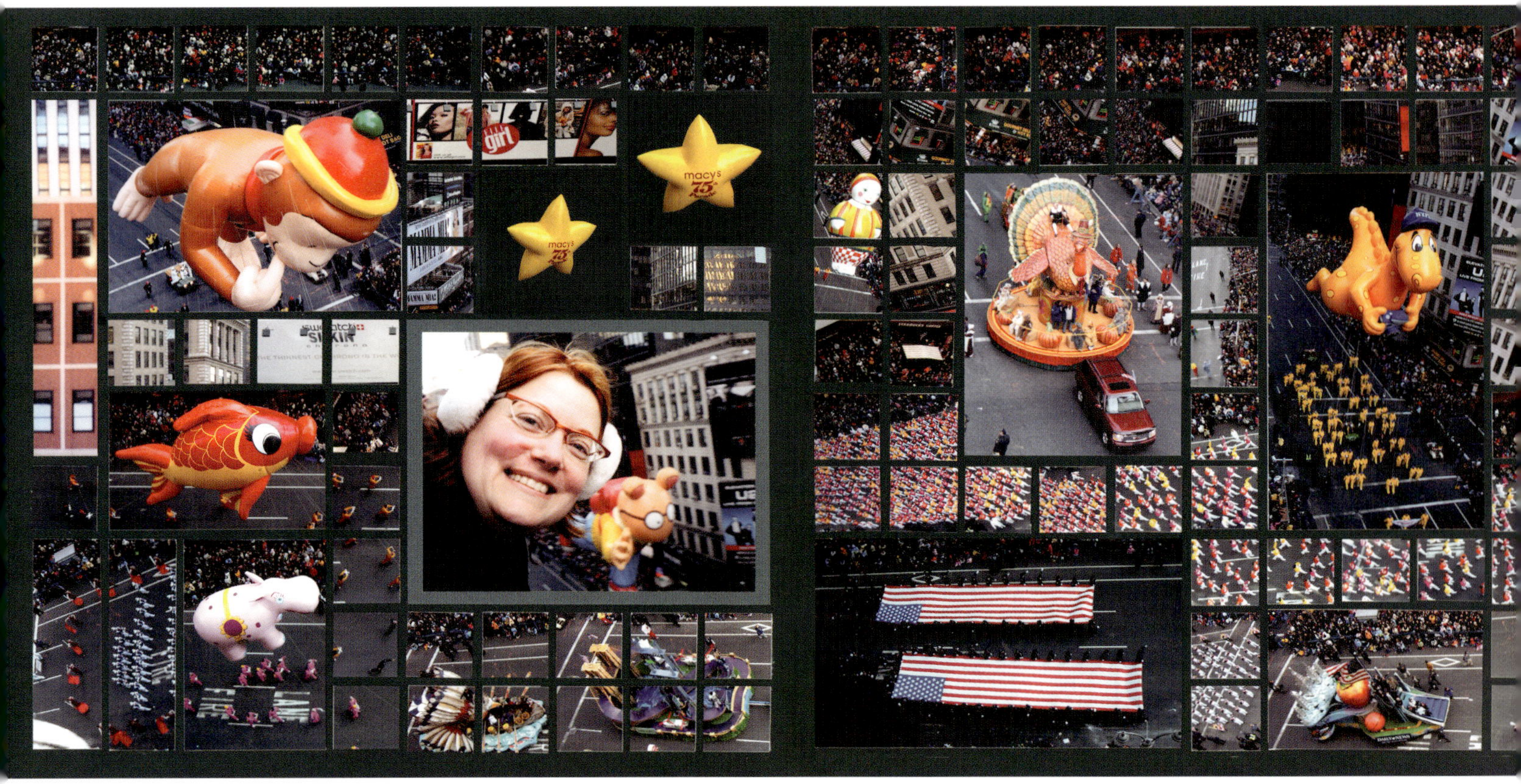

Macy's Parade: Joan Hess
number of photos: a lot

A photo mosaic creates a view like no patterned paper, sticker, or shape can. It is an excellent way to capture the sunset, a waterfall, a stadium, or the expansive shores of Florida. All it takes is a few more clicks and few more cuts.

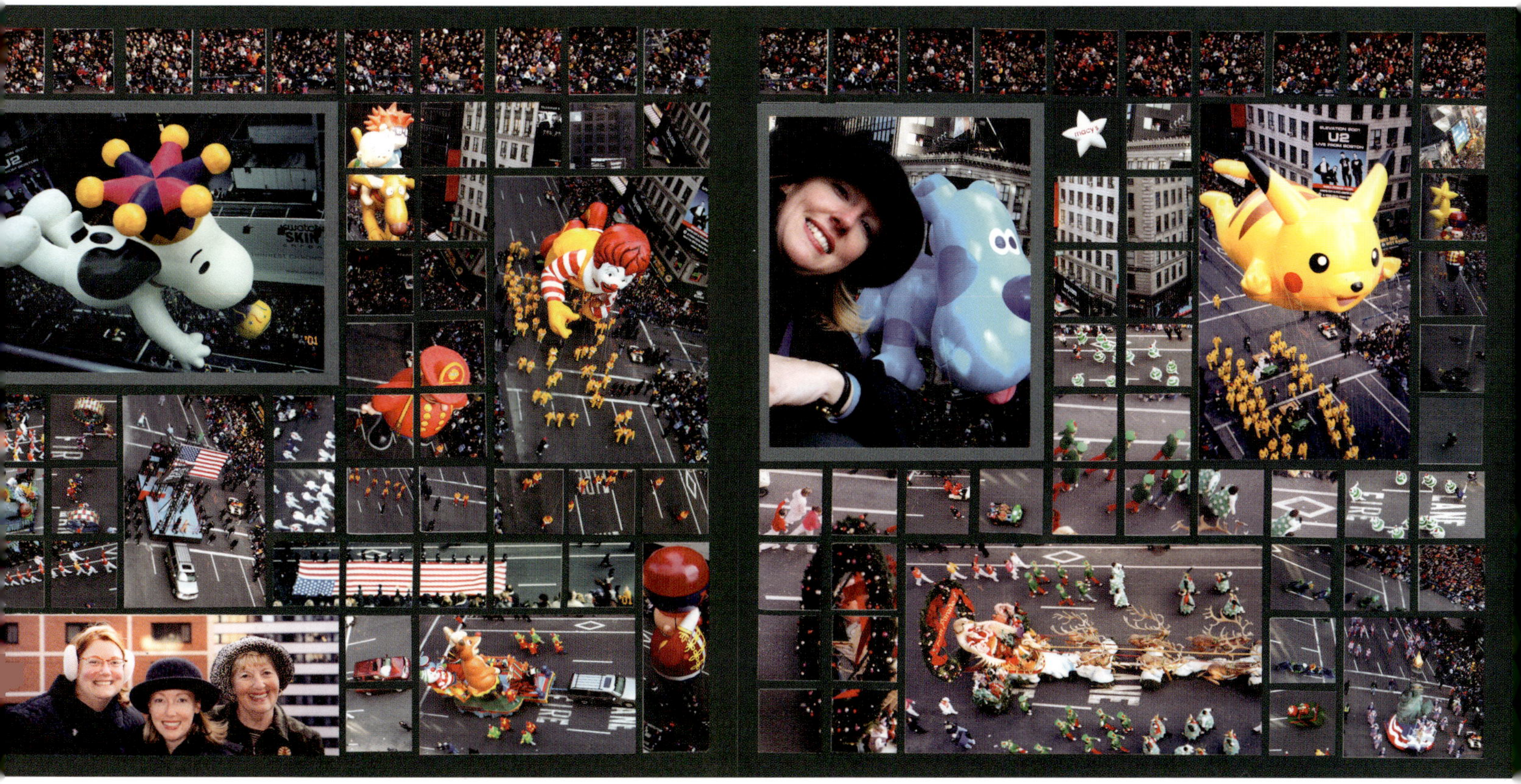

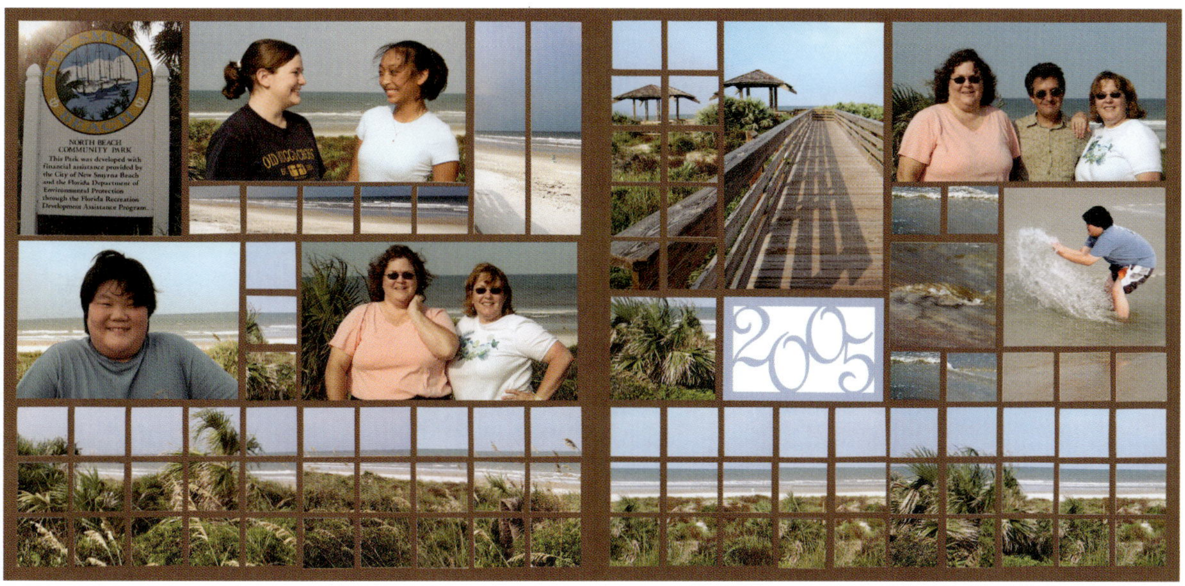

New Smyrna Beach: Sandi Keene
number of photos: 13

Gallery

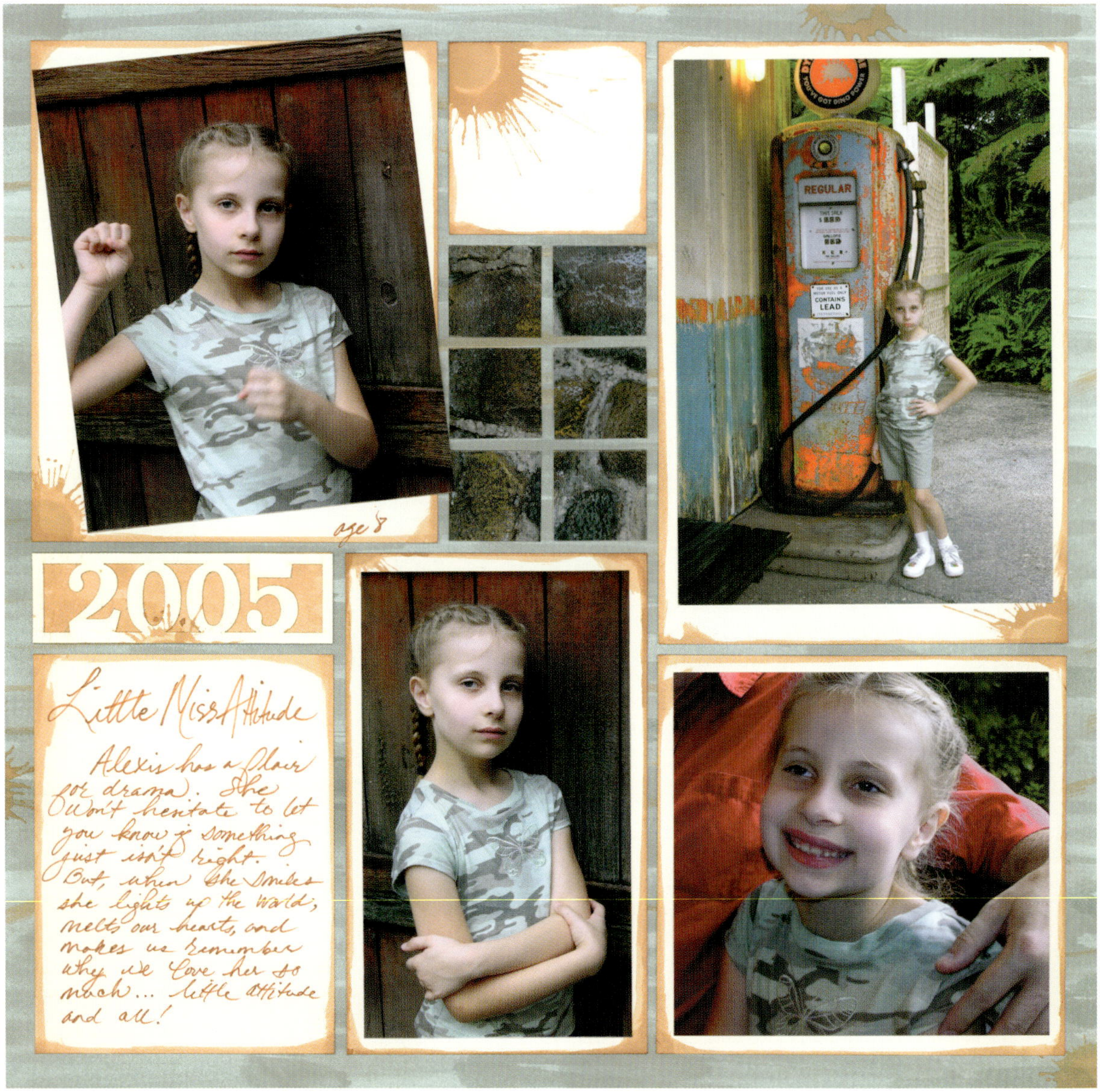

Little Miss Attitude: Tami Potter
number of photos: 4

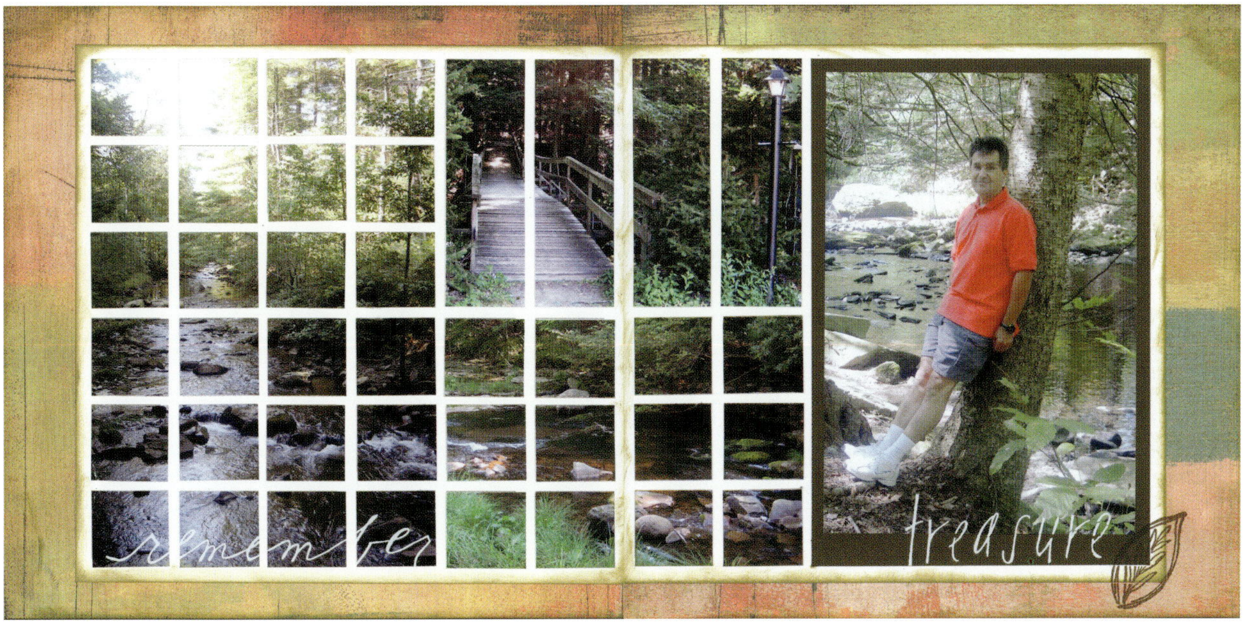

Hiking: Sandi Keene
number of photos: 5

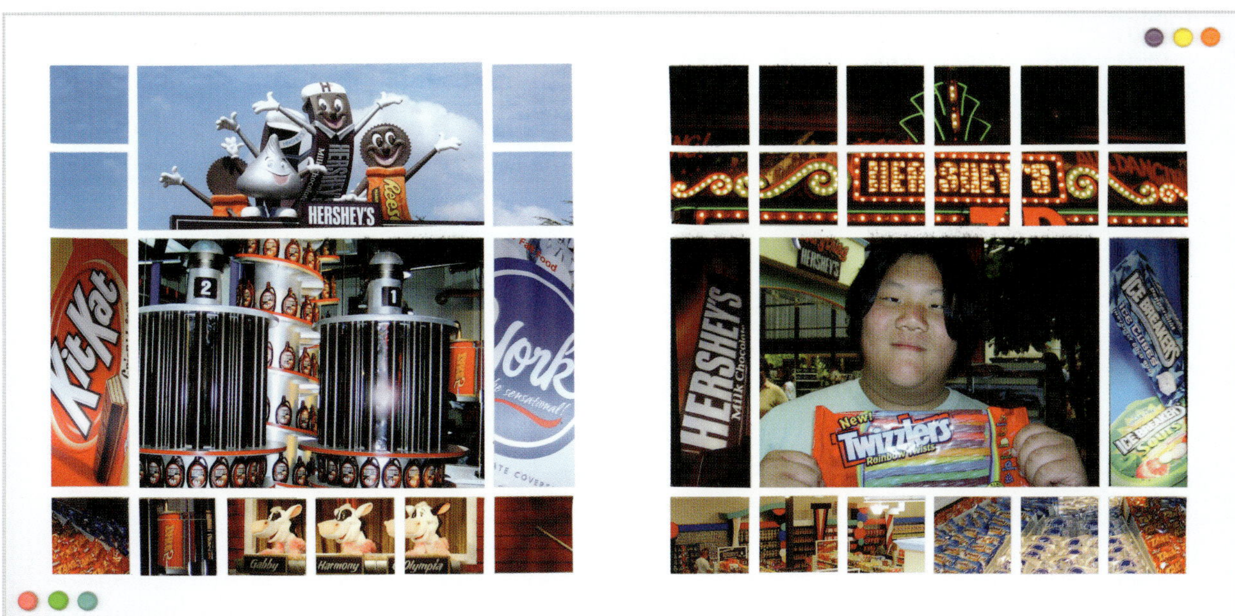

Hershey: Sandi Keene
number of photos: 8

Gallery

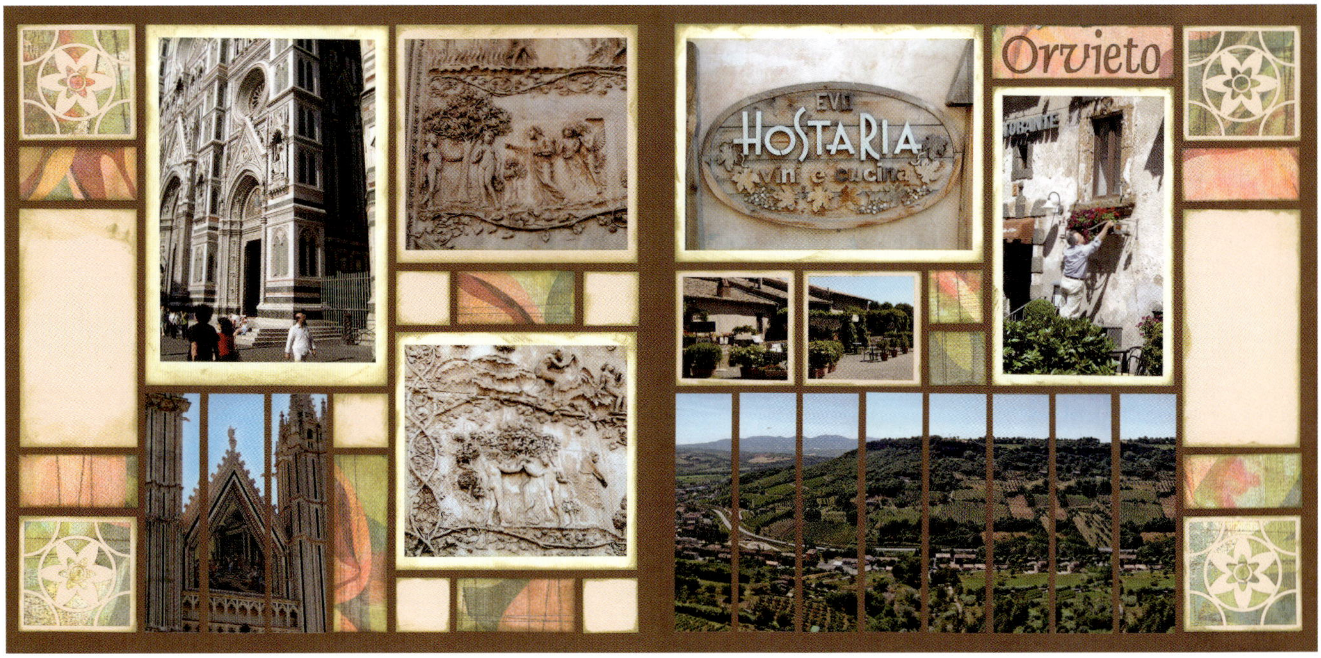

Orvieto: Sandi Keene
number of photos: 9

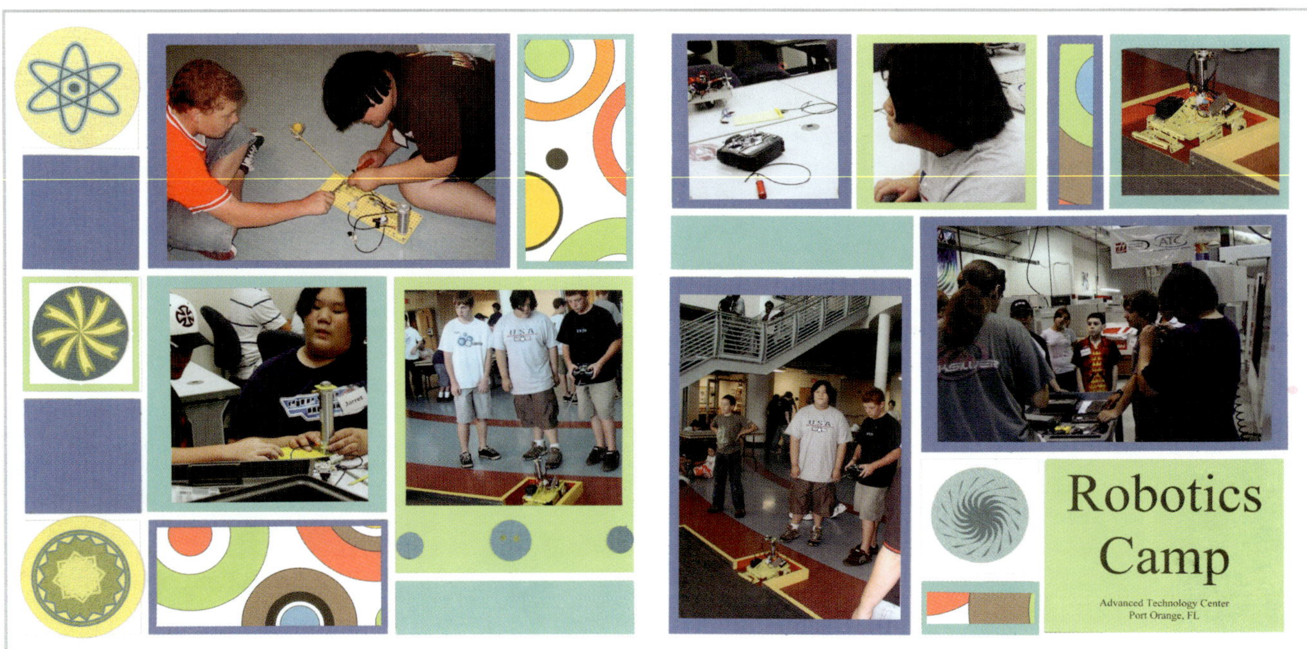

Robotics Camp: Jarrett Keene age 13
number of photos: 8

Gallery

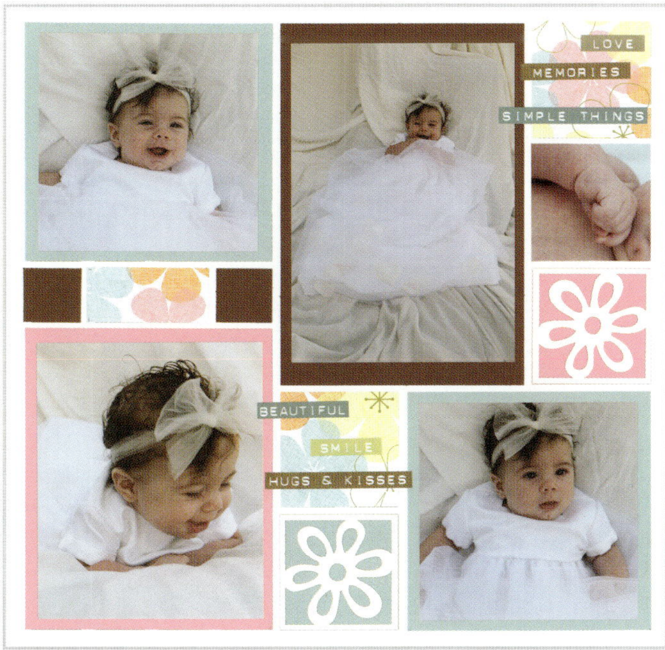

Alexa: Shannon Johnson
number of photos: 5

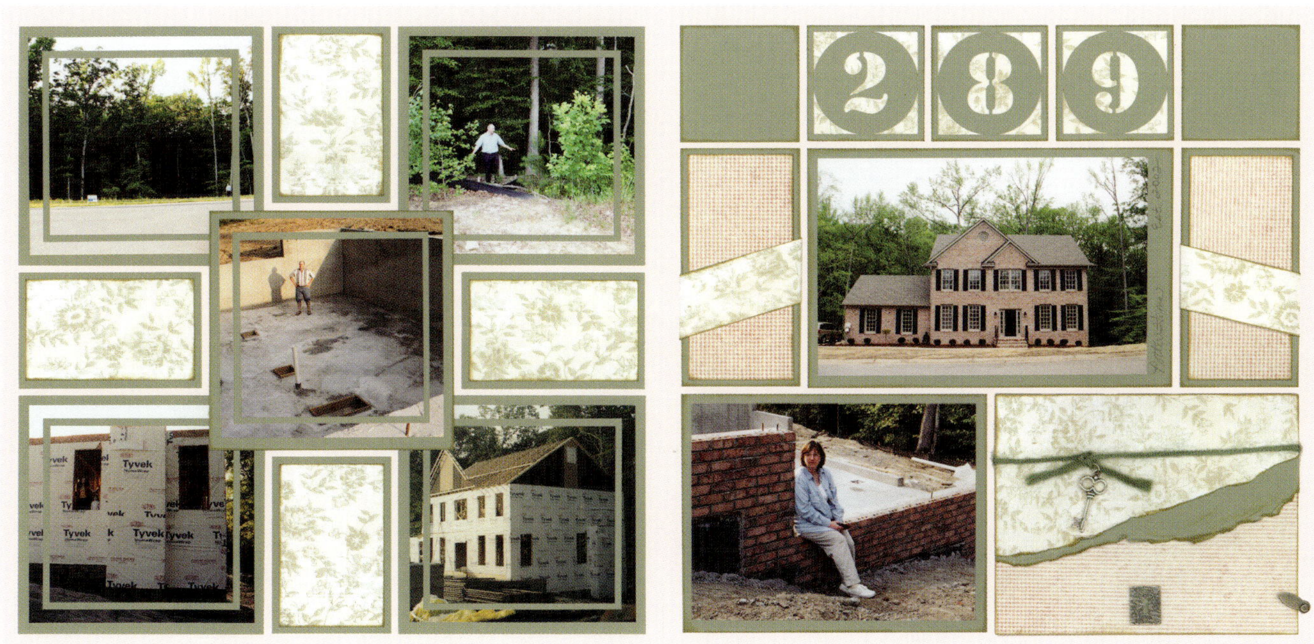

289: Tami Potter
number of photos: 7

Gallery

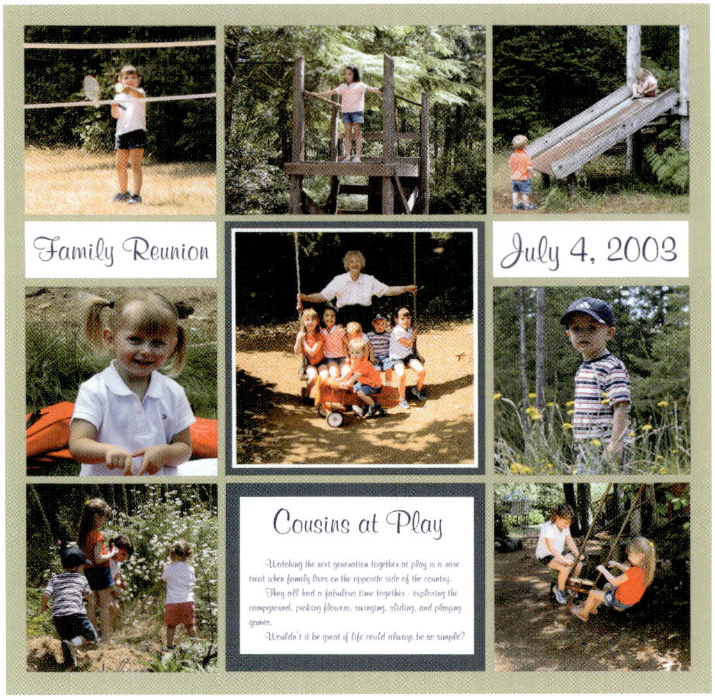

Cousins at Play: Tami Potter
number of photos: 8

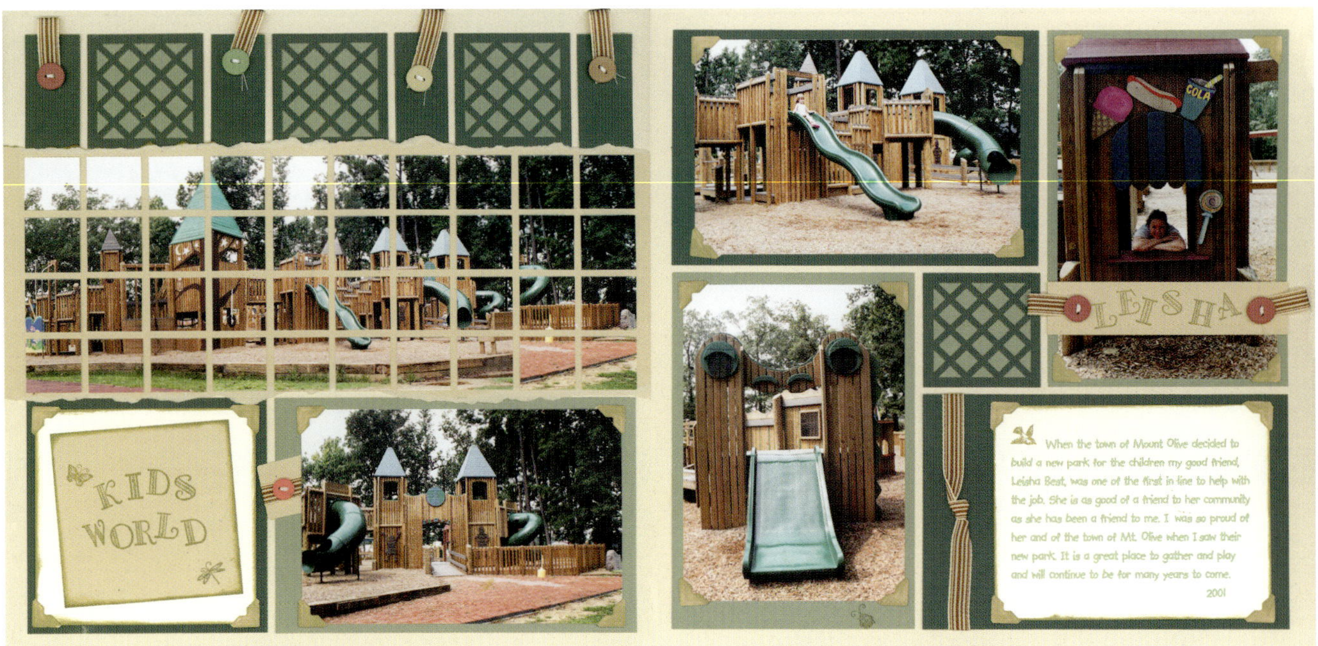

Kids World: Tami Potter
number of photos: 7

Gallery

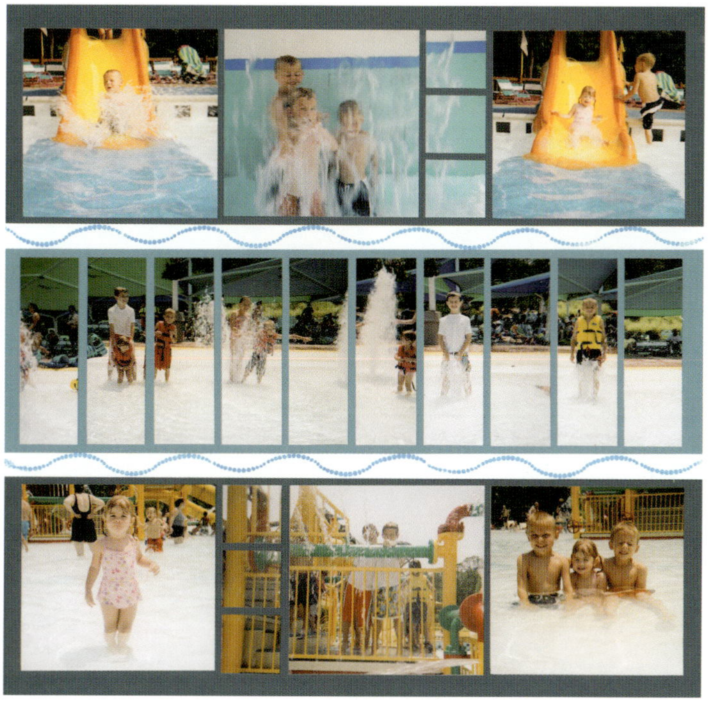

Water Park: Shannon Johnson
number of photos: 11

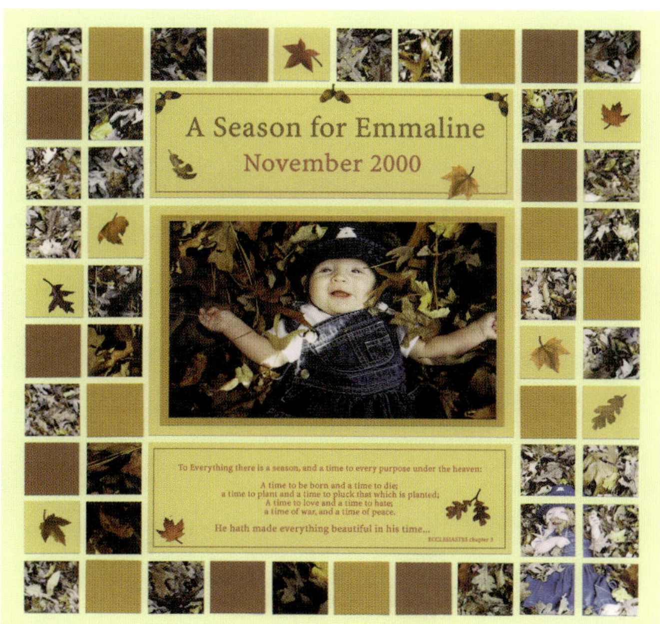

A Season for Emmaline: Tami Potter
number of photos: 2

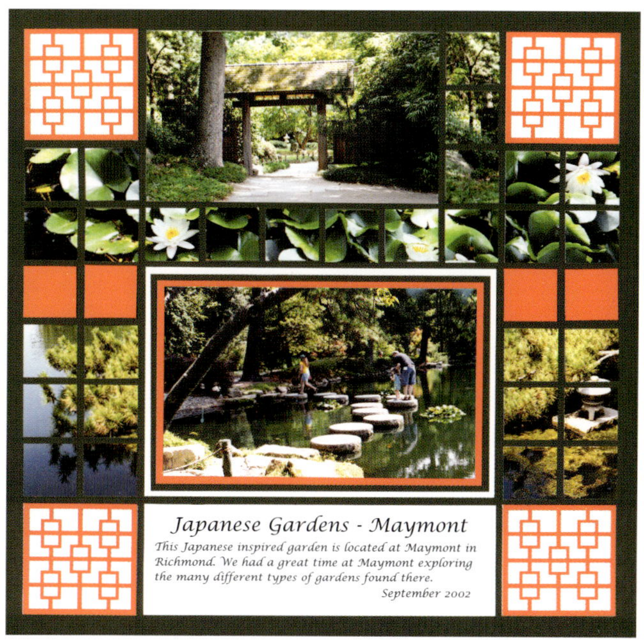

Japanese Garden: Sandi Keene
number of photos: 4

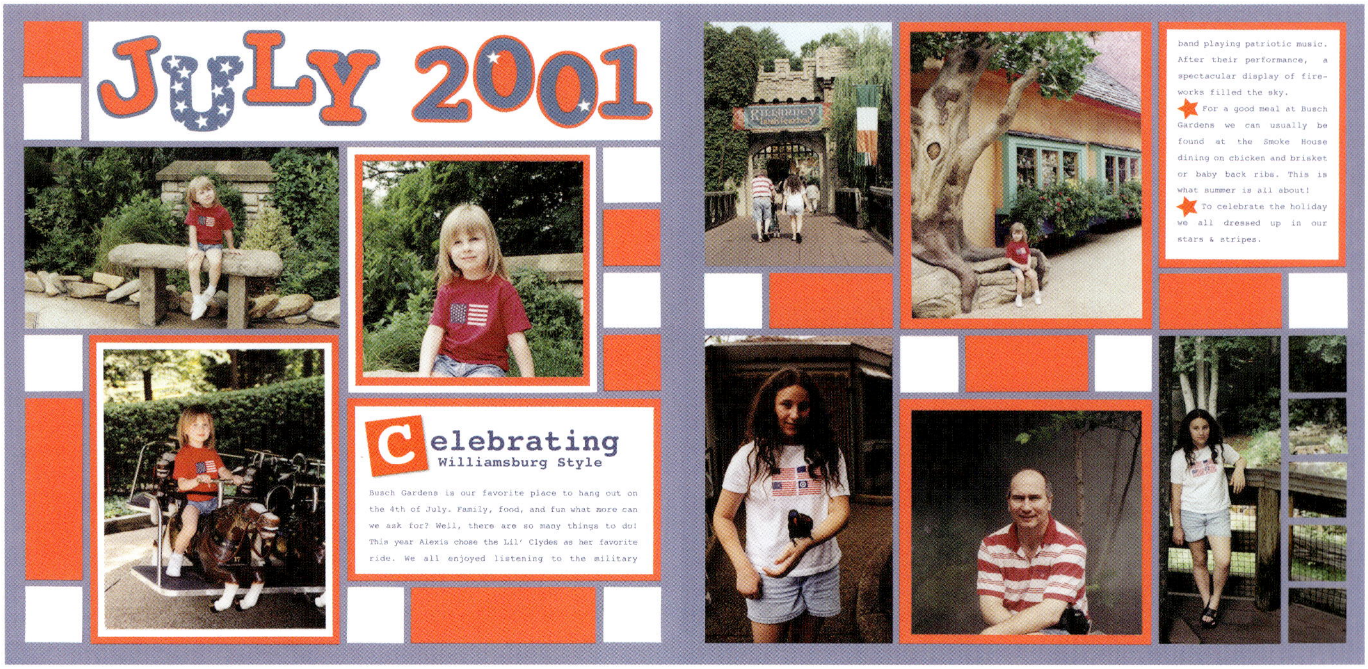

Mosaic Moments™ Quick Glance Cutting Guide

I have found it very useful to use a transparent overlay to help me determine where cuts should be made. The grid pattern pictured right can be copied (at 100%) onto transparent material to serve as your guide for cutting/cropping 4x6 inch photos to fit the Mosaic Moments grid paper.

The top grid is a guide for cutting photos into one inch squares. The bottom guide is designed to help when you are cutting photos to cover multiple squares. The black dot in the bottom left corner serves as a reminder of your starting point. You must start your measurement in this corner for the guide to work properly.

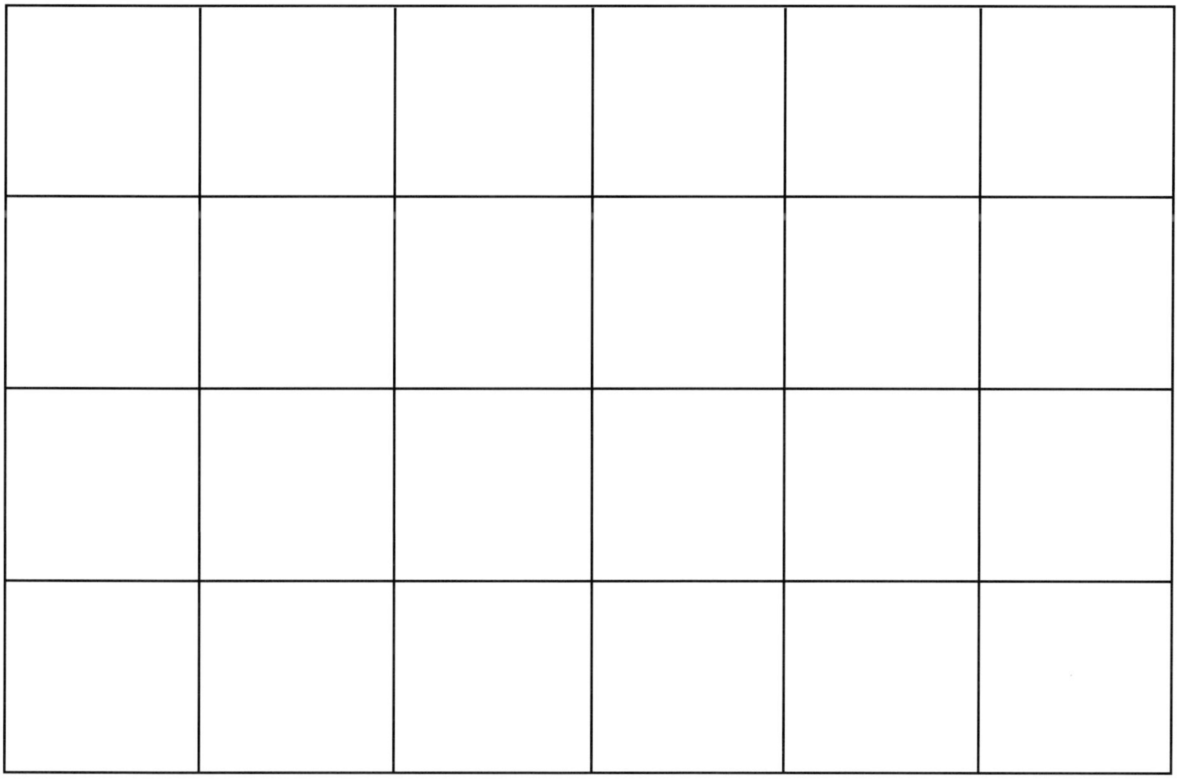

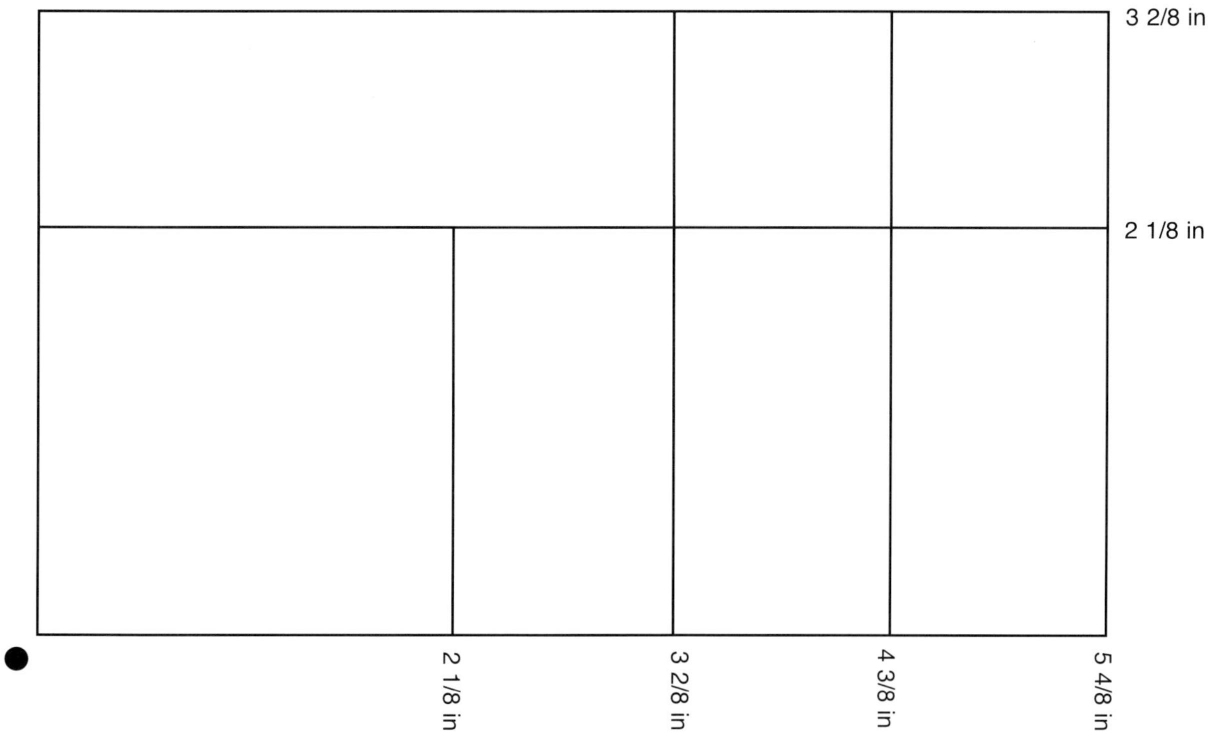
3 2/8 in
2 1/8 in
2 1/8 in
3 2/8 in
4 3/8 in
5 4/8 in

Contributors:

Sources:

All My Memories, LLC
www.allmymemories.com
embellishments

Basic Grey
www.basicgrey.com
patterned paper
rub-ons

C-Thru Ruler Company
www.cthruruler.com
metal ruler

Creative Imaginations
creativeimaginations.us
embellishments

EK Success, LTD.
www.eksuccess.com
Herma Dotto adhesive

Fiber Scraps
www.fiberscraps.com
Tintz

Impression Obsession
www.impression-obsession.com
rubber stamps

Inkadinkado
www.inkadinkado.com
rubber stamps

K & Company
www.kandcompany.com
stickers

Making Memories
www.makingmemories.com
embellishments

me and my Big ideas
www.meandmybigideas.com
stickers

Melissa Frances
Heart and Home Inc.
melissafrances.com
patterned paper

Mrs. Grossmans Paper Co.
www.mrsgrossmans.com
stickers

SEI
www.sei.com
patterned paper

Sonburn Paper
sonburn.com
patterned paper

Wish in the Wind LLC
www.wishinthewind.com
Mosaic Moments™ Grid Paper
Mosaic Moments™ Mat

Contributing artists:

Angela Andrews | pages 28, 83
Angela has been scrapbooking since 1999 and also enjoys reading, quilting, and taking photos at any opportunity. She lives in Virginia with her family.

Joan Hess | pages 84-85
Joan has been scrapbooking to showcase the decades of photos she has massed. She loves to travel to scenic places, visit with family and friends, and spend time with her grandsons. Joan lives in Williamsburg Virginia with her husband.

Shannon Johnson | pages 3, 32, 56, 89, 91
Shannon enjoys scrapbooking and making cards. She loves to travel and be with her family. Shannon lives with her husband and four children in Williamsburg, VA.

Sandi Keene | pages 28, 69, 79, 81, 82, 85, 87, 88, 91
Sandi has been scrapbooking for ten years. She loves patterned paper, Johnny Depp movies and taking photographs. She loves being inspired by other scrappers, her family, and life.

Jaime Zenger | pages 26-27
Jaime started her crafting career early, following in the footsteps of her mother. In her spare time Jaime enjoys spending her free time with her granddaughter. Jaime lives in Utah with her husband and three children.

Youth Contributor:

Jarrett Keene | page 88
Jarrett lives with a scrapbooking mom so he has no choice but to scrapbook occasionally. He enjoys computers, music, and paint ball.

About the Author

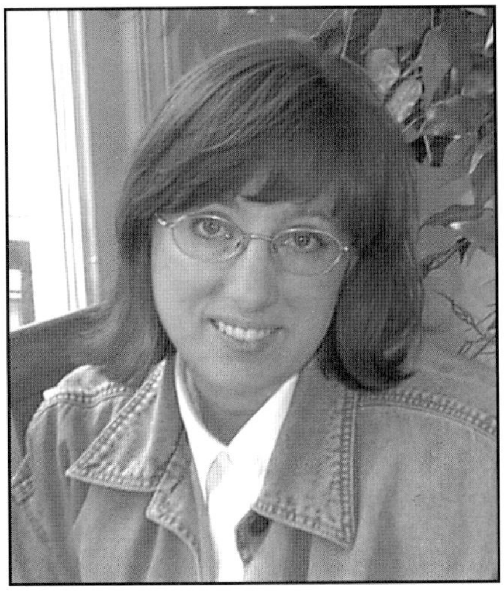

Tami Potter has been creating since she first held crayons, swapping them for the precise lines of pencil sketching, and finally graduating to mixed media and computer graphics, earning a Bachelor of Fine Arts with an emphasis in Graphic Design from East Carolina University.

Tami is the founder of Wish in the Wind, LLC., makers of the Mosaic Moments™ scrapbooking system. Mosaic Moments™ is a result of her aspiration to make the most of a moment, providing fellow scrappers with inspiring new techniques and fresh ideas.

Through her graphic approach to scrapbooking Tami has gained an enthusiastic following both at home and abroad. Tami travels extensively throughout the U.S. teaching and demonstrating her simple system for creating photo mosaics.

Tami grew up in the Pacific Northwest. She is the youngest of eight children. She lives with her husband, also the youngest of eight children, and their three children in Williamsburg, Virginia.

You can keep in touch with Tami's current designing activities through her blog, go to: www.tamipotter.com

www.tamipotter.com